Letters to N

CW00672360

Letters to My Son

A SON'S ADDICTION—A MOTHER'S GRIEF

FROSO HACIPARA SENDUKAS

RONCHRISPER PUBLISHING
Houston, Texas

RONCHRISPER PUBLISHING
HOUSTON, TEXAS 77057

Copyright © 2023 by Froso Hacipara Sendukas

All rights reserved. No part of this book may be used or reproduced in any manner whatsoever without written permission, except in the case of brief quotations in articles and reviews.
Published 2023 in the United States of America

32 31 30 29 28 27 26 25 24   2 3 4 5

ISBN: 13: 979-8-218-27527-3

Send permission requests to ronchrisperpublishing@gmail.com.
Cover photograph by Chris Sendukas

Also by Froso Hacipara Sendukas—

Bridging the Aegean: Growing Up Greek in Turkey

https://www.amazon.com/Bridging-Aegean-Growing-Greek-Turkey/dp/1508567603/r

CONTENTS

PREFACE

There are a lot of stories about addiction in social media nowadays. Unfortunately, way too many. The disease of alcoholism and drug addiction seems almost commonplace, yet every story is unique and heartbreaking in its own way. So there is nothing commonplace about that.

This is the story of my beloved middle son and what addiction did to him. Consequently, it is also a story about what happened to me as a result. My letters to him were not started to be part of a book. I wrote them because I couldn't not write them. They were the only solace I had in my desperate grief journey.

During many sleepless nights, especially in the early days of this terrible journey, they were the only thing that kept me from going off the rails and from choking on my desperation of not being able to stop or control what was happening in my life. In a spiritual, even mystical way, the letters were my only connection to a person I dearly loved and lost.

ACKNOWLEDGMENTS

I dedicated this book to The Compassionate Friends organization because I am deeply grateful for the emotional support and the safe place that it provided for me during my intense grief journey. The organization's chapter in Katy, Texas, near Houston, was a place where I could go and let out my anguish without being judged about the intensity of my feelings. The members—mostly bereaved parents like me—understood that the grief that results from losing a child is like no other grief. It goes on forever.

I am also very grateful to my therapist Robert Scott. His expertise, empathy, and compassion have been steadfast and very much appreciated during my painful journey.

I also want to thank my editor, Beth W. Allen, for her diligent and valuable help with my book and for her support.

My granddaughter Alexa took time-out from caring for a new baby to volunteer to change the names in the manuscript. She also gave me some valuable legal advice.

Contributing to the book's cover with a photograph was my son Chris. The tree shown is the one planted long ago by my late son, the subject of this book. I am grateful to Chris for this art and more.

Family members, especially my late son's children, Sam and Peter, and good friends, particularly Uğur and Verdi Adam, Virginia Brown, Pete Cronquist, and Dolly Davenport, were very important during my time of great distress. My longtime close friend Connie Curtiss (who lives in another state now) cried on the phone when I told her the terrible news of my son's passing. Her warm empathy and affection touched me deeply.

My heartfelt thanks go to everyone who helped me navigate my painful journey.

PART I
STATE OF LIMBO:
DREAD AND ESTRANGEMENT

Letters of March 27, 2017, through March 12, 2018

March 27, 2017

My Dearest Son,

It's your birthday today. A day that should be a joyful occasion for a mother. But this year, your special day is a painful one for me. I don't know how you are or even where you are. All I know is that you are somewhere in the Los Angeles area, probably homeless.

Are your legs still swollen? You told me that they were when you last called me on my birthday on the first of December. I advised you to go to the doctor and check on your legs. Did you ever go?

I called you this morning, with trepidation in my heart and a shaky feeling in my stomach. I wanted to wish you a happy birthday, even though I knew that you would not answer your phone—but I was hoping anyway. Of course, there was no response to my call. Just like all the other times I tried, even recently.

I canceled my sessions with my last remaining clients. (I am very close to retirement from my psychotherapy practice.) I just do not have the emotional energy and mental resources needed to do my job and counsel my clients. I was too depleted to offer help to them or to anybody else.

I was determined to go to my regular Al-Anon meeting at 6 p.m. today, hoping it would help my distressed mood some, and I did go; however, there was no parking designated for those with a disability available anywhere close to the building, so I had to park one-half block away. Ordinarily that wouldn't be a problem, but today it was. I have to use a cane to walk nowadays because of the pain in my left knee. This is the same knee that was on the verge of breaking last October when I came to Los Angeles to see you and read my intervention incidents, only I didn't know that back then.

The knee pain had gotten so bad after our painful meeting that I was unable to walk out of the plane when I arrived in Houston. Airport personnel had to bring a wheelchair by the exit ramp so I could leave the airplane. You may remember that I had to go to a rehabilitation center after the trip because the doctor told me that I had to spend a month in a wheelchair so as to totally rest the knee and prevent it from totally breaking. It was an ordeal, but I survived. It's better now, but it still limits my functioning because it still hurts quite a lot, especially when I walk.

Anyway, I did go to the Al-Anon meeting—hobbling—and it helped some. I talked with some people I knew and they tried to comfort me. It lessened some of the despair I was feeling about our noncommunication (especially on your birthday) and my constant worry about your situation.

I love you, Son, no matter what!

March 28, 2017

My Dearest Son,

I am still waiting to hear from you. I stayed home all day. Once again, I'm feeling depressed and hopeless. Nicholas told me that he heard that you and his mother are living in a U-Haul. Wondering how long one can stay in a U-Haul, and what kind of lifestyle you are living there. Can you even take a shower in a U-Haul? Probably not. By the way, where did you find this U-Haul? Is it stolen by any chance? Am I going to hear from a jail next? No answers here.

I am still obsessing that maybe if I had figured out the right words to say during my ineffective attempt at intervention, some months ago, that maybe I could have pierced your denial and thus maybe stopped your sad,

4

downhill slide. After all, I think that I am a pretty good therapist and have helped many clients through the years. "Why?" I ask myself, "Why couldn't I help my own beloved son?"

My rational self realizes that this is a tremendous, almost arrogant idea. My intellectual knowledge of your disease tells me that my obsession about saving you is foolish. The truth is you have to save yourself. Regardless of what I know, the compulsive thoughts still come night and day, tantalizing and torturing me!

I had a dream last night. In the dream, you were grinning at me. This was not your typical sweet, loving grin, but a weird, almost evil grin. Your eyes were bloodshot and had a vacant stare. That was a dark version of you that I hated seeing. I woke up with a startle and cried for a long while.

April 8, 2017

My Dearest Son,

I have not written for a few days. Don't know why. Maybe because I have a bad cold and the physical misery adds to my ongoing depression. I have not heard from you about the medical tests or results. You told me some time ago that you underwent medical tests for your swollen legs and some other physical symptoms. I feel so discouraged about your health and your whole situation.

I am still going to Al-Anon meetings on a weekly basis (except when my cold makes me cough a lot). The meetings help me some. I see and hear from so many people whose kids suffer from this terrible disease of alcoholism. I never thought that one of my children would be a victim. Your younger brother Constantine came close, but he was still a teenager at the time. I was able to intervene in time, get him to a treatment center, and alter his path. I used my knowledge and influence on him to get him the help he needed. It was a difficult time for both of us, but we made it through.

Unfortunately, I am not able to do the same for you. You are in your fifties and on your own, and I have no leverage to use. So, to get you into treatment, I tried to go to your wife for help, but regretfully it didn't work. I think she may be also a victim of the disease and too codependent to help you get into treatment. I keep telling you both about Alcoholics

Anonymous meetings to no avail. So, I just keep on worrying and suffering, unable to let go of the idea that I should be doing something, anything, to save you. I have endless conversations with you in my head, trying desperately to convince you to change your destructive path.

April 10, 2017

My Dearest Son,

Every time the phone rings, my heart leaps, hoping that it's you calling. I am anxiously waiting to hear about your test results. Leslie texted me some time ago to tell me that you had finally gone to the doctor because you were feeling so poorly. Now, all I get is silence. My fantasy script is that this will be the wake-up call that you finally respond to and go to get some help. On the other hand, as your mother, I don't really want the blood tests to show something terrible, just some ailment that can be cured with sobriety.

Olga just texted me that she and Spiros are going soon to Colorado to ski. They were invited by friends of theirs who have a second home there. She asked me to keep an eye on my grandsons, Stuart and Nicholas. Your younger son, Nicholas, has been living with them since January. Your brother and his wife have generously opened their home and heart to him, and I'm very grateful.

I cannot help but compare their situation to yours. I am happy for them. They can afford the numerous vacations that they take, but I feel a little resentment that Spiros doesn't go out of his way to help you in your dismal situation. He tells me that he is tired of loaning you money that is never going to be returned and that he is angry with you about your current situation, especially for what he calls "abandonment of your children." I keep reminding him that alcoholism is a disease, that you are not choosing to be that way intentionally, and that deep down you do love your children. He shrugs his shoulders and walks away. I don't think that he totally believes me. I think he still holds on to the belief that it's a matter of character and maturity and that you are failing in that regard.

Frankly, Jaime, I don't think that you believe the concept of the disease either.

During the intervention I heard you call yourself "an alcoholic" with a contemptuous tone in your voice. Your father used to say that it was all about strength of character and, unfortunately, you and Spiros were brainwashed by his ideas.

May 3, 2017

My Dearest Son,

I have an Al-Anon sponsor now. I had my first meeting with her yesterday. I think it went well. She is from England and has a delightful accent. She's been with the organization for fifteen years and is nice and smart. She confronts me sometimes in a gentle way when I sound codependent with you and your addiction. She tells me that when I am angry with your brothers about not helping you enough, I am displacing the anger I feel toward your disease and your behavior. Yes, she is probably right. I do want them so desperately to rescue you from your destructive life path. My sponsor says the truth is that you have to want to be rescued and you don't, not now anyway.

She does not want me to keep texting you or calling you when you obviously do not want to text or call me back. That suggestion fills me with despair. How am I going to stay in your life—even on the periphery—if I don't text or call? Her answer is that I need to pivot my efforts toward me. I have to get out of the way so you can have the consequences of your actions and choices. "Do not give him the message that he cannot do it for himself," she says.

It seems I am distracting you from facing your own reality of what's going on in your life. Most of all, she said, "Do not keep reminding him that he promised to get help. Reminding him is shaming, and he already feels shame."

I hear all this and it sounds like wise advice, but I know it will be hard to put the advice into practice. I am planning to buy a book she recommends, *Paths to Recovery: Al-Anon's Steps, Traditions and Concepts,* and start working on the Al-Anon steps.

7

June 1, 2017

My Dearest Son,

I finally heard from you yesterday. It was a plea for financial help. You told me on the phone that you and Leslie had items in a storage facility for over a year now (probably since your house was foreclosed) and that the owner of the facility is now threatening to sell your stuff because your account is past due. You told me that some of the items were of important sentimental value to you and you cited photo albums of the children, a Turkish carpet that my mother had sent you from Istanbul when you were a young boy, and religious icons that I had given you through the years. You said, pleadingly, that you needed to pay the guy so he wouldn't sell your items. And then you added almost casually that you had recently broken your shoulder and were in a lot of pain.

I told you that I was very sorry about your broken shoulder. I wondered if you even went to a doctor or hospital when it happened. You did not answer my question.

I then told you that I could not send you money directly, that the action would go against everything I had learned at Al-Anon, but that I was willing to send some money to the facility so that you could retrieve some of your valuable items. You thanked me and then you gave me the name and number of the facility owner.

I did not have a pleasant conversation with the owner of the storage facility. He had a lot of contempt and cynicism in his voice when he talked with me, and it reminded me of the time last year when you asked me to pay for the rental of a tuxedo for Nicholas's prom in his senior year of high school. The man at the tuxedo rental facility also had contempt in his voice, and I felt oddly ashamed on your behalf. Later in the day I wondered if I had done the right thing about agreeing to pay for the stored items and whether my new sponsor would approve of my actions. Too late to reconsider now, that's for sure.

This turned out to be a good day after all. I heard your voice!

July 2, 2017

My Dearest Son,

I finally went to see an orthopedic surgeon. I had to wait a long time for an appointment because he has such a stellar reputation. He took a lot of x-rays, and then he told me that my left knee shows all the signs of severe arthritis, is rapidly deteriorating, and is causing the pain I am feeling. He is definitely recommending knee replacement. I had guessed that this would be his diagnosis and recommendation, but hearing the actual words still shook me up.

How am I going to navigate the surgery and the long period of recovery that follows the surgery, especially with my family being against the idea of surgery? This is major surgery, no *ifs* and *buts* about it. I have to make plans and make them rather quickly. I have to find a new rehabilitation center. I was not happy with the one where I spent a month last year, in a wheelchair, because of my semibroken knee bone. I was not impressed by their physical therapy department. Therefore, finding a dependable center will be very important to the recovery process.

I also will have to make arrangements for my dog, Skye, since I will not be able to take care of her for quite a while. At this point, I am beyond worrying about the surgery itself, even though quite a few people—including my cardiologist—warned me that a lot of pain was involved with this type of surgery.

I told my Al-Anon sponsor that my head was swimming with all the difficulties and challenges I was facing in the near future, assuming that I went along with the surgery idea. My sponsor reminded me of the twelve-step principles of taking one day at a time and not worrying so much about the future.

I decided to follow her advice and prepared a step-by-step plan for the surgery and the recovery time to follow. I hope I have the strength and determination to accomplish all this because I do not see an alternative that I can live with. My severe knee pain makes functioning really hard, and I do not want to be permanently in a wheelchair or end up in an assisted living nursing home. I need to bite the bullet and go ahead—despite all the challenges that surgery presents.

Say a little prayer for me, honey, so I can accomplish all this. How I wish that you would also help yourself to get out of the mess you are in. I know for a fact that California has many social service programs—a lot more than Texas. I know this because I have made hundreds of phone calls during the past two years and have personally talked with many addiction program managers. I gave you a thorough list when I came with Olga to do the intervention last October. I included names, numbers, and addresses (after many years as a practicing social worker, I definitely knew how to obtain information and resources). You barely looked at my list and said, "I would rather go to jail than go to a rehab!" I tried to stay calm and pointed out that many of the programs were outpatient, some were quite inexpensive, and all you needed to do was go and apply in person and ask for help. I also told you that you had choices. You could come to Houston and get help here with your family's support. I had talked with addiction facilities here as well and had found a couple of openings.

"I can't leave Los Angeles," you said. "Who is going to take care of my wife and my dog? The kids are gone and doing fine"—not really, I thought, but did not want to argue—"but I have to stay here, in LA. My law career is here."

"What career?" I wanted to shout. "Your career is in shambles, and according to your partner, you no longer even have a practice. All you have are debts." I wanted to say all that, but I didn't. I was trying so hard to keep our conversation civil and not to anger you. I handed you and Leslie copies of all the resources in LA that I had compiled. You glanced at my list for a second and put it down. You shrugged your shoulders and my gut twisted in distress. I realized then that all the long hours of research that I had done on finding possible resources for you, all the endless imaginary conversations that I had in my head trying to convince you to give up your path of destruction, and all my sleepless nights worrying about you and wondering how to help you—they were all in vain. All I wanted to do was cry and cry!

You listened to all my incidents without interrupting me. I tried to keep my hands from shaking and my tears from brimming over. I tried to shut out the dingy, smelly motel room and your shoeless bare feet and just concentrate on reading my nonjudgmental, nonshaming list. I was so careful to put into practice everything I had learned through the years about addiction treatment and counseling.

The only comment you made during my reading was when I reminded you that my mother, your grandmother Anastasia, who adored you and thought you were the smartest, most thoughtful kid in the world, had told you that she was sure you would become president of the United States one day. You turned to your wife and said, "This is totally true. My grandmother did believe that I would be president someday." That's when I couldn't control my emotions anymore and started sobbing. "Don't cry, Mom," you said. "I promise you I'll get help. You came all the way to help me. I will do it, I promise." I wanted to believe you so badly, I asked you to make a plan and choose how you were going to get the help you needed. You shrugged your shoulders and said, "I'll get help my way, don't worry about me. I know what I'm doing." Once again, I had that sinking gut feeling that nothing would be done and that those were empty words.

We took Leslie to lunch. You refused to come, saying that you were going to watch the University of Michigan football game that our arrival had interrupted.

All I remember from that fateful lunch was Olga and I desperately trying to convince Leslie to commit you to a psychiatric hospital for seventy-two hours (that's all that the law allowed) so that you could get some help, despite yourself.

Leslie said she couldn't do it! She added that she was scared of you and your reaction. I practically begged her to not be afraid to do the right thing. She retorted that you would be very angry, and she could not bear the consequences. I could not understand her resistance. I asked her if you had been physically abusive to her. "No," she replied. "He has not, but there is verbal harassment when he is drunk," she said. She continued to talk about that for a while. I was so overwhelmed at what I heard that my mind went blank and drifted away. I didn't hear the rest of what she was saying.

You seemed clueless. You talked about the Michigan game and we just listened. We spent the afternoon on the patio of the motel with you and Leslie. I didn't say much of anything. I felt as if I was in a foggy state, barely functioning. The feeling was one of total defeat.

Before we left the motel, I told you that I needed to go to the ladies' room. "I'll take you, Mom," you said. And like the gallant son you used to be, you got up to walk with me. As we passed a woman who was sitting by herself on the patio, you stopped and said to her, "Hi, Alice. I want to introduce you to my mother. She came all the way from Houston to see me!" I nodded to her, went to the ladies' room, and cried and cried.

11

We left and joined Nicholas for dinner. He had refused to come with us to the motel but had told us how to find you. He spent the night with us in our hotel room. Poor baby, he seemed so in need of affection. He is staying with a friend's family.

We told him that he would be very welcome to come to Houston and live with me or Spiros and Olga. He said he would think about it. By the time we boarded the plane to come back home, I was limping and in a lot of pain. Some of it was psychological, I'm sure. I had to use a wheelchair to exit the plane.

Right now, as I'm writing this, I'm dreading the future for both of us, my son.

August 2017

My Dearest Son,

How are you? Are you all right? Foolish of me to ask, I know. You probably don't know yourself how you really are.

Last time I heard from you was when you called me to ask me to pay your past due cell phone bill. I hesitated some before agreeing to do it, but then I realized that I would be doing myself a favor as well. The cell phone is the only way I can reach you, even if you don't answer my calls most of the time. So I stopped wondering whether my behavior was codependent or not and just paid the bill.

I haven't heard from you since then, so I endlessly worry about your welfare. I keep hoping for a miracle.

Houston has been in the middle of a disaster of major proportions—Hurricane Harvey. There's flooding and devastation about everywhere you look. We are in the midst of a huge hurricane and have been in national news over and over again. I have heard from quite a few people worried about my safety. It hurts my feelings that I have not heard from you, my son. I tell myself that maybe you are in jail and that's why you have not heard about the hurricane that's affecting Houston. After all, the last phone call I received about you came from a bondsman asking for bail money on your behalf.

I followed my sponsor's advice and did not return the phone call and/or offer any bail money, but it broke my heart to turn down the request and to realize once again that you are heading to jail. I hope and pray that you turn your life around before it's too late. If you ever do, then you'll understand and hopefully forgive me for not giving you bail money.

I have loved you with all my heart since I saw your little wrinkled face and bald head when you were born. You looked so small and so vulnerable! You instantly touched my heart, and you have been there ever since. I know there's a deep connection between us, despite everything, that will never be broken. You told me so yourself last year when you were in a better place emotionally.

I am so sorry that I cannot help you with the bail money. The idea of your going to jail and suffering all sorts of indignities makes me feel miserable. It keeps me awake all night. I know that you will be angry about my refusal. Last time the same thing happened, you told me, "Mom, how can you say you love me and then let me go to jail?" Your words stabbed my heart, and I was too choked up with tears to even manage a reply.

September 14, 2017

My Dearest Son,

It's 4 a.m. and I cannot stay asleep. I keep having fragments of dreams or, rather, nightmares about court verdicts, driving under the influence violations, stolen U-Hauls, and your being in jail.

I have never been in jail, but I have learned of and read many accounts of jail life and have seen plenty of shows about it. I try not to focus on harsh or even brutal jail conditions that you may be experiencing, but my mind refuses to obey and wildly wanders.

As a retired therapist and addiction counselor, I know a lot about the misery of detoxing. I also know that currently there are some medications that can make the process more bearable. My hope is that, maybe instead of abandoning you to agonize alone in a cell, the jail authorities will show some compassion and take you to a jail hospital or at least get you some medical help. I have no doubt that you will have to go through the process of detoxing—one way or another—and I dread it for you. How I wish I could spare you the suffering! The truth is I don't really know what's going on, and that's killing me! All I have is your heavy silence and my overactive imagination.

"Please, God," I keep praying, "take care of my son and help him in his hour of need. Help me as well to be able to bear this ordeal and stay mentally strong, and help me practice tough love for both of our sakes, even though it's far from easy."

This past week has been terrible for me. I know in my head that I am doing the right thing in refusing to send money for bail, but my heart keeps protesting and wanting to rescue you from your mistakes and actions. I want to say, "Principles be damned. This is my child we are talking about," but something holds me back.

It helped some to go to church today and light a candle for you.

September 21, 2017

My Dearest Son,

This is so damn hard! I sit here watching TV but unable to concentrate on what's going on in the screen. Distractions don't seem to work anymore. My Al-Anon sponsor keeps telling me that I need to detach from you and your addiction and concentrate on myself, but this is a very hard concept for me. I still have fantasies of wanting to rescue you, of doing something—anything—rather than helplessly watching you destroy yourself.

I constantly get mental images of you in jail, guessing that you are there unless you found somebody willing to bail you out (which I doubt, based on the many phone calls from friends of yours telling us that you owe them a lot of money).

At times, I'm still angry with my family for not trying to help you, even though my sponsor tells me again and again that I should be angry instead with your disease of alcoholism. She tells me all this, and I know deep down that it's wise advice; however, I still hear in my head the desperation in your voice as you ask me to help you. It got so bad that I couldn't stand it anymore. I disconnected all my landline phones yesterday.

I never dreamed that I would come to this. That one day I would have to disconnect the home phone so as not to weaken my resolve by your desperate attempts to stay out of jail. I am not even sure why you are facing jail. Is it because of your multiple DUI violations, or is it because of the U-Haul that you and Leslie may have kept after the move from your foreclosed house? Nicholas told me in the past that you lived for a while in that U-Haul. Or are there fines that you did not pay that were due? I don't know the answer to the above questions—I keep wondering and worrying. I am almost too afraid to ask any more questions about your life for fear that I will not like your answers, assuming that you do answer me truthfully ("truth" being a commodity unfortunately lacking in the last few years).

My head is swimming with all the above, and I have a fast heart rate—I can tell. I am going to turn off the TV and try to go to sleep. Maybe this time I'll succeed and get some much-needed rest. I hope that you are able to rest as well, my boy.

Sending you love!

Mom

September 25, 2017

My Dearest Son,

It's my "name day" today, and I am spending it in a hospital—Texas Orthopedic Hospital, to be exact. I had a knee replacement surgery two days ago, and I am recovering now. Remember what I told you about name days? How we used to celebrate them in the Greek community in Istanbul when I was growing up? I wrote an essay about them in my memoir about growing up Greek in Turkey. Did you ever read my memoir? I gave you a copy as soon as it was published.

Greeks all over the world cherish name days and celebrate them a lot more than birthdays. Almost every calendar day is named after a particular Greek Orthodox saint, and Greeks celebrate as name day the one linked to the saint for which they were named and with which they were baptized. My particular saint name is Efrosini, after a young woman who was a nun and became a martyr during the Roman Empire because of her faith.

I gave up on the custom of celebrating my name day when you were a young child because it was hard to get American friends to remember the day. It seemed easier to go along with the flow and just celebrate

15

birthdays. However, the day still holds a sentimental importance for me, and it pleases me a lot when somebody in my world remembers it and says, "Happy Name Day, Froso!" (or Frosula, as my mother would say). This year it was my oldest sweet granddaughter, Victoria, who remembered. She surprised me today and came to the hospital loaded with flowers and pastries. It was a wonderful surprise. She was a treat for sore eyes and I teared up with joy. Nobody else remembered, but it didn't matter. Her visit made up for the lack of the rest.

I had another surprise yesterday, of a different sort. You called me to ask about my surgery. I was shocked that you remembered that I was having surgery and even more shocked that you called to see if I was doing okay.

Just as I was rejoicing about your call, you threw in the conversation—almost casually—that they took away your license to practice law. You didn't say why you lost your license, but I presume it was because of your DUI conviction and/or time in jail. I was still too foggy from surgery to ask any pertinent questions. You added, "Mom, I think I can eventually get it back. I would need $300 to reinstate it."

I didn't reply. The pleasure of having you call was diluted, and I couldn't help wonder if that was the real reason behind your call. You kept on talking, "Mom, how am I going to earn a living without my license? I can't believe they did this to me." I did not answer you. No words were coming out of my mouth. I was still in a lot of physical pain from the surgery, despite the pain pills, and now I felt deep emotional pain as well. Instead of responding to what you said directly, I tried Al-Anon's "detachment" theory—not my natural style at all. "I'm sorry about your license, Jamie," I said, "The doctor just came into my room, and I have to go."

It was a lie, of course. I apologize to you for the lie. I hate indirect conversation and untruths, but I couldn't bear our painful conversation any longer. "OK, take care of yourself, Mom," you said. "You, too, honey, you take care of yourself as well," I replied. After we hung up, I started sobbing. I cannot write anymore, Jamie, I'm hurting too much.

November 3, 2017

My Dearest Son,

Did you get my text? I wrote it a few days ago. I had been thinking of doing it for a couple of weeks before I actually did it. I have not heard from you for quite a while. Since the day after my surgery in late September when you told me that your license to practice law had been taken away.

My ongoing fear is that when I practice Al-Anon's detachment principle, that you interpret it as not caring, and I definitely don't want that between us. I want you to know that no matter how I disapprove of and dislike your alcoholic behavior, my love for you is always there, constant and strong! I tried hard to delete any parts of the text that sounded like interrogation or scolding. Did not even ask (even though I badly wanted to) how your "antidrinking" class—that's what you called the Alcoholics Anonymous meetings required by your parole conditions—was going. I did not ask, "Are you doing better?" because I was afraid that you would interpret it as "Are you drinking and drugging?"

I merely reported on how hard I have been working on my recovery from knee-replacement surgery. I spent 20 days at a rehabilitation center doing daily physical therapy exercise that at first hurt like hell. The payback of all that work is that I'm doing much better now, even though I still have occasional knee pain.

At the end of the text, I wrote about your younger son, Nicholas, how he has been adjusting to Houston (since he moved in with Spiros and Olga) and how well he has been doing. He is going full-time to a community college and having a part-time job as a parking valet at a fancy restaurant. I hope you shared the news with Leslie.

I tried not to attach any expectations to the text—as Al-Anon teaches—but I have to admit that I'm still very disappointed that I had no response from you. Before I wrote, I had a fear that I was setting myself up to hear painful news. Now I am full of sadness that I did not get any response from you whatsoever.

Late November 2017

My Dearest Son,

The worst part of your noncommunication with me is that I have no idea how you are. Are you okay? Are you following the terms of your parole? Are you still drinking or even doing cocaine? Your friends and even your wife told me that you used to do cocaine earlier on. When I came to LA for the intervention last year, you swore to me that you didn't touch cocaine anymore. Your wife mumbled, "Because you can't afford to buy it anymore?" You gave her a dirty look but didn't respond to her. I don't know what the truth is and it's crazy-making. I even texted and tried to call Leslie numerous times, but her cell phone number is not working anymore. My anxiety about you is getting out of bounds.

Please don't get angry with me for saying this, but I had even hoped for a while—terrible as the prospect is—that going to jail for a month (like you did) would do the trick and shake you out of your denial about your situation and addiction. Sort of like the scared straight program that used to be trendy at one time about exposing delinquent youth to the harsh reality of a life of addiction and getting them on a straight path. I wonder if the concept would work for middle-aged addicts like you?

Unfortunately, I don't think that the jail term has changed your life for the better. Your continued estrangement and lack of communication with me and your sons is an indication of that.

I am so sorry, my son, that your chaotic, sad, homeless lifestyle is still going on. I don't know what else to do or how to help you. I feel so desperate and helpless!

December 1, 2017

My Dearest Son,

It's my birthday today. I'm trying valiantly to be grateful for all the birthday wishes from my family and my friends and for feeling less pain in my knee that the orthopedic surgeon replaced, my "robot" knee, as I call it.

18

Despite all my efforts, I can't shake off my sadness about your situation. Spiros told me that you asked him the other day to send some money to your storage unit. I thought, "Here we go again." I remembered that you had asked me some months ago to send money to that same storage facility. This time around you told Spiros that you asked Robert to come to LA from his college in San Francisco so as to retrieve some important family documents and photo albums from your unit. I presume you are having another deadline because of nonpayment of monthly rent. Spiros said that he sent a thousand dollars to Robert so he could retrieve some of your possessions.

Where is all this going, Jamie? Pretty soon, you'll lose all of your belongings. Do you really want to keep going down that rabbit hole? I feel so bad for you and for the rest of us who are witnessing your terrible fall!

The family and I went to Relish for my birthday. That's the restaurant where your nephew Stuart is a sous-chef for bread and pastries. Stuart made some nice desserts to honor my birthday—mainly his famous brownies that I love.

Nicholas did not mention Robert or the retrieval of objects from the storage place. He hardly even talks about you or his mother, but one can see the sadness in his face and demeanor. He has been dealing with the loss of his immediate family for some time now, and that must be traumatic for him—no matter how well he is treated here in Houston—especially by Spiros and Olga, who have opened for him not only their home, but also their hearts. I am very glad to see that, and I'm sure that deep down you are as well.

I came home from the restaurant around 10 p.m. and looked at my cell phone to see if I had any messages from you (I had tried hard all evening to avoid looking at it). My heart sank. There were no messages.

I took a mild pain pill (for the knee pain) and went to bed. I woke up at 1:30 a.m. and was awake for a couple of hours. That's kind of my normal pattern nowadays. I spend the time writing letters to you, like this one, that you will probably never see. My hope is that maybe one day I can talk to you in person and connect with you without needing to write letters for comfort or emotional relief.

I'm sending you all my love, wherever you are and whatever you are doing!

December 20, 2017

My Dearest Son,

Now I understand why I have not heard from you for a while. My granddaughter, Victoria, who is a practicing lawyer, called me to tell me that she looked at court records for Los Angeles and found out that you were given a jail sentence for forty days, but got credit for twenty of those days, because you were incarcerated for nonpayment of bail money. So now I know what transpired in November when I had numerous calls from bondsmen asking for bail money. During those calls, I would hear your voice in the background, saying, "Mom, please, Mom!"

It broke my heart to hear you pleading, but I had to turn you and the bondsmen down and close my ears to your urgent pleas because I knew that I had to keep practicing tough love and not rescue you from the consequences of your alcoholism and addiction. I paid a heavy price for my stand, spending the rest of the day in anguish and dread every time the phone rang, until I disconnected all the landline phones in the house.

A few hours after Victoria's call, your brother Constantine called me to tell me that he had looked at the Ventura County (Los Angeles area) website online and found out that you had been released on parole and had to go to DUI classes and undergo random urine tests and had until June to pay a $3,700 fine to the court. You were listed as a "multiple offender."

I was flabbergasted! I texted Victoria the information that Constantine had given me and said I was confused about the conflicting data. Are you still in jail or out on parole? After texting back and forth for quite a while, I finally told both of them to let the matter go. The truth would eventually come to the surface. All of a sudden, I had realized that all three of us were in an uproar, trying to figure out which version of the data was the correct one. It came to me—kind of like a revelation—that in the long run, it didn't really matter that much what the complete truth was. It really wasn't up to us to figure out where things stood in your life. There was too much chaos to navigate through. You are the one who has to decide whether to save yourself or not. Maybe the anxiety and distress will come back to me later (perhaps in the middle of the night), but right this minute I am remarkably calm. That feels like a miracle to me. This is the first time that, in the middle of chaos and despair, I can emotionally separate from your disease of alcoholism and realize that you are the architect of your destiny—not me, your wife, or your sons. Could it be that I finally am making some strides toward what Al-Anon and my sponsor call "detachment"? I hope so.

Please understand that this is not abandonment or the absence of love. I will love you until I die!

New Year's Day, 2018

My Dearest Son,

Wondering where you are and what you are doing today. According to the information that Victoria obtained from the legal website, you are probably a free man today. Your month-long jail sentence was over yesterday. I question the wisdom of a justice system that would allow an addict of substance abuse to leave jail on New Year's Eve—the biggest drinking day of the year—but I guess they don't consider these matters. Like Pilate, they wash their hands of any responsibility regarding your drinking and using drugs.

I am sure you are very happy about not being locked up anymore. You always hated to be cooped up indoors. While you were still in jail, I sent you a long letter (Victoria found the address for me). I tried to explain to you in the letter why I had to refuse to pay bail for you. I also implored you to change your bad habits and move toward sobriety, maybe by attending AA meetings.

I know more than ever that there's nothing I can do to change your lifestyle and situation. It's your situation after all, not mine. I keep trying to put the "Serenity Prayer" of twelve-step tradition to practice, and I finally accept (most of the time) what I cannot change. It's damn hard, Jamie, because I love you so much, and it's agonizing for me to watch you, even from a distance, destroy yourself.

God knows what your health is like. I found out that you were in the jail hospital for a week. You told me that you were there for a whole month. Hard to believe anything that you are telling me. Where is the truth? Who knows? I realize that even a week doesn't sound good. Was it detox or some serious illness? I don't think that they would have kept you in the hospital for a week if it was a minor problem. As my sponsor keeps reminding me, I can't believe anything that you say because it comes from a place of addiction.

I know I have to focus on myself instead of you and get emotionally healthier and less codependent, but it's such a struggle! Despite our recent history and your noncommunication pattern, I kept hoping that you would answer my letter. I thought that maybe the thirty days in jail would have cleared your head some and given you enough clarity so you would see the love contained in the pages of my letter and answer me.

I should have known better. You are probably still angry with me for refusing the bail money. "I'm never calling you again, Mother," you said. I have noticed through the years that you call me "Mother" instead of "Mom" when you are angry with me. Your hurtful words reverberate in my mind and break my heart. I despair about our being estranged and fear that you'll always see my tough love behavior as a betrayal and abandonment of you. If only you knew, my dear boy, how much I love you and how I daily despair when I see you wasting your life away and giving in to your disease of alcoholism. Oh, how I hate your disease!

January 2018

My Dearest Son,

Here I am again, in the middle of the night, unable to sleep. This letter—like all my other letters—will probably never be read by you (to whom it is addressed), but it gives me a little solace to keep writing to you.

Funny how so many things trigger me to think of you and remember happier times. I was listening to a music show that I like—"Austin City Limits"—and the Neville Brothers from New Orleans were the musical guests. The show reminded me how we both love that kind of blues.

Remember when we went to see the great B. B. King many years ago? You were in your twenties, staying with me for a while and studying for the bar exam. I bought tickets for the show because I liked B. B. King, and I knew that you loved guitar music (you always had an old guitar with you that you kept playing). You and I went to the concert, and it was such a wonderful, unforgettable evening. We always had a musical connection, and you would often remark on that.

I was slow dancing in place during the show, and you looked at me and laughed and said, "Mom, I knew that you were a pretty good dancer, but I didn't know that you could groove so well. You really feel this music, don't you?" (As I am writing this and remembering your laughing face, tears are flowing from my eyes.)

Another day, another memory. I went to the Greek church on Sunday for services. As I was reciting a prayer with the rest of the congregation, a thought flashed through my head. It was so clear, I thought you were standing next to me. I have heard you say, more than once through the years, "Mom, you really do pray louder than anybody else in church!" I knew you didn't mean the remark as an insult—you were smiling as you said it—and I laughed with you. As the memory came, my voice faltered with emotion. I had to stop reciting the prayer because I was crying again, thinking of our current wounded relationship.

Unlike your father, my ex-husband, you were never critical with me. I always loved that about you, because criticism was a very sore point in my marriage. I had figured out from personal experience how criticism can affect relationships in a very negative way, even before I was in my School of Social Work graduate classes.

You were such a sweet son, except for the last few years, when substance abuse and addiction altered your behavior. I took such joy in your company. Unlike your brothers, you were not a cuddly baby or a particularly affectionate young child, but there was a big role reversal when you grew up, and you became my most affectionate son. What a special child you were! Your teachers and Boy Scout leaders all praised you as the perfect student—attentive, curious, and a noncomplainer. The only flaw they would mention was that you talked too much during class. (They used to say the same thing about your brothers.) The truth is that I also would get in trouble when I was young for the same offense. I guess you all inherited my trait!

I miss the old Jamie so much. This may sound crazy, but I wish I had recorded you in the past so your words would give me some comfort during the present difficult days of our estrangement.

I remember vividly how you apologized profusely a few years after my divorce from your father. "I am so sorry, Mom, that I rarely visited you early on," you said. (You were in college at the time.) "I feel so guilty now that I listened to Dad and stayed away. He told us kids that we needed to stay away from you so you would feel lonely and miss us and that would make you come back home to marriage and family life. How foolish I was—we all were—to believe him. Can you ever forgive me?"

I hugged you and told you that I understood and there was nothing to forgive. What I did not say then or ever was that I cried myself to sleep for months and months after I separated from your father because none of you boys would come over to see me much. (I had moved to an apartment because your father refused to leave our house, and I was tired of his shenanigans.) I had no idea, of course, of his strategy and how he brainwashed you with his lie.

Well, his selfish strategy backfired on him. What he didn't realize was, that despite the emotional pain of separation and divorce, that the more obstacles he placed in my way, the more determined I became to cut the tie and stay away. He underestimated my emotional strength and resolute determination big time. After twenty-four years of marriage, he really did not know me after all.

The divorce was a long time ago, but it's still hard to forgive my ex-husband for trying to keep my boys away from me.

February 3, 2018

My Dearest Son,

It's 1:30 a.m. and I can't sleep. As always, you are on my mind. No matter what I do or where I am, I think of you and wonder where you are and what you are doing. Even when I am watching a movie on television, there is a constant background tape running in my head and it's all about you. I used to have endless, imaginary debates with you about your addiction and situation—trying to convince you to get some help and stop drinking/drugging before it kills you.

At Al-Anon they would probably say that this compulsive habit of mine proved that I was addicted to you, just as much as you are addicted to chemical substances. So, nowadays, I try to refrain some from these constant head trips and one-sided debates.

Now I am writing letters to you instead, letters that you will probably never see or read. Is the behavior better or worse regarding my own recovery from codependency? I don't know the answer to that question. All I know is that I have to communicate with you somehow, even if it is only on paper. The important truth here is that these letters bring me a little emotional comfort, enough that I can have a tiny bit of peace in my troubled soul and I can and eventually go back to sleep.

You never responded to the letter I sent over during Christmas when you were still in jail. I'm not even sure that you received it, even though Victoria says that she obtained the right address of the correctional facility from the legal website.

In addition to the letter, I also texted you twice, after you were presumed to be out of jail. I did not receive a response to any of my communication initiatives. My sponsor tells me to stop these endless texts because all I get is disappointment and despair when you don't answer.

According to my legal source (Victoria again), you are supposed to be "on parole" and have to go to classes. I presume these are the "antidrinking" classes that you hate and that you mentioned a couple of months ago in one of your rare texts. You also—as terms of the parole—have to undergo drug tests to show that you are not using. There is also a big fine to be paid by June.

Are you doing all that and saving money for the fine? I surely hope so, but forgive me when I say that I have my doubts that make me agonize about your present and future. I wish I could give you some emotional support about all this. How can I do that though, since you are not even calling me or texting me? I assume this is your idea of punishing me, or at least showing that you are still angry with me about not giving you bail money, like you wanted me to do. I couldn't do that, Jamie. How I wish that you could understand that my behavior was an act of love. True love—not enabling love—that in the long run causes more harm than good.

Do you really think that it was easy for me to deny you bail? My heart ached for you. The idea that you were to spend Christmas in jail was a horrible thought for me. At the same time, I know that I cannot support your disease (alcoholism) by rescuing you from its consequences like jail. That would go against everything I believe in as a therapist and as an Al-Anon member. Yet, it kills me inside every time I have to say no to your financial demands.

Maybe one day a miracle will happen, and you will understand the reasons behind my actions. What keeps me going during these days of anxiety and despair is the hope that one day a light will flare in your head—despite the fogginess brought on by excess alcohol and drugs—and that you will move toward sobriety and recovery. Then, only then, you will get to the truth, that I never stopped loving you and never will, no matter what!

February 12, 2018

My Dearest Son,

As I watch an Astros game (I don't know if you remember this, but the Astros are Houston's professional baseball team), I am remembering all the hundreds of Little League baseball games that I attended through the years when you and your brothers were kids.

You were an excellent student and a very musically oriented child (you would practice for hours on the clarinet and later saxophone and were in a marching band in middle school and high school), but not very good at sports. From a young age, you learned to play baseball like your older brother, Spiros (who excelled at the sport), but, unfortunately, to your father's despair, your skills did not match your desire.

You tried and tried, but your balls went mostly out of bounds and you couldn't score. It was painful for me to watch you play, especially because you kept being compared to Spiros, who was a skilled pitcher, even at a young age.

One summer, coaches placed you on the same Little League team as your brother, even though you were seventeen months younger, and I cringed when I found out. I guessed that it would be a hard summer for both of us. It was so painful for me to watch you miss ball after ball and look so small and miserable on the mound. Incredibly, one evening you hit a home run. I couldn't believe it and neither could your dad. We jumped up and down with glee and applauded you until our hands hurt. I was so happy that you had that one moment! It never happened again, but we kept hoping.

Another memory about baseball came to mind tonight, but that was not a happy one. It was the end of the season, and your (and Spiros's) team was in the playoffs. Your brother was very excited because he was the starting pitcher for the team. My fear was that you would stay on the bench during the game as one of the relief players. What happened next always gets me tearful, even now, many years later. I didn't see the drama that happened behind the scenes, but your father, who was the assistant coach of the team, told me what transpired. It seems that Spiros, being, I presume, nervous about that day's important game, had spilled a cup of lemonade all over his baseball uniform, right before the game started and was too embarrassed to play in a wet uniform. Your father who was sitting next to him giving him last-minute advice (like he was prone to do), immediately sprang into action. He called you to his side and asked if you would do Spiros and the team a big favor. Would you exchange uniforms (you were close in size to your brother) so he could pitch in your clean uniform?

You, always the dutiful son, immediately complied and put on Spiros's wet uniform and sat on the bench. What your father was of course implying in his request was that he knew you were not likely to play in the playoff game and so did not need a clean uniform. You sat, stone faced, on the bench the whole game and never got on the field.

Despite your important sacrificing act, your team lost that playoff game. When I found out later what had happened behind the scenes that day, I was stunned. I was also speechless. I ran to the car, crying, furious at your father for what he asked you to do and seriously thought—not for the first time—that I needed to divorce such an insensitive man! (I did divorce him, ten years later.) I was so miserable for you and so angry with your dad, that I couldn't even talk with you about the incident at the time. I didn't even have the emotional strength to comfort you.

I tried to approach you the next day to talk about what had happened, but you brushed me off and told me that you didn't want to talk about the incident. "It was no big deal, Mom," you said, but I noticed that your eyes got misty. It was always hard for you to talk about your feelings. I hugged you as much as you would let me and tried to hide my own tears.

February 24, 2018

My Dearest Son,

As I watch the Winter Olympics, I fantasize that you are watching them as well, and I hope you are in a warm and nice place. I know that you like cross-country skiing. You told me more than once how you loved the snow during winters in Michigan, while attending law school there. I know that you went on cross-country ski trips whenever you had the chance. I realize as I'm writing this that my vision of you watching the Olympics in a nice warm place is indeed a fantasy, not based on truth. How can you? As far as I know, you and your wife live somewhere on the streets of Los Angeles, if you can call that living.

In my fantasy vision, you are sitting or half-reclining on a couch in your old home (the one that was repossessed about two years ago), and you have just come back from a dip in your swimming pool. After all, you used to take numerous dips throughout the day year-round, whenever I visited you in LA. In my fantasy, you would watch the games on and off and brag about the bench in the middle of your backyard that you kept painting and repainting. Leslie used to tease you about the bench, telling me how you found it discarded on somebody's sidewalk. "It is a perfectly good bench," you would retort in an indignant tone of voice, "I don't know why they would throw it away!"

It was too heavy for you to lift, so you came back to the house and picked up your boys so they could help you move it to the house. You painted the bench multiple times so as to give it an antique look, you said. Leslie said that it was more like a street look, and you glared at her. How ironic that you and she would be on the streets yourselves a short while later! I told you that day that I liked what you did with the bench and that indeed it had a vintage look to it after you painted it dark green. I am crying as I am writing this. I dearly loved your house and my visits there. In my view, your house perfectly matched its surroundings and the very pleasant California weather—(such a relief from the heat and humidity of Houston). Summers visiting you and your family there were definitely a highlight of my life! I especially liked your backyard and your tall trees. Nothing fancy, but that was part of its charm. When I semiclosed my eyes and used a little imagination, your trees reminded me of Mediterranean views and my travels to the Tuscany region of Italy.

I told you about all that and asked you to make a promise of never cutting the trees down. You looked at me with a big smile on your face and said, "OK, Mom, I promise I'm never going to mess with them or cut them down!"

February 28, 2018

My Dearest Son,

It's late at night, 2 a.m. to be exact, and once again, I am not able to fall asleep. As I lay in bed, tossing and turning, I had a flash of a memory from the past, and I had to get up to write it down so as not to forget it. It is a few days before my birthday, and our whole family is in the car. You are about six or seven years old. You and your older brother have been shopping in the mall for my birthday while I babysit your brother, Constantine, a toddler at the time. You seem really excited after the shopping trip. You can hardly contain your enthusiasm, a demeanor that is not typical for you, a rather calm and even-tempered child.

"Mom, you will really like what we bought for you," you are practically shouting, "especially my present. It has a lot of pockets and holds stuff, and you can really use it when you are sewing or decorating things with holes" (you meant needlepoint). Your father frowns and says, "Jamie, you just spoiled your mother's birthday surprise. Don't say another word!"

I immediately turn around from the front seat and look at you, sitting in the back of the car. Your big, expressive soft brown eyes are brimming with tears and you look crestfallen. I feel so bad for you! Trying to undo some of the damage of your dad's scolding, I quickly say, "It's OK, honey, don't worry. I have no idea what you bought me, and I'm sure I'll love it, whatever it is!"

Hearing my words, your face takes a more hopeful expression, but I can tell that you are still on the verge of tears. My heart aches for you. Spiros pipes in, "Boy, oh, boy, you're such a baby, Jamie, you don't know how to keep a secret!" I look at him sternly and tell him to be quiet and to stop teasing you (a frequent occurrence).

I also glare at my husband, despairing about his lack of sensitivity. I try to bring to mind all the nice things he does for you and your brothers and to remind myself so as not to stay angry with him (another frequent occurrence) that he does love you all.

I have to be fair and acknowledge the nights that he willingly massaged your legs for a long time. Do you remember the painful leg cramps that you had as a child and how you would cry about them? Your pediatrician kept saying they were not serious and were just "growing pains," but you often suffered from them, and you welcomed your father's massages.

As for the sewing basket that you chose for me for my birthday, I kept it for many years—even though I rarely sewed. It always reminded me of your love for me.

March 8, 2018

My Dearest Son,

It's the middle of the night again. A disturbing dream—more like a nightmare—woke me up. I don't remember the exact details of the dream, but I know that it involved your health. One image that kept coming up was that of your hands. They looked weird. The origin of the dream was probably the memory of the last time I looked at your hands; they startled me. They looked very rough and dark red in color, almost purple. They did not look like normal hands. I remember telling you then that you needed to show your hands to a doctor. "Don't worry about my hands, Mom," you said. "It's nothing bad. They are just very sensitive and get red in the cold!" (At the time of this exchange, we were in Los Angeles, and the weather was a balmy 60 degrees!) When I came back to Houston, the image of your hands stayed with me. I googled the color and condition and all sorts of worrisome physical conditions popped up as a possible reason for the texture and color.

I told my sponsor about my bad dream and the flashback of your red-purple hands. I started crying at the coffeeshop when we met for an Al-Anon meeting. "I don't know how other parents live with this kind of pain and constant worry," I said. "Here I am, a retired psychotherapist of forty years, and I should know how to cope with this emotional pain; however, when it comes to my child, I know zilch! I feel as helpless and despairing as any other parent of an addict!"

Everything I do lately, even the simplest everyday things, seem to have a deeper darker meaning, a double layer so to speak. For example, I was taking a shower just a little while ago and my thoughts went to you as they often do. I wondered, since you live in a tent (Leslie called it "camping out"), how do you two take showers? I was immediately flooded with sadness. Your whole existence seems so grim and joyless to me. Maybe it doesn't seem that way to you, but how can it not? This lifestyle is your "normal" now, and I still have a hard time believing that my lawyer son lives on the streets. If nothing else, I'm sure that you miss your house and the swimming pool that you used to take dips in all day long!

Jamie, when I think of how your law license was taken away, I feel like crying. I know how important it was to you and how proud you were of being a lawyer. When one's mind is foggy with an excess of alcohol and other drugs, does all this not matter so much? I wonder about that. My sponsor keeps wanting me to attend some AA meetings so I can understand your present situation a little better, but I cannot bring myself to go. Maybe one day?

Sending you love as usual and prayers for your safety and health!

March 9, 2018

My Dearest Son,

I have a message from you on my cell phone from September 2017. I am afraid to delete it because I don't know if you will ever call me again. You have been angry with me for a while now, ever since I told you that I wouldn't pay for your bail. You said, "I'm only asking for $500, Mom."

"I can't believe that you will let me go to jail. You used to say that you loved me. If you really loved me, surely you wouldn't let me go to jail. You told Leslie that you see me as a worthless alcoholic drunk and that I deserved to go to jail."

I tried to protest. I told you that I never placed negative labels on you and did not tell your wife what you said that I did. I admitted to you that I did say that you had a terrible disease and that it drove your life out of control. I did add that all this had nothing to do with character or the worth of a person. You were not listening. You kept ranting and repeating the same accusations over and over again.

I finally was crying so hard and my heart was racing so wildly that I hung up the phone on you. I refused to answer the ten or so times that you kept on calling. I also heard on voicemail numerous calls from bondsmen to whom you must have given my phone number. That's when I disconnected all the phones and they stayed disconnected for weeks.

Victoria, your niece who is a lawyer, as you know, told me that she looked at the online information for Ventura County Courthouse and found out that you are supposed to be on parole now. The official offense listed was "public intoxication and missing a court hearing."

Are you keeping the rules of the parole? No drinking and going to AA meetings?

There is also a late fee fine that needs to be paid by June fifteenth or (I'm afraid) you'll end up in jail again. How are you going to pay this fine, I wonder, without any visible means of support and no law license to boot? The sad truth is that you are probably not in any condition to practice law, even if you still have your license.

I wonder about all of the above, and I constantly worry about you. I guess I'm not following the Al-Anon detachment theory very well right now!

March 12, 2018

My Dearest Son,

I talked with an old friend today. We used to both attend the YMCA water aerobics class for many years, but I had not seen her for a while because my knee problems and the recent surgery kept me out of the class for the last few months. She called to tell me that her son died two weeks ago. I was sad to hear her bad news, and I felt sorry for her.

"Was he the one with the alcohol problems?" I asked. She answered with a yes but then added that he had recently stopped drinking but died from throat cancer.

By the time I hung up the phone, I was in tears myself. Her phone call stirred up strong feelings in me. Of course, I felt bad about her loss, and at the same time, a great sense of fear took hold of me as to what your future might be. Usually, I push these kinds of fear deep down, and I try to stay in the present, as much as I can. Since only God knows what the future may hold, I tell myself not to leap into scary scenarios and to take one day at a time. I tell myself that, but then I hear something like what happened to my friend's son, and my fears jump right up front and center. I find it hard to hold them back.

What helps me some during those difficult times is going to an Al-Anon meeting or trying to focus on happier times and happier memories. I think of your graduation day from law school and how happy and proud you seemed on that day. You introduced me to your girlfriend, who was also in your school and told me that she had one more year to go before her graduation. You two looked at each other with affection on your faces and I rejoiced. You looked so handsome in your graduation gown. I have a small framed picture from that day that I treasure. The two of us are sitting on the grass, in the pretty lawn of your school, with your arms around my shoulders, and we are both smiling. How I wished that day that your grandmother could have been alive to see you graduate from law school! You were her favorite grandchild, and she adored you. She often told me you were smart enough to become president one day.

Somebody during a meeting told me once after I spoke up about my distress about your addiction situation that "the disease sure seems to grab the brightest ones!" The statement seemed true enough, even without the specific statistics. The sad truth about all this is that I know as an experienced therapist that after many years of substance abuse, that the brain cells—like those of the liver and other organs of the body—start dying, and the natural intelligence of a person who is an addict of those substances fades and disappears. The slang term *junkie* then becomes a reality.

What a terrible waste of life and its infinite possibilities! What a terrible waste of my own son's intelligence and talents!

I feel so sad as I'm writing this.

PART II
THE YEAR OF
ENDLESS, UNFATHOMABLE GRIEF

Letters of March 15, 2018, through March 18, 2019

March 15, 2018

My Dearest Son,

Now I know for sure that you are never going to see these letters that I'm writing to you. My darling boy, you died two days ago on March thirteenth, two weeks before your fifty-eighth birthday.

To the very end I clung to the hope that you were going to get professional help and finally stop drinking and drugging. I was wrong. The addiction won and we who love you lost you. I am eighty-four years old. No parents should outlive their children. I should have died instead of you.

"Heart failure," they said. "Alcohol and drugs," I said.

I spent the last three days at Spiros and Olga's house. They insisted that I stay with them for a while, not wanting to leave me alone in my townhouse. At first, I refused, but then I gave in, realizing that they were wiser than I at this very emotional time in my life. I know that right now I don't have the energy to take care of myself or Skye, my little dog. The only positive aspect of these three terrible days has been the long talks I've had with your younger son, Nicholas, who has been living with them for the past two years.

You know how Nicholas is. He is usually quiet and very private. He keeps his feelings locked in ordinarily, but he is hurting right now. He came to me while I was sitting alone on Spiros's patio, crying. He showed me a picture of the two of you and shared with me a memory about his childhood. He told me how you used to put him to sleep when he was little by playing and singing George Strait country songs, instead of lullabies, on your guitar. We shared memories of you, back and forth, and cried together for some time. We even laughed a little, thinking of how you used to love to imitate Peter Sellers playing an incompetent French police inspector in the Pink Panther movies.

The truth is that I am so angry with everybody for not saving you. At my more rational moments, I am mostly angry with your disease of alcoholism, but there are not too many rational moments right now. I am angry with myself, as well, for not having been able to save you from destruction and the iron grip that your terrible disease had on you.

I also blame myself for not sending you bail money, even though I still know in my head that it would have been enabling you to avoid facing the consequences of your addiction. You see, I kept hoping that eventually you were going to reach bottom (in Al-Anon terms) and turn your life around. To my dismay, not even jail proved to be your bottom.

Now that you're gone from me, the same agonizing thought keeps occurring: if I had known that you had advanced cirrhosis of the liver (as the autopsy showed), would I have sent you bail money? Honestly, I don't know, but the thought of your being in constant pain tortures me. What kind of mother would willingly let her child suffer in jail?

March 16, 2018

My Dearest Son,

I am back home, alone in my desperation. I went to an Al-Anon meeting today, and it was somewhat comforting. My sponsor came to my house, picked me up, and took me to the meeting. She told me that she didn't think that I had enough emotional and physical energy right now to do it on my own. She was right.

Quite a few members came to my side afterwards, after they heard the sad news of your passing. Some knew me from previous meetings;

some did not. They told me words of sympathy and some gave me hugs. I couldn't concentrate on their words. They kind of washed over me, but I did appreciate the hugs.

I am sorry you never got to the point of experiencing the fellowship of AA and Al-Anon people. They really understand the pain of addiction. Many of them have had similar journeys of grief in their lives, past or present.

Olga came over later in the day to bring me some food. She didn't say this, but I'm guessing she was also checking on me to see how I was doing. She also told me some news. Robert is coming to town next week from San Francisco. Spiros and Olga sent an airplane ticket to your older son, thinking that it would be a comfort to your two sons to grieve the loss of their father together. I appreciated the gesture, as I'm sure you do also. It seems that the boys are also worried about their mother, thinking that she may die as well.

Forgive me for this, Jamie, but I refuse to worry about your wife right now. Frankly, I'm too busy trying to heal the awful pain in my heart about losing you. I don't tell your boys this, but the truth is I'm too angry with her right now. I hung up on her a few days ago when she called me after your death, because she was ranting on and on, spouting clichés and platitudes. All I could think of was how she had refused two years ago to have you committed after the intervention and did not even join Olga and me when we were urging you to get professional help. Without her aid and participation, we had no leverage and no way to help you.

I know this is not rational, but I'm angry with the whole world right now (at least, my world) and blame everybody for not saving you, including the American justice system, which jails addicts instead of rehabilitating them. The only entity that I'm not blaming right now (and this will surprise some people) is God. My idea of God is that of a merciful being, and I deeply believe that you were taken by God because you were suffering an awful lot with no apparent hope of redemption.

They are cremating your body in California, probably today, maybe as I'm writing this. Spiros asked me tentatively if I wanted to travel to Los Angeles before the event. I told him that I had no desire to see your lifeless body, that I couldn't bear it. I truly believe that your soul (i.e., your spirit) has already left your body and flown away to some other place or alternate reality that we don't know anything about. Hopefully, it's a nice place, my son.

A part of me (a small part) is relieved that you no longer have to suffer from your addiction and its consequences. No more cirrhosis of the liver or broken shoulder or severe hip pain, let alone financial and legal worries. It must have been so awful for you to be homeless on the streets of LA and to lose your law license, which was such a big part of your identity.

I know you, my child; at least I used to know you. You were always a person with *philotimia* (pride), as my fellow Greeks would say. Proud of your Greek-American identity, proud of being a Californian, proud of being a lawyer, and especially proud of being a dad.

Well, you are no longer homeless or a hopeless alcoholic. So sorry that your life had to end this way!

March 17, 2018

My Dearest Son,

I still can't believe that you are gone. At times, it still feels like a nightmare and that when I wake up your death will only be a bad dream. Then I realize, one more time, that it is final and very real. That's when the anguish starts again, and I burst into tears. As I'm writing this letter an old Greek song keeps running through my mind—*"Me Piasane ta Klamata!"* ("Crying Has Gotten Hold of Me"). That is how it feels—like the crying will never stop. I keep having flashbacks of you before the alcohol and drug era that changed your personality so drastically.

One of your all-time favorite movies was *On the Waterfront,* a 1954 classic that won lots of awards during its time. (The movie is significant to me as well, partly because it was directed by Elia Kazan, a Greek from Turkey like me.) There is a scene near the end of the movie, when the emotionally broken protagonist—played by Marlon Brando—shouts, "I could have been a contender!" You loved to play that scene from the movie over and over again and to repeat the phrase while imitating Brando's voice. I can still see you in my mind, hear your enthusiastic emphases on the words, and then enjoy your unique booming laugh.

You know, honey, that particular movie phrase could sum up your life, as well. Did you have a premonition—I wonder—and is that why you loved it so? If it weren't for your addiction, you could certainly have been a contender for a successful career and life. The potential was there.

Olga told me something yesterday that she found out from talking with Leslie. Despite all your financial struggles of the last two to three years (that I know of) and your losing your home and ending on the streets, you never sold the valuable Greek icon that I gave you. It had belonged to your grandmother Anastasia, the one who loved you so much. When I gave you the icon, I told you that it was very old, authenticated to be from the sixteenth century, and valuable. I asked you to guard it well and not ever to sell it. And you did and kept your promise.

I cried when Olga told me about that. What that tells me is that there was still some glimmer of honor and family loyalty left in you, despite the ravages of the disease of alcoholism. Amazingly, you didn't sell the icon or pawn it, even when you were desperately seeking bail money so as not to go to jail while awaiting trial.

Thank you, my dear son.

All my love,
Mom

March 18, 2018

My Dearest Son,

Everything reminds me of you. I just saw a TV show character riding a motorcycle, and I started crying. I do that a lot lately. My tears are very close to the surface.

I remembered how much you loved your motorcycle. You bought it right away, after law school, when you moved to LA for your first job at a big law firm. How you loved living in California! You told me that, with a semiapologetic smile, knowing that I would have preferred for you to find a job in Texas so as not to be so far away from me. I did not reproach you for your choice because I quickly saw how you fell in love with California living. You kept telling me about the wonderful weather and being outdoors a lot and how you loved to whiz around in heavy freeway traffic with your motorcycle.

Some years later, our whole family came to LA for your wedding, even Constantine's new baby, Stacy. I marveled that you and your bride chose to get married in a beautiful old Greek church. I was touched by the familiar liturgy, and, of course, I cried. Those were tears of joy. You even gave me a special ring with semiprecious birthstones of you and your brothers. I cried one more time.

A few months later, tragedy struck your idyllic surroundings. A big earthquake hit LA, and you were one of many who felt its consequences. When U.S. Highway 101 cracked in some spots, you were on your beloved motorcycle and flew over a car (you told me all this later). If it weren't for your new helmet that you hated wearing (a gift from your bride), you would have died right then and there or been paralyzed for life. The doctors at the ER told you that you were very lucky to be alive. You broke your hip in several places and had multiple other fractures, but that was small stuff compared with what could have happened.

Later, you confided to me on the phone that you had been really scared when you couldn't get up after the fall and even more scared when you couldn't lift your right hand to make the sign of the Greek cross. You added that you then asked for Grandmother Anastasia's protection from heaven, and you were convinced that she heard you and helped you because you were then able to slightly move.

I was frantic with worry, hearing all this. Spiros called me to tell me about the accident, adding that you were alive and that I shouldn't panic. All my instincts told me to immediately get on a plane and fly to your side, but my whole family, including your wife, told me not to do it. They told me that the aftereffects of an earthquake would make it dangerous for me. I listened to everybody and did not come to see you and or take care of you. Now, looking back, I deeply regret my action. I wish I had come!

You had to have complete rest for a month after the accident, and they told you in the future you would have to undergo more hip surgeries. Your wife couldn't take time from work, but a close friend from law school and his wife stepped in and took you to their home to take care of you. I have always been very grateful to them for what they did. You were again lucky to have such good friends (that same friend is now holding your ashes until Robert and Nicholas can go pick them up).

Listen to this, honey: your younger son already has plans for some of these ashes. He wants to save them until he goes to a football game at the University of Michigan—your beloved law school alma mater—and distribute them there in your memory. Nicholas loves you very much and is quite distraught about your untimely death, so I didn't want to burst his balloon and talk about the legality or particulars of his plan.

Don't you love it? He is his father's boy, that one!

As he was telling me about his plans, I remembered one of the last phone conversations that I had with you before you got angry with me and stopped communicating. I told you then of an episode about Nicholas from his early days in Houston. He was staying with me for a week while Spiros and Olga were out of town. One day, he volunteered to clean my car. After working on it for quite a while (I admit, the car badly needed cleaning), he said, "I never knew anybody to disrespect a car like you, Mema." I got a little defensive by what he said, so I immediately replied, "Only people can get disrespected, not cars!" (Later, I went to him and told him that he was right about the car being messy and that I appreciated his efforts.)

You laughed in your hearty, big way and said, "That sounds like something Nicholas would say." I joined you in the laughter, happy that I could still make you laugh, even in your desolate situation. I remember thinking, "He must really miss his boys!"

A vivid memory came to my mind. I had said to you during my attempt at an intervention, "Jamie, the way things are going, I'm afraid you are not going to live long enough to see your future grandchildren." (It was a rather mean thing to say, but my excuse is that I was trying desperately to break your denial about your disease.) Your response to my confronting statement was to shrug your shoulders and say, "Forget the grandchildren, Mother. I would just love to see my two children and hug them!"

I swallowed my tears and walked away. Later, in the intervention, you told me that you knew you drank too much (those were your exact words), and you promised me that you would get professional help.

I looked at you as you said those words and felt a stirring of hope, even though my head was saying something different: "Froso, you know he's not going to do it. He's lying so as to get you off his back. Addicts lie all the time. Remember? It's part of the disease."

My heart was trying to fight back, telling myself that maybe you meant what you said. After all, some addicts do get sober and recover, though not many. What I really wanted to do that day, more than anything, was to take you by the hand and lock you up somewhere until you recovered from your addiction and came back to your senses. Of course, I couldn't do that. How I wished that I could!

As I was reading my intervention incidents, trying (as I had learned many years ago in my profession) not to be angry or judgmental, my voice quivered once or twice, but I thought I was doing a pretty decent job in piercing your denial and defenses, until you interrupted me. "I know you mean well, Mom, but it's not alcohol or other drugs that caused our unfortunate situation, made us lose our home, and end up in this motel. It was some bad breaks and bad luck, that's all." I was incredulous! I could not believe what I had just heard. I kept on reading, but my heart sank pretty low and I felt despair. I knew then that I had lost the battle against your addiction. You just refused to believe that alcohol and drugs were ruining your life. That's when I told you in desperation that alcohol was killing your brain cells as well as your other organs. For the first time, that day, you got visibly angry with me. I must have hit a vulnerable nerve.

"There is nothing wrong with my brain cells, Mother," you shouted. "I don't want to hear you say that again. I am still a damn good lawyer, probably the best lawyer in LA!" I did not respond to your statement. I didn't think that it would help my mission to antagonize you any further.

After the intervention, as we were sitting on the patio of the motel, a woman walked by and you introduced me to her by saying, "This is my mom. She came all the way from Houston to see me!" I thought I heard some love and even pride in your voice, and it warmed my numb, wounded heart some. I thought, "Despite everything I told him today, he still loves me!"

March 19, 2018

My Dearest Son,

I am having strange conversations with you in my head. I keep asking you during my crying bouts for a sign that you are OK and still around, albeit in another reality, but I don't see any signs. Later this afternoon, after a morning spent mostly crying, I tried to watch some of my old recordings of favorite TV shows in a desperate attempt to get distracted from my terrible grief over losing you.

A part of me realizes that you were in a lot of physical and emotional pain. You told me numerous times of pain in your hips and of severe anxiety attacks. You didn't mention this, but I'm sure that you were superdepressed, especially about living in a tent on the streets of LA. I know and truly believe that now you are at peace and no longer suffering. However, what my head tells me is small comfort for my aching heart.

Anyway, as I was watching television and trying hard to concentrate on the plots of the shows—plots that seemed to my current state of mind nonsensical—I heard your name mentioned twice, in two different shows by two different characters. I gasped. Even though your first name is not rare, it's not that common either. OK, I thought to myself, maybe that's the sign that I have been looking for! It must have helped some, because afterwards, I was able to go to sleep for a few hours. Truth is, Jamie, sleep eludes me on most nights, and I lie awake for a long time, just tossing and turning, thinking of you and crying.

Tell me what to do, my son. Please tell me how to manage and live with this massive pain that tears up my insides. Will it be like this until I die?

March 20, 2018

My Dearest Son,

I tried reading tonight (you know how much I love to read), but I couldn't concentrate. That's a common occurrence nowadays. To my surprise, I discovered that reading poems brings some solace to my acute grief, and once in a while, I can still tolerate music (another activity that I used to love).

So I turned the TV on to one of my many recordings of *Austin City Limits*. It's an iconic musical show from Austin, Texas, that features diverse artists, mostly alternative musicians. I immediately thought of you and how much you loved music, all kinds of music. When you were young and still at home, the Beatles and rock music were your favorites. Nicholas told me that you used to sing country music songs to him when he was little. Obviously, at different phases of your life you liked different kinds of music.

I still remember all the times your dad and I looked for you and followed you as you marched with your high school band, playing the clarinet and the saxophone, all over Houston. You seemed at the time to really enjoy doing that. You always excelled in music, no doubt about that. Many a time you asked me to take you to music stores after school, so as to shop for new reeds for your instruments and also to look through their collections of vinyl records and CDs. There were times when I had to drag you out of the stores so I could go home and cook dinner.

When you and Leslie were newlyweds and I came to visit you in your new apartment in LA, you and Leslie surprised me by having planned a trip for the three of us to Mexico. The only thing that you bought on that trip was an old guitar that you saw in the windows of a store. It didn't look that great to my eyes, but you instantly fell in love with it and had to have it. Later, I saw you playing that guitar for hours, teaching yourself how to play. You loved that guitar and played it for many years. When I mentioned the trip and described the guitar to Nicholas, he told me that he remembered it well and often saw you playing it throughout his childhood.

I started crying again when I thought of our trip to that border town in Mexico. How carefree we were, how happy you seemed. I loved it that you had planned that trip as a surprise to me, knowing how much I loved traveling, especially by train. We reminisced about our family trip to Mexico when you were twelve. I had proudly paid for that trip from my first year's income as psychiatric social worker at Hermann Hospital (a hospital in Houston with a big psychiatric department at that time). I had been a housewife until I attended graduate school and then went to work for the first time in my life at age fifty. I was determined to take the family on a big and unique trip, so we went by train from Houston to Mexico City (not easy to do, then or even now). I had always loved trains, so this was my project.

The kids were a little dubious about my plans, especially when we had a train wreck somewhere along the way and the dining car of the train went down a ravine in the middle of nowhere. We were not hurt by the wreck, but we did stay without food or water overnight until we were rescued the next day. As we watched the dining car sliding into oblivion, your brother Spiros turned to me and said, "Mom, why would you have planned this trip? I don't know of any other kids or families that take a train to Mexico! What about cars or planes? They exist, you know!"

We laughed, you and I, thinking about that adventurous but ill-fated trip of ours. You remembered it well and how we raided Constantine's crackers because we were all starving.

There was a funny incident during our trip to Mexico and I told Nicholas about it. Remember how I bought a bottle of Mexican raspberry liqueur and put it in my suitcase and how it broke during the trip and colored all my clothes, including my lingerie, a weird pink color? I laughed, in between my tears, as I remembered the incident, and Nicholas seemed to enjoy the story as well.

Thank you for that trip, honey, and for all the other times and happy visits when you always made me feel welcomed and loved! I'll always remember your big smile and booming voice, greeting me at the Los Angeles airport with the same words every time I arrived, "I'm so glad you're here, Mom. Thank you for coming."

March 20, 2018 (Late at night)

My Dearest Son,

I toss and turn in bed and keep thinking that you must have been in a precarious financial situation for some time before they foreclosed your house, but I had no clue. You made a big effort to hide your problems from me, and I fell for the deceit.

During my last visit to your home, I did notice that your house needed some urgent repairs, but I had no idea about the magnitude of the problem. One strange thing that I did see was that one of the bathrooms was locked, and I was told not to enter it. Leslie explained to me that it was cluttered and that the toilet was broken. I immediately offered to pay for the repairs, but my offer was refused in a very firm tone. I was baffled by the resolute refusal to get things fixed, but not wanting to start an argument, I let the matter go.

I still can't figure out what the deal was about that bathroom, but I view it now as a manifestation of the dysfunction and malaise of the family disease of alcoholism. My own denial at the time prevented me from seeing the truth.

I did get concerned when I would see you and Leslie awake around 2 a.m. or 3 a.m. watching television. This happened every night, and I told you my concerns. That's when you told me about your anxiety attacks. You even asked my professional opinion about having insomnia around 2 a.m. I tried to explain to you as gently as I could that alcohol could be a contributing factor to that occurrence. I had no idea at the time of how things were (I never saw you drunk) and did not have a clue about your past history of cocaine addiction. I made that remark about alcohol based on some empty wine bottles that I would see in the morning in your kitchen. I did not even figure out that your wife also might have had a problem. I thought that she was depressed. Period.

Here I was, a therapist and alcoholism counselor, and I missed all the signs! How ironic and sad that I helped dozens and dozens of clients through the years, and I couldn't save my own son. I know what Al-Anon and my sponsor would say. They would remind me of the three *C*'s, an important Al-Anon principle—"I didn't cause it, I can't control it, and I can't cure it!"[1]—but my bleeding heart stubbornly believed otherwise. I feel angry with myself for having failed you, and I feel guilty.

When we talked that night about your anxiety attacks, you told me that alcohol helped make them better. I explained to you how alcohol works. That it acts as a flimsy Band-Aid for anxiety and that the help is only temporary. The condition comes back after a few hours, and this time it is stronger. In the long run, it increases the anxiety attacks. And the cycle goes on and on.

You looked at me as I explained all this and you nodded, but I could tell from the look in your eyes that you didn't believe me or didn't want to believe me. I got a sinking gut feeling, but I tried hard not to take your disbelief personally. I knew that you loved me and that at different times and about different issues, you respected my ideas, even when we disagreed on the issues. Looking back, I realize your alcohol and drug addiction stood in the way, and that's why you did not want to believe what I was saying or even consider its truth. Oh, how you always loved to debate! We had endless discussions through the years about social issues and politics. You hated wearing a helmet while biking, but always agreed with me about social justice and civil rights. You were a committed Libertarian and defender of individual rights, but rejoiced with me when Barack Obama became president, telling me that Robert and Nicholas were shocked by those opposing him and did not understand about racial prejudice.

Even when you were a little kid, you would question everything and ask hundreds of questions. "Why, why, why," you would say over and over again, to your father's and my annoyance. That would be the only complaint that we would hear at parent-teacher conferences. "Your son is an excellent student and his behavior is exemplary, but he does ask a lot of questions during class," they would say, and we would secretly smile, knowing very well what they were complaining about. Your natural curiosity was a positive trait, but it drove us crazy sometimes!

We figured out from early on that you were probably going to be a lawyer and we were right. You were a National Merit Scholarship Program finalist and got lots of scholarship offers. We were surprised and rather dismayed that you turned down a full scholarship at Rice University, a prestigious college in Houston, and chose instead to go to Washington University in St. Louis. I think you must have wanted to get away from home, even though you never said that.

Your father and I were not surprised at all when you told us that you decided to go to law school. We had always assumed that you would end up a lawyer. You were so proud of being a lawyer! Despite all the silly jokes about lawyers, you always thought that it was an honorable profession.

It is rather significant that the only time that you reacted in an angry way while I was reading intervention incidents was when I mentioned the probable deterioration of your brain cells due to excess alcohol and other drugs. You then became visibly angry and yelled at me (a very rare occurrence).

You didn't know this then, and neither did I, that a few months later you were going to go to jail for a second DUI citation and violations of parole, and that would cost you the loss of that law license that you were so proud of.

I'm so sorry, honey, that your disease and addiction gave you so much heartache. You deserved a better life!

March 21, 2018

My Dearest Son,

I'm doing one of my compulsive behaviors again. I keep thinking about my past efforts to save you from your destructive path of addiction, and I keep wondering how I could have done things better. I know, in my rational mind, that it doesn't matter anymore. You are gone and nothing can bring you back, but I can't help thinking, "What if?"

What if I done this? What if I had done that? I know it's foolish of me to keep playing this tape in my head, and yet I keep doing it.

I had spent countless hours on the phone in Houston, before the last fateful trip to LA, calling all the mental health services and resources that I could locate so as to get the right kind of information to give you and Leslie (my previous professional training and experience as a social worker were useful here). I found out that there was help available in Ventura County, California—where you lived—but you had to go ask for it. We (Olga and I) told Leslie that we couldn't do it for you two. You had to do it yourself; it was required. I gave Leslie a list with specific addresses and phone numbers. She took the list and placed it in her purse, without even looking at it. At that point I realized that she was not going to follow through on any of that information, any more than you were going to. That's when I lost even the small hope that things were going to change for the better.

Later, when we were alone with Leslie, she told us that you were verbally abusive to her when drunk and that you even threatened a few times to kill yourself! Hearing that, I got even more scared than before and immediately told her that she needed to commit you to a hospital, at least for seventy-two hours (the legal limit at the time). That could be the way for you to get help and treatment, I said, and Olga backed me up.

Leslie's reply was that she couldn't do that—you would not like it and would turn against her. I practically begged her to think about it, stressing that it would help both of you in the long run. I said all that but deep down, my heart sank one more time. I could tell from the expression on her face that no action would be taken.

When we brought Leslie back to the motel after lunch (you had refused to come, saying you wanted to watch the Michigan football game), I tried one more time to convince you to get professional help. I said, "Please come to Houston. The whole family will support you and pay for your expenses." I mentioned that I had talked to many rehabilitation centers in Houston and found two places that had openings.

You looked at me with a stern face and said, "I have to stay here in LA, Mother, and work. Remember, I have a wife and a dog to support" (by that time your two boys had left home). "Besides all that," you added, "I would never go to a rehab place. I'd rather go to jail!"

That's when I started crying. Your face softened a little, and you said, "Don't cry, Mom! I'll get help, but I have to do it my way. I have to tell

50

you, though, you are wrong about your conclusions. Alcohol did not cause this situation."

I didn't reply. I was too desolate. At that moment, things really felt hopeless. I could see and hear that your denial was too strong, and my efforts were for nothing. Unfortunately, that was very evident by now. That was one of the lowest points of my life, if not the lowest. I felt so defeated!

March 22, 2018

My Dearest Son,

I don't know how I can bear the pain of losing you. I am even angry with your late father, my ex-husband, that he died before you did and was thus spared the pain of losing a child. A friend told me that it was crazy to be angry with a dead person, but I don't care. He died, if you remember, two years ago from Alzheimer's disease. He must have had a dying man's premonition about you because when he asked to see me a couple of weeks before his death, one of the things he said to me was, "Don't let Jamie drop out of school."

I thought at that time that he was confused because of his illness. After all, you were a grown man, not in school anymore. Now, as I'm thinking back about his words, I do believe that he meant for me not to let you drop out of normal life. How I wish that I could have done what he asked me to do. It was soon after my last meeting with him that I found out that you had lost your home, were estranged from your boys, and were living in a cheap motel.

For many years after my divorce from your father, I was angry with him for the way he was treating you. You had been his favorite child—the obedient, rule-following good student. Always superorganized to the point of even alphabetizing your books. You became an Eagle Scout and a National Merit Scholar, two achievements that your dad deeply admired.

By the time you graduated from law school and moved to California, your dad and I had divorced and he had remarried. I remember that he and his new wife came to your wedding when you married Leslie a few years later. However, according to what you told me through the years, he never visited you after the event. He never saw any of your houses, and he only saw Robert and Nicholas twice in his life, when you brought them to Houston for visits early on. As a result of that, you and he had not spoken for many years.

Every time you complained about your dad and his seeming lack of interest in your adult life, I tried to explain to you from what I knew of his roots and his personality that your father believed in the old-fashioned notion that it was the children's duty to visit the parents, not the other way around. You never accepted that explanation or saw it as an excuse for his behavior. You pointed out that I came from the same roots, yet I visited you in LA many times through the years—often annually. "You grew up in the same place," you said, "part of the same community and its values. How come you acted differently and he didn't?" I told you that your dad and I had very different personalities and had different values and beliefs. I made an attempt at feeble humor and added, "That's probably why we divorced after twenty-four years of marriage!" You didn't laugh and you didn't seem swayed by my argument. You always seemed bitter and hurt by your father's actions.

A few months before your father died, I was in LA on one of my visits to your home. (I didn't know it at the time, but it would turn out to be my last visit to your house with your family intact and my grandchildren still there with you.) I told you at that time that your father did not have long to live. That's what your brothers had been telling me. I also told you that he was in a skilled nursing facility and that it would be important for you to visit him before he died. You balked, telling me again about your resentment about his lack of visitation through the years. You said, "We haven't even spoken on the phone for more than ten years. Why should I visit him?" I told you that I thought that if you didn't see him before he died, you would probably have regrets and guilt later on. "Please, Jamie," I said, "Go see him." You nodded your head and told me that you would think about it. You did come to Houston a couple of months afterward for a very short visit, and you did go see your dad. I was very glad that you did.

Later, after he died you called me to thank me for urging you to visit him. I was glad that I had and that you listened to my advice. I, too, went to see him before he died. I had to do some forgiving of my own prior to my visit. He had told your brother Constantine that he wanted to see me. Your brother and I went to the skilled nursing facility where he was staying. I was a little apprehensive about our meeting, but it turned out to be a positive—rather amazing—experience.

Even though your brother had prepared me some beforehand, it was still a shocking experience to see how your father looked. I hardly recognized him. He had a long white beard, and he looked very gaunt and fragile, much older than his actual age. There were quite a few tubes on his body, some sticking out from under the sheet covering him.

It was clear during our visit that your father knew exactly who I was. To my surprise, he seemed very happy to see me. His mind would wander from time to time (after all, he was suffering from Alzheimer's disease), but he responded to me both in English and Greek in a tone of voice that was quite affectionate. I was astonished to observe that all his postdivorce anger seemed to be gone, and he even called me "baby" a few times like he used to do during our courtship and early marriage. The whole visit was kind of shocking and eerie but in a positive way.

Your phone call, thanking me for urging you to visit your dad, reminded me of when you were younger—before alcoholism and addiction dug their claws into you—and how complimentary and affectionate you used to be. You often told me how I looked younger than my age. On one visit, you and Leslie told me that I looked like a Greek Sophia Loren. I laughed at that remark, but secretly I was vain enough to be pleased about your compliment. You would put your arms around me and tell me how nice I looked in my clothes, and I would bask in your admiration.

I miss your old self so much! After your passing, Nicholas told me something that I never knew. He told me that he remembered that when you used to argue with his mother, you often told her that you wished she had some of my better qualities. I was stunned! Not a good thing to tell a wife, Son. Many years of experience as a marriage therapist taught me that a husband should never compare his wife to his mother—at least not in a negative way. Bad strategy for marital peace and harmony. It's a wonder that Leslie was nice to me during my yearly visits!

Sending my love as always,

Mom

March 23, 2018

My Dearest Son,

We had a small prayer service for you today at the chapel of the Annunciation Greek Orthodox Cathedral where you used to go to Sunday School with your two brothers. Your sons came to the service. Robert came from San Francisco where he lives. Spiros sent him an airplane ticket, so he could come and be with Nicholas so that the two young brothers could grieve together and console each other some.

I held hands with Robert during the short but meaningful (at least to me) service and cried throughout it. I noticed that both Robert and Nicholas had tears in their eyes. I think you would have been fine with the service. I don't believe that you ever lost your faith, even though you did not attend services on a regular basis. That went by the wayside with the addiction—along with a lot of other things in your life.

A few times through the years, when I was in LA during Easter or other religious holidays, you offered to come with me to church, and we went to St. Sophia—one of the two Greek churches in LA. Every time we went, you told me that you wished you were going to church on a regular basis. I believe you were sincere about that.

Nicholas was ambivalent about the memorial chapel service and was vocal about his ambivalence. Olga and I convinced him that it was a good idea for all of us, especially so during Robert's visit to Houston. It has been really hard for Nicholas to lose you. He's also worried about his mother's safety and welfare. He keeps saying that he's afraid that she is going to die as well.

Despite my grief, I was able to observe that your two boys were affectionate with each other during their own grieving process. I saw Robert place his arms around Nicholas's shoulders a couple of times. I was glad to see the closeness between them. I know you must be glad, also.

The prayer service was in the small chapel of the church instead of the main church sanctuary because of the issue of cremation. It seems (I just found out about this) that when there is no dead body, church clergy cannot conduct a Greek Orthodox funeral service. I was so upset to hear that. It seems to me that this is an outdated notion that should be abandoned, especially given the large number of people nowadays who choose cremation instead of the traditional burial. I am one of those people. I guess they won't give me a regular funeral service, either.

I don't understand the church position. I was told that the church position is based on biblical injunctions. Oh, even the Catholic Church, not exactly a proponent of innovations, has changed its position and is accepting cremations.

I have been a lifelong member of the Greek Orthodox Church, except for attendance for some years at the Unity Church, but I refuse to be buried underground. When I was a child in Istanbul, Turkey, I read some scary stories that are supposed to be true of people accidentally being buried alive, and ever since then, I have been determined not be buried underground.

Now there are environmental principles as well to add to that old fear. Since you always hated the idea of being cooped up in small places, Jamie, I think that cremation would probably have been your choice, also. You did not leave a will and did not tell anybody about your choices, so all we can do is surmise what you would have preferred.

I keep having some crazy thoughts about your death that are somewhat confusing. One thought that came to me this morning was at least you don't have to worry about going to jail anymore! According to your niece, Victoria, you had a judicial deadline in June. You had to be sober, keep the terms of your parole, and pay a large fine, or you would have had to go back to jail! Well, honey, you don't have to worry about the June deadline anymore or about going back to jail. Your two times in jail must have been so dreadful. I shiver to think about that, about your pleading voice that keeps reverberating in my head, asking me to post bail.

I'm so sorry, my son, that your life ended this way, with constant fear of jail and estrangement from your loved ones. I kept hoping that jail time was going to be your bottom (as they say in Alcoholics Anonymous and Al-Anon circles) and that you would turn your life around. Unfortunately, it never happened. Your ongoing denial and—maybe a stubborn streak that you probably inherited from your dad—prevented you from seeing the truth about your circumstances and your life.

I will ache about that as long as I live. Be at peace, my baby. You were and are dearly loved!

March 24, 2018

My Dearest Son,

It's evening time and I'm alone at home with my little dog, Skye. Most days and nights, he is my only companion. A tide of grief is engulfing me again, and writing to you is the only way I push the tide away a little and I can breathe better. There is a tightness in my chest since eleven days ago when I heard the terrible news that you left our earthly home.

Yesterday, after the prayer service, Olga and I were in her car alone for a while, and I finally got the courage to ask for more details about the end of your life. I had been told previously that you had died in your sleep, that your heart just stopped. I was too distressed then to ask more questions as to why a fifty-seven–year–old's heart suddenly stopped beating.

Olga told me that you died asleep on a park bench after a drinking binge with a buddy. It seems you two had a shoving match a little while before your demise. The man involved told Leslie that you and he had an argument earlier in the evening, you fell during the argument (or maybe he pushed you down?), and you hit your head. It seems that he then took you to the emergency room—you must have complained of your head hurting. The staff examined you, he said, and then they released you. I don't know how or why you ended up back in the park on your own, but that's where they found you early on the morning of March thirteenth. At first, they thought you had passed out from drinking, but then they realized that you had died in your sleep.

I wonder about all this. Did your fall contribute to your death? I don't know. Did the ER doctors do a thorough examination, or did they just assume that the fall was part of a drunken brawl between two addicts and not to be taken seriously? I don't have the answer to that either. The coroner in his autopsy report cited "advanced cirrhosis of the liver and a weakened heart, with considerable amount of alcohol in the body."

The diagnosis of advanced cirrhosis hit me like a ton of bricks. Of course I suspected it, but I did not realize it was advanced or severe. I guess I was in denial about that also. You must have known! Probably that was the reason you spent a whole week while in jail in the infirmary. You did not tell me or the rest of the family about your illness. Maybe if I had known, I would not have denied you bail money, despite my Al-Anon principles.

Oh, my son! It pains me so greatly that you died alone on a park bench, nobody to hold your hand and no loving goodbyes! Passersby must have seen a homeless drunk bum. They didn't know or think that this homeless drunk was you, my precious child, a person dearly loved who had at one time all the potential to become a successful human being. Somebody who graduated from a prestigious law school and was a practicing lawyer for many years. How terribly sad and wasteful it all sounds.

I am so angry at the disease of alcoholism! That's what killed you in reality, because that's what caused the liver disease and the weakening of your heart. At the same time, I have to admit that you are not totally blameless and neither are we, your family. You turned a blind eye to all the signs that the universe planted along the way, and you refused to listen to people who loved you and tried to warn you about your dangerous path. As for your family, we share some of the blame as well. Your father dug a hole for himself with his pride and old-fashioned ideas and refused to visit you in California through the years, causing you a lot of hurt feelings. The rest of us stayed in denial for quite a while and missed the early signs of addiction. The two jail incarcerations (short, but real) and the loss of your home as well as the estrangement from me and your boys must surely have been a big red flag, but you chose to call it all "bad luck" and stayed in a state of big denial.

Victoria had shown me the Ventura County website recently. I had read that you had not paid your fines and assumed that you had not kept the conditions of your parole. I knew that you were still drinking excessively, maybe even drugging yourself. I was so afraid that you were heading back to jail. The deadline of June was fast approaching.

You had sounded so desperate last September when you called me after my knee-replacement surgery and told me that your law license had been taken away by the license board. I heard the desperation and huge sense of loss in your voice—despite my postsurgery pain and discomfort—and I ached for you and for the way your life was going.

And still, you kept drinking and drinking, despite your losses. You texted me, at one time that you were attending "antidrinking" classes (as you called them). I presume they were dictated by your parole board. So, I should give you some credit for making a feeble effort to change. I'm sorry if I'm sounding sarcastic—and even angry—at you, my dear son. It's just that I am hurting so much! I hope your soul or spirit is at peace, because the ones you left behind who loved you with all their hearts are not at peace.

I hope that one day we will be, but not yet, not now.

March 25, 2018

My Dearest Son,

Here's some news that I believe you will like. Olga told me today that she arranged for a tree to be planted in your memory at Hermann Park. You always loved nature, especially trees, didn't you? I told her that I was touched by her gesture and that it was a wonderful and fitting memorial for you. I still remember how you and Verdi (our lifelong friend from Turkey) planted a tree in the front yard of our old house at Ashford Place.

You were ten years old at the time, and we had just bought and moved into the house after we moved to Houston from Baltimore, Maryland. I didn't care for its colonial architecture (I preferred modern), but you kids loved the big front and back yards, especially after the smaller and more confined space of our duplex in Townson, Maryland. Your two brothers loved running around in all the outdoor space, but you couldn't stand it that the yard was bare of vegetation. You kept bugging your dad to plant bushes and trees. He, busy as he was establishing himself in the engineering firm that he had been hired by, kept telling you to be patient: "I am too busy to worry about trees right now."

A month or two after our move, our friends Verdi and Uğur came to visit us from Baton Rouge, Louisiana. Verdi heard your lamenting about the lack of trees in the yard and asked you to go shopping with him. You did and brought back a seedling of a tree that our friend said was his housewarming gift. You two immediately planted that tree in the middle of the front yard. That was many years ago. We don't own the house anymore. Your dad and I, as you probably recall, were divorced ten years after the tree planting.

Your dad died two years ago from Alzheimer's disease, but the tree stands—tall and regal—in the front lawn of that house. It's so big now that it covers one third of the front yard. Good job, honey! Obviously, the tree was planted with a lot of love. That's why it survived all sorts of weather in Houston, including two major hurricanes! I cried when I went by our old street and saw your tree recently, but also I smiled at the memory of your ten-year-old self, a boy who cared so much about having trees in his family's yard!

Your tree lives on, but I don't know how I am going to live without you in this world. I keep telling myself that other parents have lost children through the years—some a lot younger than you and thus more vulnerable—and somehow they have survived the terrible grief. I tell myself that, but it's a small and hollow comfort. Right now, the thought of living without you seems like an impossible task.

I remember when Debbie Reynolds (a twentieth-century movie star) lost her daughter Carrie Fisher (of *Star Wars* fame), who also died from addiction-related problems. Like you, Fisher died from sudden heart failure and was about your age. It was reported at the time that Reynolds said that she did not want to live anymore without her daughter. Sure enough, she died of a stroke the next day. They called it "death from a broken heart" and buried mother and daughter together.

At the time I thought that she must have been too enmeshed with her adult daughter. How smug and judgmental of me! Now that I find myself in similar circumstances—except for the fame—I understand Reynolds's immense grief a lot better. I am not suicidal, but I do notice that when my blood pressure goes high (that happens more often lately), I don't panic anymore like I used to. Now that death has touched me closely because of your passing, it does not frighten me like before.

March 26, 2018

My Dearest Son,

Tomorrow is your birthday, and I don't know how I am going bear it! Maybe I'll die from a broken heart, too, like Debbie Reynolds, and I'll join you where you are.

Yes, I know I am being melodramatic now. James, an ex-boyfriend, used to say that I was full of Greek drama! I am very serious though when

I say that I don't know if my heart can bear any more pain. After all, it's a damaged heart. I don't know if you remember this, but I was diagnosed with congestive heart failure and atrial fibrillation in 2010. I've had a tightness in my chest for days now, ever since I heard the news that we lost you. The tightness comes and goes, but the immense internal pain is always there.

By the way, why did your heart suddenly stop? You never said anything about having heart disease. I know that excessive drinking and substance abuse affect a person's organs—including the heart—but the circumstances of your death still shocked me and caught me by surprise.

It's true that when I last saw you, a year and a half ago, you did not look well. You were thin but with a bloated stomach. I thought to myself that maybe you had cirrhosis of the liver—the classic disease of alcoholism—but how did your heart get so weak? Remember I am the older person here with the heart condition. I should have been the one to go first, not you. I am wondering if you died because of the fall you had in the park that day during the brawl with your so-called friend. Did the doctors miss something important in the emergency room? Did they see only the appearance of a drunken middle-aged homeless man and not examine you carefully? We'll never know, will we?

I don't know the point of all this ruminating and lamenting. I am probably tormenting myself with questions that will never be answered since you are already gone from this earth. I feel like I'm bleeding inside and I'm alone in all of this. I am trying to help myself, Jamie, I really am. I truly believe you loved me, and you would not want to see me wallow in misery and self-pity.

I am seeing a therapist on a regular basis. I started attending meetings of an organization called "The Compassionate Friends" that holds grief groups, mainly for parents who have lost children of any age. They are not in Houston per se but in Katy (about thirty to forty minutes from my house), but I don't care about the distance because the people in the groups understand my pain and are truly compassionate.

Somebody approached me after an Al-Anon meeting and told me about another group called Bo's Place. It is not close to me either, and despite my not liking to drive far anymore, I will try that group as well. I am desperate for emotional support. There are limits to how much grief family and friends can tolerate.

The irony of all this is that I used to lead grief therapy groups myself some time ago. I especially remember the ones in the Annunciation Greek Orthodox Cathedral in Houston, where I would go for services.

The priest at that time was named Father Lou, and I found him to be a wonderful man of God, full of empathy and compassion. Knowing that I was a therapist and having referred some parishioners to me earlier, he asked me one day if I would be willing to form and lead some grief groups in the church. He told me that the need was definitely there, but that Greek-born members of the church were reluctant to go outside the church for therapy.

He told me this about twenty years ago, and I did as he asked—recruiting another therapist as well. Our task was not easy. As a whole, our church was new to this kind of help, and there was initially a lot of resistance to the idea. There was a trust issue as well. Members had a hard time believing in the therapeutic principle of confidentiality and were afraid that all the church members would learn about their private issues. I finally convinced some after many private conversations to attend the grief groups, and we got started. I was very gratified to hear later that the members who did attend those groups told Father Lou that they got a lot of emotional help from the grief group process. I never dreamed that the day would come when I would be the one asking about grief groups as a participant—not as group leader—not in my worst nightmares!

Jamie, you have to help me survive your birthday. I'm serious.

Send me a sign or something—please, honey.

I need you to help me live without you, and I cannot do it by myself!

March 27, 2018

My Dearest Son,

Happy Birthday, sweetheart! I hope your spirit (soul) knows that it's your birthday today, here on earth. Maybe the occasion doesn't mean anything anymore, except to me and your kids.

Yesterday evening was really hard. I have a strong tendency to have anticipatory anxiety anyway, so I just crashed with grief. I tried to reach out to people—I really did. I called my sponsor, but she just started a new job and did not have any time to talk. I then called my best friend of many years, Connie, who was not home but visiting her son in California. I was happy for her but sad for me and you because her visit immediately brought to my mind the remembrance of the many trips to California through the years to visit you. She couldn't talk either.

I took an antianxiety pill and tried to distract myself from grief. Of course, it didn't work. Lately, I cannot for the life of me focus on what's on the television screen. I watch the shows but cannot concentrate on plots. I have no idea what's going on, so after a while, I turn it off. Reading books—an activity that I usually love—is pretty impossible as well. I tried desperately to figure out what to do.

I was experiencing such immense emotional pain that I didn't think I could bear it. Images of you kept popping into my head. I saw terrible scenes: you beg me to post bail, I say no so as not to enable you in your disease, and then I hang up the phone and sob for hours.

At 10 p.m., I finally couldn't stand my miserable mood anymore, and I called my friend Betty who had lost a son some time ago. He died of leukemia but had had some substance abuse problems in the past. My friend is a retired psychotherapist like I am. I thought that she would understand my distress and listen to my pain for a while, maybe even tell me something comforting. I hesitated some before calling her because she lives in an assisted living facility and because of the lateness of the hour. However, I was desperate for some kind of help, so I called.

It turned out to be a good move on my part. She was still awake and willing to respond to a needy, grieving friend. She reminded me of all the things you had accomplished in your life before the downhill descent into alcoholism. She talked of your scholastic achievements and how proud I was of you when I went to Michigan to attend your law school graduation. She added that she remembered how excited and happy I was before my many visits to LA to visit you and your family.

"Froso, you always had a deep connection with your son," she said. "It was amazing that we came upon him and his girlfriend—in Paris, of all places, on a remote hill—with absolutely no prior knowledge that he was visiting Paris at the same time that you and I were!" I laughed, despite my tears. I remembered well that crazy surprise reunion.

My friend Betty and I had left our hotel and were walking downhill when we saw two people, in the distance, coming up the hill. Betty turned to me and said, "Froso, doesn't that guy look like your son, Jamie?" I looked and, to my great surprise, it was you walking up the hill. What are the odds of a mother and son meeting on a hill in Paris, one coming from Houston and the other from LA? Betty said she would never forget the incredulous, shocked look on my face that gave way to joy about the unexpected reunion.

After talking with Betty for a while, I was able to calm down a little and go to bed.

April 1, 2018

My Dearest Son,

It's Easter Sunday today for most Christians in the world, but for me and other Eastern Orthodox folks, it's Palm Sunday.

I went to the Antiochian Orthodox Christian church close to my house. I could not bear to go to a Greek church. I was too afraid that I would run into some people I know—not that I know that many, but still—and would have to explain you had died recently. It seemed less emotionally draining to be amongst strangers.

I had gone to that church a few times already. I like its proximity to my house and the very diverse congregation. People from all over the world attend this church—different home countries, different ethnicities. I love hearing the exotic (at least to me) languages and accents. Many of the women attending—unlike Greek women—wear scarves on their heads. They remind me of my Grandmother Eleni.

I remember that when I was a little girl, my mother and grandmother would often quarrel about my grandmother (Yiayia) wearing a headscarf in church. She used to explain to me that when she was growing up in a Turkish village by the Black Sea that everyone she knew wore headscarves. The Greek girls (like Yiayia) being part of a Christian minority would imitate the Turkish Muslim girls and wear scarves as well. Looking back, I'm guessing that they probably did not want to stand out as different.

My mother, who grew up as a member of a much larger Greek community in Istanbul, couldn't stand to see her own mother wear a headscarf and kept reminding her that she was no longer living in a village but in a big city. I regret now that I never asked her why she liked wearing that scarf. I guess kids don't ask those kinds of questions or care about those things. The habit probably reminded her of her childhood and of her parents who were deceased. Anyway, it would irritate my mother to no end to see a scarf on Yiayia's head, and she would tell her to take it off. Yiayia would refuse, and then I would be a witness to another battle royal! I remember those two arguing a lot, even though my grandmother lived in her own apartment in a separate place. I was her only grandchild and she doted on me, so she would visit us a lot.

My mother and grandmother were both strong, opinionated women with a stubborn bent who did not give in easily. Looking back with an adult, therapeutic perspective, my guess would be that there were deeper roots to those quarrels. I believe that my mother, who was the kindest person I ever knew, had some unresolved feelings of resentment toward my grandmother because of old history. When my mother was nine years old, her father (my grandfather) killed himself or was killed in a labor camp during the Turkish-Greek war of the 1920s. My grandmother, who was left a widow with two young children, placed my mother in an orphanage run by Catholic nuns. Mother was always bitter about the fact that my grandmother chose to place her in the facility while keeping her brother, Christos, at home. Yiayia's explanation to me was that my uncle was only five at the time and too young (she believed) to leave his mother's side.

I don't believe that my mother ever forgave that placement and her mother's choice. "I would rather die than place you in an orphanage, Frosula!" were my mother's words to me. She would tell me that numerous times during my childhood years.

I am pretty sure that I have already told you the above family story, Jamie, but maybe you have forgotten the details. It's important to remember that children never totally get over abandonment or what they perceive as abandonment. That's one big reason why your brother Spiros has been angry with you in the last few years. He told me that he has tried to understand about your disease of alcoholism but finds it very hard to understand and to forgive you for abandoning your children. I tried to explain to him that people under the influence do a lot of thoughtless and crazy things because they aren't thinking straight, but he shook his head and walked away. He and Olga are taking care of Nicholas now, so I hope you forgive him as well—for his attitude and for the past when you two were young.

Our family did not get together for Easter (or "American Easter" as I call it). We are all too depressed about your sudden death to make any plans to get together! Even Olga, who is the unofficial hostess of the clan and who usually loves to cook and entertain people, could not bring herself to cook for the occasion.

We also had some further bad news that your wife (I guess I should call her your "widow," but I hate the word right now) is somewhere in LA, but nobody knows her whereabouts. We heard that she was arrested for a public disturbance. I am sorry to have to tell you the above news, but I have a feeling that you already know and are not too surprised. In fact, some months ago—before you stopped talking with me—you had told me on the phone that you were worried about her. I wish you had been more worried about yourself, my son, but we both know by now that denial is hard to overcome, don't we?

April 2, 2018

My Dearest Son,

I'm trying everything I can think of to help myself through this journey of terrible grief, but nothing is working. I just came back from an Al-Anon meeting. This group was nice enough to send me a sympathy card after they heard of your passing. I know they mean well and I thanked them, but, unfortunately, all the kind words and intentions bring only a smidgen of comfort, no more than that. As for distractions, I cannot concentrate on anything. Being an avid reader, I have a big stack of books at home, but neither books nor television shows (not even the BBC dramas that I love) are able to lighten my mood or engage me. The truth is that the only real comfort I get currently comes from writing these letters to you— the letters that you are never going to see or read.

You told me—in the days when you were still communicating with me—that I did not love you anymore because I refused to send you money to post bail. I tried to explain to you, again and again, the reasons behind my refusal, but you wouldn't listen. You and the bondsmen you went to called me too many times, and my anxiety and distress became so severe that I had to disconnect all the phones in my house so my blood pressure would not go any higher. I cried and cried and hoped that I was doing the right thing. I kept hearing the desperation in your voice, and that made me desperate as well.

Since that fateful day, there was no communication from you. Your niece Victoria, my granddaughter, found a website and an address for the correctional facility where you were detained, so I wrote and sent you a long letter. She also sent you an email advising you how to plead. I trust her legal advice and hope that you did also. I didn't keep a copy, so I don't know exactly what I said in my letter; nonetheless, I know that I spent a lot of time on it, trying hard to be nonjudgmental and lovingly supportive. I avoided using labels like "alcoholic" and encouraged you to go to AA meetings while in jail (I hope they have those). I urged you to take advantage of the detoxing in the facility and to get some help for your problems from the county and/or the justice system of Ventura, California.

For a long time, I did not even know if you got my letter. I did not get a response. Even though I did not logically expect a response, there was a tiny hope in my heart that I would hear from you, despite your anger at me about the bail. Unfortunately, the only thing I heard was that your heart had stopped completely on that eventful day in the park in LA.

When I heard the terrible news, it was such a jolt that my own heart almost stopped as well. In the midst of the shock, a family member (I have no recollection of who it was) handed me the phone, telling me that your wife wanted to talk with me. I asked her if you had said anything about the letter I sent you while you were in jail back in December. She said that when you left jail a month later, that you had my letter in your pocket and that you told her about it. I told her that you had been angry with me and how painful that was for me. "Don't worry about that," she said, "Jamie always loved you!"

Despite my immense grief, I felt a touch of gladness that you had kept my letter and had not torn it up or thrown it away. I am hopeful it meant something to you.
All my love,
Mom

April 3, 2018

My Dearest Son,

I had lunch today with Virginia, a friend I met at the YMCA while we were both attending the water aerobics class. She has recently become more important to me because she and I are on a similar nightmarish journey—she also lost a son recently. He died a couple of weeks before you did.

She came over last week—after hearing of my terrible news—bringing me lots of food that she had cooked—I guess to comfort me some. I appreciated her visit and did not tell her that my appetite was lacking currently and I really doubted that I could eat all that food. I thanked her and told her my truthful feelings—that the food was less important than her company. She understood the depth of my grief a lot more than other people for a simple reason: she is feeling a grief similar to mine. She brought along pictures of her deceased son, and I showed her some of your pictures. We talked about our two lost sons and cried together. You might say that we had our own little memorial service.

Her son, Keith, died of throat cancer. Virginia told me that he had suffered a lot before he died. He also had a history of alcohol abuse. At least, Jaime, you didn't suffer a lot before you died (or so I hope). I was told that your heart just stopped that fateful day in the LA park. I hope and pray that you did not know what was happening to you.

I had been terribly worried this last year that you were going to have some horrible disease because of the neglect and abuse that your body was subjected to. I am glad that you were at least spared that and, crazy as this may sound, glad that you no longer must worry about returning to jail, especially since you were not meeting the terms of your parole (sobriety and payment of your fine).

On second thought, dealing with homelessness must have been a constant mental and emotional strain. My first sight of you during my last visit was your barefooted self, looking gaunt and kind of lost, walking your dog around the crummy motel where you were staying. It brought tears to my eyes. I know how much you loved your dog. I hate to tell you this, but he is missing as well. We don't know where he is. Don't worry. We'll keep calling shelters and other places and try to find him.

I have to say, honey, I never expected that you were going to die so young. You were fifty-seven years old when your heart stopped, certainly young nowadays, especially when compared with my eighty-four years. If I had had an inkling of knowledge a year and half ago that my intervention trip would be the last time I would set eyes on you, I would have definitely hugged you longer and tighter, and I would have kissed your unshaven cheeks a lot more times. If I knew or had even suspected what the future would bring, I would not have wanted to leave your side. As it was, I left our last encounter with a lot of fear and a lot of sadness. Some of your last words to me were reverberating in my brain over and over again, words like "I can't imagine, Mom, not ever drinking again!"

Later in the evening when I couldn't stand the despair anymore, I would try to remember the love in your voice as you introduced me to one of your friends in that shabby, grim motel. It warmed my aching heart a little to hear the pride and affection in your voice. This was a couple of hours after I read my intervention list of incidents and after you had said, "I'll get some help, Mom. Please don't cry!" Just as I felt a touch of hope, you added, "The truth is, Mom, I'd rather die or go to jail than be locked in a rehab facility!" And my heart sank again.

Deep down—during that whole visit—I knew in my gut that you were not going to get any help—no matter what you promised. You did listen to me—I will grant you that—as I listed (as nonjudgmentally as I could) the dangers of the path you were on. The only time you interrupted me with anger in your voice was when I told you that your brain cells were probably dying because of the alcohol and drug assault on them, along with the other organs in your body.

"There's nothing wrong with my brain cells," you shouted. "Don't say that again, Mother." I did not reply. I looked at you and realized how strong your denial was and how powerful the hold of your alcoholism disease. I knew that there was no point to my replying. Deep in my gut, I also knew that this was hopeless, that I had lost you.

The day was so traumatic for me that by the time the plane reached Houston on my return, I was not able to walk out of the plane. My feet would not hold me up. The crew had to secure a wheelchair for me.

A few days later my orthopedic doctor told me that a major bone on my left knee was on the verge of breaking. I had to stay in a wheelchair for a month to give it time to heal. The news was shocking, and it did sound as if there was a physical reason behind the fact that I couldn't walk out of the plane. However, I just knew that the events in California had contributed greatly to my knee problem. My many years as a psychotherapist convinced me that stress and emotional pain can play havoc with one's body.

The knee debacle symbolized to me the breaking of my heart.

April 5, 2018

My Dearest Son,

Yesterday we celebrated your younger son's birthday. Nicholas is such a mature, fine young man. You would have been so proud of him. He goes to college here in Houston while also handling two part-time jobs. He is very smart and very resourceful. He managed on his own to be hired by a company that owns some of the most prestigious hotels and restaurants in Houston, despite the fact that he had no prior experience as a valet attendant.

He still lives with Spiros and Olga and Stuart. Stuart treats him like a younger brother. Spiros and Olga are very fond of him and think that he is great. Olga tells me that she cooks a lot more nowadays because she wants to make sure that Nicholas has nourishing meals.

On the occasion of his birthday, Spiros took the family to a steakhouse of the restaurant chain that Nicholas works for. It was an elegant, superexpensive place. I gulped when I saw that the cheapest steak on the menu was $48. I had a hard time containing my tears. I was thinking of the contrast between us dining here and the penniless, homeless state that you were in before you died.

I was angry at Spiros for a while because of his refusal to come to LA with Olga and me when I tried to rescue you from your alcoholic fate with my pathetic intervention. I was also angry at him for not offering to pay for a private, expensive rehabilitation facility. I couldn't afford that, but he could. Maybe it was my own denial that made me think that you would have been willing to go to rehab, but I still wanted Spiros to at least offer.

To be fair, I must remember he did bail you out financially quite a few times in the last few years—the latest one being two months before your passing when you called him, pleading with him to pay past due rental fees for a storage unit so that your son Robert could retrieve some family memorabilia.

I wonder why you did that, particularly at the time. Did you have a premonition that you might not have long to live? I wish I had more answers about your life and death. I have a hard time calling and talking with your wife because she doesn't always make a lot of sense. I wonder why. I was told that she had been arrested for a public disturbance and had a court hearing coming up in May. Does all this sound familiar, Jaime?

I have to admit that I am still holding some resentment toward her for not helping us to get you to treatment back in October of last year.

Nicholas is so afraid that his mother is also going to die that he is saving money so he can hire somebody to represent her in court. Poor child, in addition to grieving for you, he is also trying to figure out ways to try to save her. Last week he told me that he was thinking that he and Robert should go to Los Angeles and kidnap her so as to take her to a hospital, whether she wants to go or not.

I told him that it sounded like a desperate plan, and he admitted that he did feel desperate. He is so afraid that his mother is going to die also and that he will be a total orphan.

"My life sucks anyway," he told me, "but I don't want it to suck more than it is already." I felt for him and hugged him, trying to bring him a little comfort.

You know, Jaime, I thought I was in pain before in my life. After all, I'm in my eighties now and have gone through some pretty tough times: leaving home and parents at age twenty-two; coming alone to the United States for a better life; enduring a divorce twenty-five years later; having to hospitalize a hostile teenager (your brother Constantine) using pot and acid; and surviving thyroid cancer and later a heart condition.

All these events were painful for me, but nothing compares with what happened to you. When I heard that you were gone from this earth, that you had died, I felt like my heart was torn out of my body and trampled.

April 6, 2018

My Dearest Son,

I start my days with crying, and I finish them the same way. In between, I semifunction—as much as I am able to—and do what I have to do to take care of myself (sort of) and Skye, my little dog, who depends on me. Sometimes taking care of her is all that keeps me going.

I attend all the Al-Anon meetings that I can. Going out takes more physical and emotional energy than I have nowadays, but I push myself to do it, with the hope that it will bring me some internal comfort and relief. The effort is often in vain. Once in a while somebody says something in a meeting that touches my heart, and I get to breathe normally for a few minutes. That kind of special moment makes my going worthwhile.

Anything and everything make me cry. Today, Nicholas texted me to ask about your wedding to his mother. I am guessing that he needs the date because he's filing out some forms for college. By the time I looked at the back of your wedding photo, looking for a date, I was in tears! You and Leslie are looking so young and handsome in that photo. You are both smiling and look so happy! Hard to believe that twenty-two years later, you would be dead and your wife would be unreachable, somewhere in LA!

I remember your wedding day so clearly. It took place in a woody, beautiful resort outside of Los Angeles. It was December and the weather was crisp and lovely. You and Leslie chose to be married in a Greek Orthodox church located on that site, and the choice of the church was a delightful surprise for me—a surprise because your bride was raised a Lutheran. The ceremony, flower crowns on the head and all, was of course familiar to me and very touching. I cried then too, but those were tears of joy. How I wished that your grandmother Anastasia, who loved you so, could have been alive and seen you on your wedding day!

The reception was charming, albeit a little awkward for me because my then partner Lou and I had to be seated at the same table as your father (my ex) who seemed very uncomfortable about our sudden proximity. He barely said a couple of words to me.

There were lots of surprises during your reception. You and Leslie danced the first dance in an obviously well-rehearsed fashion (it seems you had secretly taken dance lessons just for this occasion). Later in the evening (it was an afternoon wedding), you two gifted me with a nice ring that had three birthstones on it, one each for you and your two brothers. You said it was for my birthday that happened to be three days before the wedding.

Your lovely, sentimental gesture touched me deeply. Especially because you two made time—during the hectic prewedding days—to think of me. You were both so thoughtful and loving back then. How I miss the two young people that you used to be!

April 7, 2018

My Dearest Son,

Yesterday I went to Good Friday services. You remember how I always liked Good Friday and midnight Easter Services at the Greek church? Amazingly, I made it through the Lamentations sections without sobbing. I had been afraid that I would make a spectacle of myself. My voice trembled some, but I was able to sing the whole segment.

I don't know if I was the loudest person in the church (as you used to tease me), but I did notice that I was one of the few parishioners singing the Greek sections. I sadly predict that one of these days in the near future, the Lamentations will be sung totally in English instead of mostly in Greek. The church congregation seems to get less and less fluent in Greek as the years go by. I really have no right to complain. Your father and I, being afraid that you would be confused when young, did not teach the Greek language to you and your brothers. Now I regret what we did— or didn't do—and think it was a mistake. I remember you reproached me once about this matter.

Tonight, at midnight, it will be Greek Easter. (Most years, Orthodox Easter falls on a different Sunday than Protestant or Catholic Easter.) You probably remember this. There are various factors that determine the date. You have asked me about this more than once through the years, and I have tried to explain it to you. The issue is rather complicated but has mainly to do with following a different calendar.

I had not planned to go to church tonight for the traditional midnight service. The Good Friday Lamentations service was in sync with my current sad mood, but the Easter service with its theme of resurrection did not fit my state of mind. However, three of my grandchildren (one of them being your son Nicholas) changed my mind. They insisted that they were coming to pick me up and take me to church. They told me that they wanted to attend the Pascha service with me. They probably want to cheer me up because they see the grief and distress that I am in. Bless them! They are good-hearted kids—young people, I should say—they mean well, and I love them for it. So, I guess I am going with them (despite my earlier resolution), even though my heart says no to such festive celebrations.

I'm starting a new grief group next week. It was full, but the leader of the group attends one of the Al-Anon meetings that I go to and is making an exception for me so I can attend her group. In the meantime, I'm planning to go to a balloon-release ceremony in a few days. That one is sponsored by Compassionate Friends, a grief group in Katy, Texas. I think I mentioned that one to you before. As you can probably tell from all of this, I am so desperate for any and all kinds of emotional support and relief, that I am trying out as many grief groups as I can find.

Stan is taking me to the balloon ceremony. He offered to help, and I asked him to drive me there and come with me to the meeting. You may remember Stan. He's Lou's son. He still calls me his stepmother, even though his father and I broke up about nine years ago. By the way, I have not told Lou about your passing. I'm sorry about that, honey. I know that you and he had a good relationship and that he liked you a lot.

You see, I'm afraid to tell him because he may use your passing as a way to immerse himself into my life again. This is not something that I want. He has a cognitive disorder—similar to Alzheimer's—and his behavior is unpredictable and can be quite difficult. The truth is that I wish I could tell him about your death and have him share some of my grief. I am so needy for that right now!

Contrary to society's belief, I do like talking about you, not just to talk about my sad feelings but also to remind people of the person that you used to be—smart, kind, and honorable—before alcohol and other drugs destroyed you. Unfortunately, I don't have much of an audience for the above. Either because the subject of death is deemed unpleasant or because people have the mistaken notion that it upsets me, they get that look in their eyes and try to stop me by saying, "Let's not talk about the unhappy past. Let us focus on the present and future!" That kind of disavowal leaves me hanging, distressed by unexpressed feelings and unconsoled.

I guess that must be one big reason why I like going to see my therapist. He doesn't mind hearing me talk about you. In fact, he encourages it. Yes, I know what you are probably going to say—that I pay him to hear my feelings—but I still feel comforted by his active listening. In fact, he gave me an assignment last week—to write a eulogy to honor you and your life. Would you like to know what I wrote?

A Eulogy for Jamie

This is a toast to the real Jamie, not the victim of addiction of the last unhappy years, but the earlier version.

To the shy, serious, studious child, full of curiosity about the world. The one who loved music and intellectual debates and books. The one who practiced his clarinet and later saxophone for hours on end until he got it right. The teenager who idolized the Beatles and inspired his younger brother Constantine to do the same.

Also, a toast to the fine young man that he became, getting a law degree like he always wanted, and later—when practicing law—charging less (or nothing) to people unable to afford high legal fees. A toast to a person who loved nature and the outdoors with a passion as well as the motorcycle that took him wherever he wanted to roam.

How he loved the Boy Scout camping trips. He had two parents who grew up in urban apartments in a foreign city—Istanbul—and were totally clueless about camping. Furthermore, they couldn't care less about outdoor living. So, Jamie embraced the whole Boy Scout experience with gusto. He stayed in it until he achieved the Eagle level. (When Constantine later on was asked if he wanted to join the scouts, his response was "I already did the whole thing with Jamie!")

A toast to the fine young man who became a Merit Scholar and received four full scholarship offers and accepted the one from a prestigious school (Washington University in St. Louis).

A toast to the handsome boy who became a handsome man—inside and out—but who was a late bloomer about dating. He fell in love with a very attractive and intelligent woman in law school and stayed committed to her for quite a few years. He suffered deep pain when his girlfriend left him, and he came to Houston to be with family after the breakup. He came to me, anguished, telling me about his pain and asking me if his late grandmother Anastasia would be angry with him about his using her in a lie—telling his new legal firm that she had died—so he could get a week off to come to Houston. "I'm sorry I lied, Mom. I hope she won't mind in heaven!" he said. I told him that since she adored him in life that I was pretty sure that she would forgive him for his white lie. Later on, he found a new love and decided to marry her in the Greek church to my delight!

A toast to the son, who told me when his two boys were born—two years apart—that they were the light of his life and that he loved them dearly.

A toast to the man who loved animals all his life and would feed his cats on fine china, telling his annoyed wife that they were just as important as people and part of the family. During his trips to Houston, he would always tell me to not forget to stroke the dog of his brother Spiros because in his words: "Animals need a lot of affection, Mom!"

Last, but not least, a toast to the affectionate son who used to tell me that I looked like Sophia Loren and cooked *keftedes* (Middle Eastern meatballs) better than any Greek restaurant. The son who always welcomed me at the LA airport with a big hug and the words: "I'm so glad you are here, Mom!"

April 8, 2018

My Dearest Son,

We just had Greek Easter. Hard for me to find joy this year in the traditional celebration. I did not have the heart to attend the annual Easter picnic that the church sponsors. My granddaughter Victoria asked me about that—I usually invite her and Michael, her fiancé, to come with me. I told her that I was sorry, but I couldn't bring myself to go this year. She said she understood. I have not bothered with the Greek Easter bread that I always bake on this holiday or even the dyed red eggs!

Remember how I used to send you a big loaf of Easter bread every spring? I used to send the bread via overnight mail so it wouldn't get stale, and postal workers teased me about it. I especially remember one year when a postal worker looked at my package and asked me what it was. When I told him that it was loaf of bread, he smiled and said, "You know, lady, they do have bread in California. You don't have to spend twenty dollars to send it there!"

I would smile and shrug my shoulders and carry on with my mission. I was happy to do it, regardless of the cost. I would happily send dozens and dozens more loaves if you were only there to receive them.

I would happily sell everything I own, if only I could hear your wonderful, booming voice tell me one more time—"Hey, Mom, it's your son Jamie calling!"

April 12, 2018

My Dearest Son,

I have neglected my letter writing in the last few days—sorry. It's not that you haven't been on my mind. To the contrary, it is because I grieved for you in more diverse, communal ways.

On Tuesday evening, two days ago, I attended the balloon ceremony that I previously mentioned to you. True to his promise, Stan took me. He has been steadfast in his association with me. I have to admit that I like it when he still introduces me as his stepmother.

Anyway, we went to the ceremony, and it was very meaningful and touching. There were about thirty people there, all grieving their deceased children of all ages. We wrote love notes and attached them to the individual balloon. Then we formed a big circle outside, holding hands and then, one by one we named our lost loved ones. But why am I telling you all this? I believe that you were there in spirit. As I stood there, holding my balloon, I was crying—like most of the bereaved parents in the circle. There were bagpipes playing—you, the big music lover, would have loved that part of the ceremony, I'm sure.

Jamie, the reason that I said what I said earlier about your being there in spirit is because of what my balloon was doing during the ceremony. Hear me out! I am not going crazy, I assure you! My balloon was hitting me in the face and on my head nonstop while everybody else's balloon was flying straight! I was and still am convinced it was your spirit telling me that you were there with me and trying to console me. Am I right, honey? Was that a sign from you that your spirit lives on? I hope so.

Today I took Uber to go to another grief group, Bo's Place. It's about forty-five minutes from my house, and I didn't want to get lost (you know me and my shaky sense of direction). The first driver who came to pick me up addressed me with, "*Salaam alaikum*" ("Peace be upon you") in Arabic, and I answered him in English since my knowledge in Arabic is limited to just a few words and sentences that I remember from my childhood in Istanbul. His response was "No English, sorry," and he canceled the ride immediately and asked me to leave his cab. I was stunned. How on earth this guy became an Uber driver without knowing the English language at all was a mystery.

I can just hear your booming laugh at this point, Jamie. I knew you would get a kick out of my Uber story. You always used to laugh at my funny stories. Nowadays it's your younger son, Nicholas, who tells me that he enjoys my "funky stories" (as he calls them)!

I finally got a driver with whom I could communicate, and he took me to the group. It's rather far from me, and I'm not sure that it's the right group for me. Not all the attendees are bereaved parents, but I'll reserve judgment until I give it another try.

I'm so desperate for any kind of help, honey! I don't know what else I can do to bear this unbearable grief of mine.

April 13, 2018

My Dearest Son,

Today is a month since your heart stopped, and I lost you. It's so strange that there are times when the past month feels like a year—a terrible year—and there are some other times when it feels like only yesterday.

I still wake up in the morning and for a few blessed moments I feel that the past month was a bad dream and that you are still alive. Then the awful truth hits me, and I start crying. Unfortunately, reality is not a dream. You are gone forever, and I'll never see you again unless there is life beyond death. I cling to that belief because to not do so is too painful to bear.

I went to see my cardiologist today because I've had chest pains on and off the whole month. To tell you the truth, it's a wonder to me that my heart is still beating and has somehow survived this terrible month. I have alternated in my feelings between wanting to die and join you (wherever you are) or wanting to live some more, primarily so I can keep writing these letters to you and maybe help other bereaved parents. I guess it's the psychotherapist inside me wanting to counsel and give some solace.

Both my cardiologist and my therapist are telling me that I am stronger than I think I am, but I have had a hard time believing them, knowing how broken and vulnerable I feel. When I went to the first meeting of Compassionate Friends, I talked with some parents (mostly mothers) and realized that other people, in similar situations, had feelings similar to mine. A couple of them admitted to me that when they first heard of their children's deaths that they, too, wanted to die. It didn't matter what the age of the child was. The reaction was the same. I admit there was a little comfort in realizing that I wasn't alone with my feelings.

I really like this group. Too bad it's far from me and only once a month. I'm still glad I found it.

April 16, 2018

My Dearest Son,

I haven't written in the last three days, but you have been constantly on my mind. I still continue my habit of talking to you in my head.

I went to a teenager's birthday party yesterday. I wasn't planning on going, but Stan convinced me to go. He told me that it was the sixteenth birthday party of Rachel (his niece) and that she would love to see me, since I have not seen her for quite a while. "She'll be over the moon if you come," he said. Rachel, being Lou's grandchild, has been part of my life since she was a baby.

I hesitate a lot nowadays before going out and socializing, primarily because of my fear that people are going to ask me how my family is doing. Then the dam will burst and I will start sobbing.

Sure enough, a few minutes after I arrived at the gathering, somebody asked me how my kids were. They probably meant my grandkids, but I immediately thought that they were asking about you and your brothers, and I panicked. I got up without answering and practically ran to the restroom. I cried and cried, and then I calmed myself some and returned to be with the guests. After that incident, nobody asked me any more questions about my family. I was glad for the event to be over and for me to come home and be alone with my grief.

On Sunday, your brother Constantine came over with his girlfriend. You never met her. She was born in Vietnam and her English is not perfect, but she is a very nice person. I can tell she has a good heart—and that's very important to me. A few weeks ago, she insisted on bringing me her big, fancy exercise bike so I can exercise my robot knee (as I call my replaced knee). She thought that my little, inexpensive indoor exercise bike was too wobbly and unsteady. That was kind of her.

I was happy to see Constantine. In the last few years—as I've gotten older—he has been superattentive and solicitous, and he comes over pretty often to see me. He is also willing to help with household chores that are too difficult for me, and I really appreciate that. I'm always glad to see him.

Unfortunately, lately, he has been avoiding me some. Your older brother, Spiros, is avoiding me as well. They don't know how to deal with my emotional pain, and they seem awkward and uncomfortable about facing it. I am resentful about the fact that they don't want to talk about you, either. Maybe it's the societal taboo about talking about the dead person. I am presuming that they think—wrongly—that it would upset me too much. My therapist says to give them some slack. They are probably grieving as well, he says, but doing it in their own way.

One day last week, your wife called me. I had refused to talk to her in the past because (a) I am angry with her for not doing more to help you while you were alive and (b) every time she called her words were slurred and hard to understand.

This time around, her voice sounded almost normal, so I accepted the call. She said she wanted to say hi and see how I was doing. I took the opportunity to ask her if you had received my letter in December when you were in jail. She said you had. It seems you told her about it and still had my letter in your pocket. You also told her that my granddaughter Victoria—the other lawyer in our family—had emailed you some legal advice about how to reduce your time in jail.

I was glad to hear that you had received my letter and that you kept it and not thrown it away. I had spent so much anxious time on that letter. I was so careful not to put labels on you and/or preach to you on how to behave. I told you in my letter that I loved you dearly and tried to explain to you why I couldn't post bail. I tried very hard to explain tough love to you without sounding like I was preaching or scolding.

I had the rather naive (or foolish) hope that while in jail, since you couldn't drink alcohol there or take illegal substances, that maybe your mind would be a little clearer and you could understand my reasons and not continue to be angry with me. Unfortunately, it didn't work. The days of incarceration, terrible as they probably were, must not have been enough to change your attitude. You never called or texted me after that. It breaks my heart not only that I lost you forever but also that we were estranged for about a year.

I know in my therapist head that addiction can and often breaks families, but it still hurts like hell!

April 19, 2018

My Dearest Son,

I went to my second grief group meeting today. We were supposed to bring pictures of our loved ones who had passed on. I took to the group a picture of you on the lawn of the University of Michigan on the day of your law school graduation. In the picture, you are wearing a graduation gown, and you are smiling. Such a handsome face, full of life and promise. I look at it and smile, and then I cry.

I also took to the group a more recent picture of you. It's the last picture I have of you. It was taken at Nicholas's high school graduation of two years ago. This was the only high school graduation of a grandchild of mine that I was not able to attend. It deeply disappointed me that I was not invited by you to come to Los Angeles and go to the graduation. You told me at the time not to come for the occasion. That it wasn't convenient. You did not give me any further explanation. I was so hurt by your words.

Later, I found out the real reason why you didn't want me to come: your house was being repossessed. Things must have started falling apart. You must have been in a lot of distress. Were you embarrassed—even ashamed—to tell me the truth? I don't know. I wish I had known at the time that your life had started unraveling. Maybe I could have helped you then—in the beginning—before it was too late.

What a contrast between the two pictures. Yes, I know that a period of thirty years has elapsed, but you look so different that it's hard to tell that it's the same person. You are smiling in the second picture as well, but the smile looks pained and you look bloated. The promise and potential of the first picture are all gone. Understandable when one considers the circumstances. You were on the edge of homelessness and trying to keep the decline of your life a big secret from me and the rest of your family.

A few months after the picture was taken, the mortgage holder foreclosed and evicted you and Leslie and your boys. You started drifting from one cheap motel to another. Eventually you lost your law license and ended up in the streets of LA in a stolen U-Haul van and later in a tent.

You told me about the loss of your license one day after my knee-replacement surgery. I was in a lot of physical pain at the time, despite being doped up with antipain pills and muscle relaxers. My mind was kind of foggy, and I did not have the physical or emotional energy to ask for details. I hurt too much. Despite my pain, I was surprised and happy that you called.

Communication between us had been sparse in the last year after you told me not to come for Nicholas's graduation. All you had said at the time was that your situation was complicated, and you couldn't welcome me to California. Of course, you omitted the vital information about your house foreclosure and the reasons behind it. After the postsurgery phone call, things went from bad to worse. Your brother and I started getting phone calls from longtime friends of yours, telling us that you were on a dangerous path. With each phone call, my concerns for you kept increasing, and I started having sleepless nights and terrible nightmares.

I felt so helpless about your situation. Here I was in a rehabilitation center, trying to recover from my knee surgery and enduring daily painful physical therapy, occupational therapy, and more. All I wanted was to come to LA and see for myself what was going on, something I definitely could not physically accomplish at that time.

I told myself I had to buckle down and faithfully follow the medical regime so as to get physically stronger and then go to see you. I needed to figure out exactly what was going on in your life. At the back of my mind was the thought: "I was a competent therapist for over forty years. Surely I can help my own son!" I know now how foolhardy that thought was, but it didn't seem so at that particular moment in time.

I had my weekly meeting with my Al-Anon sponsor yesterday. She urged me to talk with my grief groups and my therapist about what is obsessing me and tormenting me at the same time. It's this same thought that goes endlessly on in my head and tears me up inside—the idea that I helped a lot of people during my years as a practicing psychotherapist, but I was not able to help you—my beloved son!

I have been hesitant to talk openly about my tormenting thoughts, except with a couple of close friends. I believe that my reluctance is partly due to not wanting to appear arrogant—"Who does she think she is?"—and partly because I can guess what Al-Anon folks would tell me. They would probably quote the first step back to me: "I admit that I am powerless over alcohol." The truth is, I don't want to hear their argument, even if they have a valid point. My sponsor is right. I have to take the plunge and talk about my particular anguish about failing to push you toward recovery and sobriety. Otherwise, I know that I will not be able to heal my pain, which is loaded with regret as well as immense sadness. I certainly tried to help you, hence my trip to Los Angeles in late October to do an intervention on your addiction and situation. The fact that the intervention did not succeed in steering you from your destructive path will haunt me until I die.

My therapist head tries to point out to my tormented heart that there were important factors missing from the intervention. There was no leverage to be applied (financial or emotional) to push you into treatment. There were no possible threats of loss of marriage or family or even loss of a job. Your two boys had already left home—and I could not even convince them to join Olga and me in doing the intervention. As for your wife, she refused to ask you to go for help, no matter how much we implored her.

I know the logical facts, but it still hurts a lot to have failed in my mission to rescue you. I guess deep down you did not want to or were not ready to be rescued. My only consolation is that the intervention pierced your denial some, and you admitted you needed help. Unfortunately, you never pursued that—as far as I know—and there was no action, no follow-up, on the admission of need.

Later on, I thought that jail would give you the necessary push and motivation to change your life. Surely, that would make you reach bottom. The times in jail didn't do the job either. Were they too short (twenty days each) for a change in attitude? I don't know. I just agonize and keep pondering and speculating.

It breaks my heart to realize that you must have had cirrhosis of the liver when you did go to jail. I found that out later when Nicholas shared the results of your autopsy with me. How painful jail must have been, physically as well as emotionally. There are times when I wish I had set aside some of my tough love principles and posted bail for you. It wouldn't have kept you out of jail, but it might have spared you some suffering and you might not have been so angry with me. How I hate the fact that you died while estranged from me. Even while angry, did you remember how much I loved you?

I cannot write any more. The pain that I am feeling is literally choking me, and I cannot swallow. I need to stop. Good-bye, my love!

April 25, 2018

My Dearest Son,

I did not go to my grief group today because of chest pains. I had them—off and on—all night long, so I decided not to go to group. I have had these kinds of pains before for many years. After many trips to the ER, I finally got it that they are due to a thickening of the chest wall and not dangerous. However, when they do occur, they still worry me some and cannot be ignored.

I mostly rested during the day and talked with Connie, who currently lives in Florida. You do remember my close friend Connie, don't you? We went to California together a few times, and you welcomed us at the LA airport. She has a son who lives outside of Los Angeles, whom she is visiting presently. I am happy for her but feel sad for myself that I no longer have a son to visit there as well.

Oh, how I miss you, sweetheart! It's been six long weeks since I lost you, and I still have moments when I think that this is all a bad dream and that I'm going to wake up any moment and get a phone call with your booming voice saying, "Mom, it's me, Jamie!" I would go to the ends of the earth to see you, my dear son, one more time, but, unfortunately, it's not to be. I have to wait awhile and hope that my faith is right on, and I will see you again someday, in another form and another kind of existence when I also leave this world and become a spirit. In the meantime, all I have is memories of you and cherished photos. I also have the last two texts that you sent me. I asked Nicholas to undelete those texts so that I could keep a small memento of you by hanging on to your voice. I have not been able to listen to those texts yet, but it comforts me a little to know that they still exist.

I also have some pictures of you on my cell phone. I can't bear to look at the one from my last visit to LA, during your older son's high school graduation. (I am not counting the intervention trip as a regular visit.) It's a picture of the whole family—including myself—and we are all smiling.

It was all a lie, of course, but I had no idea what was brewing in the background and that life events were soon to be crashing down on all of us. There were a few alarming signs, but I turned my head away from the truth, being in denial myself. You managed to keep the mirrors of deception going, at least for the two weeks I spent at your house.

You did admit to me one day that your anxiety had gotten worse and it woke you up every night around 2 a.m. You couldn't get back to sleep for hours, you added. I gently suggested that maybe you could curtail the wine drinking at night.

You looked at me and curtly said, "I don't think that's the reason for my anxiety, Mom," and walked away.

Later, I tried to explain to you that alcohol had a Band-Aid effect on anxiety. That it seemed to quiet it down for a while, but then the anxiety came back later, stronger. I told you that alcohol was not a good solution to the problem. I suggested that you talk to a doctor about antianxiety medications.

You shook your head and said, "It's my wife who needs to go see a doctor, Mom, not me. She is the one with the problem. Haven't you noticed the unusual number of naps she's taking and all the food that she is burning?" Leslie overheard your remarks, and you two started loudly arguing about which one of you most needed medical care. I tried to intervene—and mediate a little: "Maybe you two can go together to see a doctor," I suggested. "We can't afford it" was your reply, and you walked away from me one more time.

Our conversation and your remarks got me worried about your health and the state of your marriage, but you reassured me later that everything was OK. Since I really wanted to believe that, the subject was dropped. Now looking back, I'm so sorry that I didn't dig any deeper to find out the truth. I guess it's true that you cannot be a therapist to your own family, but I still feel guilt and heartfelt pain about my actions or lack of them.

Please forgive me, honey, for not having been able to help you. There's a price to pay for misguided love, and I'm paying it.

April 29, 2018

My Dearest Son,

Every time I glance at the bench across the street in front of a neighbor's house, I feel like crying. It vividly reminds me of the bench in the backyard of your repossessed house—the one that you picked up from the trash bin of one of your neighbors. You saw some potential and a faded beauty in that old discarded bench, and you took it to your house (with Robert's and Nicholas's help). Your wife laughed at you, but you ignored her reaction and lovingly painted it over and over again until it took on a pleasing, vintage appearance.

"Doesn't it look like an antique, Mom?" you asked with a smile. You seemed proud of your efforts, and I was proud of you for rescuing that old bench and seeing something worthwhile in somebody else's discards.

How I wish you had been able to see the damaged beauty in yourself and lovingly tend to it—like you did with the bench—so as to bring out a healthier you! You had such potential, my boy! I am so sad that you let it go to waste and did not try to rescue it from the disease of alcoholism that ravaged you and your family—including me—and that eventually took your life.

Your wife later told me that the coroner said that your heart stopped while you slept on a park bench (how ironic that your final resting place was a bench), but I believe with all my mind and heart that your heart would not have stopped at age fifty-seven if it weren't for all the poison you took through the years in the form of alcohol and other drugs!

Well, you did try to help yourself, once that I know of at least. You told me about that time when you went cold turkey for twenty-four hours and stopped drinking and drugging. You ended up with a severe seizure, and your wife had to call 911 and have an ambulance take you to an LA emergency room. You thought you were dying, you said, and the experience shook you to your core. How typical of your personality and stubborn streak that you tried to fix your problem all by yourself. I tried to explain to you that your attempt to get sober was an ill-fated venture from the start.

"You need help from professionals," I said. "They have drugs now that can help the detox experience not be so terrible." I added, "Please get some help, honey." Obviously, a part of you wanted to stop drinking or you wouldn't have done what you did.

You looked at me with a stern look and said, "I know that the amount I drink is not good for me, but I can't imagine never drinking again. And you know what? I would rather die or go to jail rather than be locked up in a rehab place! After all, alcohol did not cause the situation that I'm in!"

I looked at you, the familiar face that I loved, looking haggard and so much older than your fifty-plus years, and I had this sinking feeling that your denial was so strong that you were not going to get any help after all.

Little did you and I know on that late October day eighteen months ago that a short time later you were going to be locked up in a Ventura County jail for the first of two times, that you would beg me to post bail, and that I would have to refuse to do so. I told you—with a sob in my voice—that I was attending Al-Anon on a regular basis and could not, in good conscience, enable your disease by stopping its consequences.

Not even in my worst nightmares did I imagine that this was the last time that I would ever see you, my beloved son. During your whole alcoholic journey, no matter how dismal things looked, I always hung on to a spark of hope that you would eventually give up your denial and get sober.

If I had thought that particular day of October was going to be the day of our last meeting on earth, I would have clung to you, kissed your face repeatedly, and not let you go!

April 30, 2018

My Dearest Son,

I thought of you a few minutes ago. Of course, you are always in my mind, but sometimes the remembrance becomes more focused. I was reading a book called *A Dog's Purpose*. It is a well-written book, though a little sentimental. Anyway, as I was reading about the fictional dog's devotion to its owners, I started thinking about Snicky, your beautiful and beloved dog. I started crying as I thought of how he must be missing you, wondering where you are. Olga told me that the dog is in a shelter. I sure hope that it gets adopted by a loving family, even though I doubt that they can love Snicky as much as you and your boys did.

I vividly remembered a day, a few months ago, when you called me—the alarm and distress in your voice palpable—asking me for help getting Snicky out of an LA shelter. The shelter personnel picked up your dog, you said, when he was roaming the streets while you were in jail. You said the shelter was asking you to pay some money before you could get him back.

"Mom," you said, "I know that you cannot send me any money due to problems with my drinking, but this is my dog that you have known and liked for many years, and he is an innocent animal. Will you please help me so I can get him back?" You sounded so distressed that I had no doubt that you were telling me the truth this time. I didn't hesitate.

"You are right, Jamie," I said. "Your dog is innocent and he needs you. Tell me who to talk to at the shelter, and I will promptly send him the necessary money to pay the fine. Don't worry. You'll get your dog back soon." You sounded relieved. "I'll call you back right away," you said. "Thanks, Mom." You called me back after a few minutes. This time you sounded happy. "Mom, it's OK," you said. "You don't have to send any money. They let me have him back. They forgave the fine."

I told you I was happy for you and your dog, and I hung up the phone. I was relieved that your latest crisis was resolved and that I had been able to say yes for once in response to one of your many requests for financial help. I marveled that despite the depths of your addiction and consequent disease you were still capable of telling me the truth, at least occasionally. You could have lied to me and gotten some money from me under false pretenses, but you didn't; you chose to tell me the truth. I was also very glad to realize that you still had the qualities of compassion and caring. I was happy that you turned to me for help, despite my previous refusals to help you financially. You were counting on my own qualities of compassion and caring, and that meant a lot to me. This whole episode proved to me that, deep down, there were still some traces of my loving, decent son—despite the ravages of the addiction that was consuming you—and that gave me a very good feeling.

How nice to experience the fact that there was still a strong connection between us and that you remembered that I loved you!

May 3, 2018

My Dearest Son,

I took a big step today toward healing. I went back to the YMCA to rejoin my old water aerobics class. It had been at least eight months since I was there last. Initially, I had to recover from a fractured knee, then from knee-replacement surgery, and then from my terrible loss of you in March. I just couldn't bring myself to face the questions of how I was. I didn't want to lie and say, "I'm fine," nor did I want to talk about your death.

A friend of mine from that group, Virginia, who also lost a son about the same time as I did, called me this morning to tell me that she was planning to go back to the Y. So, I decided to join her and take the plunge also. (I couldn't resist the pun. Are you laughing? You used to laugh at my jokes.)

I was kind of dreading my return because of the particularly painful current circumstances of my life, but it turned out to be fine after all. The group even called out my name with some glee as I approached the pool. A gratifying start!

It was good to see Virginia there. We hugged and talked for a little while. I only told one other person, Irene, about my terrible news. I have known her for a long time. She and I were two of the original members of this group about thirty years ago. She asked me only one question, "Was this your lawyer son who drank that you used to visit in California?" I nodded yes. My strong emotions made me unable to speak. God knows that I don't want that to be your only legacy—the lawyer son who drank—so it's even more imperative that I keep writing these letters. I have to show others that there was a lot more to your identity than your excessive drinking!

As I kept moving and exercising in the pool, I suddenly remembered an incident from your childhood involving water and pools. I thought of our early days in Baltimore, when you were six years old, and I took you and your brother Spiros for swimming lessons. I enrolled Spiros in an advanced class (he already knew how to swim) and you in a beginner's class. Constantine, who was a baby at the time, stayed by my side in his stroller (these were the sixties, and back then babies weren't taught how to swim).

The classes went along well for a while, even though both you and Spiros complained that the water in the pool was too cold. This was June in Baltimore, and the weather wasn't quite warm, just yet. You were used to the much warmer weather and waters of Louisiana where you were born.

About two weeks before you were to graduate from your swimming classes, you came to me one morning in the middle of the lesson, crying. I asked you what was wrong. "Our teacher just told us that she was going to have us dive from the high board today," you said, "and I don't want to do it!"

I told you that I would talk with your teacher. I took you by the hand, and we went to find her. I could tell by the expression on your face and the stance of your body that you were very tense. "Don't worry, honey," I said. "You don't have to do this if you don't want to or if you're not ready. I'm sure she'll understand and you will be fine."

Well, I was wrong. She did not understand, and everything was not fine. Her response to me was swift and tense. "This is the day for learning how to dive from the high board," she told me. "Jamie will have to overcome his fear and just do it. It's not that big a deal!"

I looked at you and your eyes were brimming with tears. I gently asked you, "Do you want to do this, honey?" You replied as your whole body was shaking, "No, Mom, please don't make me do this. I'm too scared!"

Your teacher kept saying, "Come on, come on. Let's do this. It's not going to kill you. The whole class is waiting for you to jump." I looked at her and said, "Jaime is not ready to do this today. Maybe we can try next time?"

"Oh, no," came the quick reply. "Your son has to jump from the high board or drop out of my class."

I could not believe her rigidity. I certainly did not want you to have a lifelong fear of water and pools because of her forcing you to do something you did not want to do. I calmly said, "If that's the case, then my son is dropping out of your class," and I walked away, shaking a little inside.

You seemed so relieved. You ran after me, shouting, "Thanks, Mom, thanks a lot. Just don't tell anybody about what happened today, especially not Spiros. He'll make fun of me and call me 'Baby.'" I could tell that your body had lost its tension and was no longer shaking. I never regretted that long-ago decision. I kept your secret, even though I did tell your father. To my somewhat surprise, he did not protest my decision, even though we had paid in advance for all the swimming lessons.

You went on to love water and swimming—all your life. When you were in high school, you even took Blue Cross training and became a lifeguard. You spent most of your high school summers working as a lifeguard in various suburban pools, earning a little pocket money. You told me more than once that you loved being a lifeguard.

In later years, after you married and settled in Los Angeles, every time I visited you there, I would see you dive or jump into your pool numerous times a day—either by yourself or with your two boys. Every time I saw you enjoy the pool or ocean, my heart would leap with joy, and I would thank the heavens and my own good sense for not forcing you to dive when you were six years old and scared.

May 11, 2018

My Dearest Son,

I miss you so much! It's going to be two months next Sunday since your passing. It's going to be hard, really hard, because next Sunday is Mother's Day. It's going to be my first Mother's Day with two living sons instead of three, and I don't know how I'm going to bear it! Never mind that I did not hear from you last year on this particular special day.

You actually called me two weeks before the day to tell me that you were not going to call me on Mother's Day! (When I spoke of this at an Al-Anon meeting last year, there was a lot of laughter in the audience to my surprise.) I was told that your behavior was typical, crazy alcoholic behavior! You were not going to call me, you explained, because you were angry with me. Supposedly, I had told your wife that you were "a hopeless drunk" who belonged in jail.

I vehemently protested and told you that these were not my words. I did admit that I had said that maybe a short jail term might push you toward sobriety, since nothing else had worked so far. I emphasized the fact that I never used the label of "hopeless drunk" and meant it.

You didn't sound like you believed me, and I felt so sad about our whole conversation. Later, my Al-Anon sponsor theorized that probably it was you who saw yourself as a hopeless drunk, and you were projecting that on me.

True to your word, you did not call me on Mother's Day, and despite everything I know, my feelings were hurt anyway. I felt hurt, but I understood why you didn't call me. I guessed that it was because of foggy, muddled alcoholic reasoning, and despite my sadness, I didn't give up my battered fragments of hope. I desperately clung to the idea that a miracle would occur one day and that you would eventually fight your way out of your denial and addiction.

Unfortunately, even the two jail terms that you endured did not alter your destructive path. They say one has to reach bottom to change. Wasn't jail your bottom? Or did you view yourself as the "hopeless drunk"—as my sponsor thought you did—and decide to not even try?

By the time your second jail term occurred, you must have known about the cirrhosis of the liver diagnosis that the coroner said you suffered from. You never said anything to me about that painful condition, but you must have known of it at some point. My heart hurts for you for how you must have suffered—both physically and emotionally—on finding out that you had the dreaded alcoholic disease.

I wonder about my actions as well. Had I known about your impaired liver, would I have weakened and given you bail money? Maybe. Would my principles have been firm and unyielding when placed against your suffering? Frankly, I don't know. All I know is that at least you are not suffering anymore, and I'm very glad about that!

May 12, 2018 (2 a.m.)

My Dearest Son,

Tomorrow is Mother's Day. How I dread it! This will be the first Mother's Day when I'll be on earth without one of my children. I don't know if I can bear the pain.

My daily blood pressure readings show some high numbers lately, despite two blood pressure meds as well as a 24/7 patch. Is it any wonder? Usually I get worried—and even fearful—when I see high numbers on my home monitor, but lately I feel numb about the whole thing.

I went to my grief group a few days ago. They gave me a plastic bracelet band that says "forever in my heart" and a white rose (in honor of the holiday). They also gave us some wise advice on how to survive Mother's Day without falling apart. I thank God for Compassionate Friends and feel grateful that this organization exists. I am wearing the bracelet. I plan to never take it off, and I glance frequently at my lovely rose as I'm writing. I marvel that beauty still exists in the world—even when my heart doesn't register any.

My life seems divided into before and after. I'll think of some event, and then immediately I'll try to figure out if it happened before your death or after. There's an old song that used to be popular many years ago. I think it goes something like "What a difference a day makes"—though it lasts only a few hours.[2]

The day of March 13, 2018, changed my life forever. Sometimes, when I'm deep in the middle of dark grief and emotional pain, I get angry even at your father for not being alive anymore and not able to share my pain. I'm also angry at him for abandoning you after our divorce and never going to visit you in Los Angeles to know your boys as they grew up. It was his loss as well as theirs.

I know for a fact that it hurt you deeply for him not to visit you through the years. You told me that practically every time I visited you on my annual trips. You pointed out that he did not call or write either. The truth is that you went silent as well, adding to the estrangement between the two of you.

I know that it's not rational to be angry with a dead person, but I don't care. He should have been a more caring father—divorce or no divorce. I admit that one of my shortcomings has always been to want—almost demand—a fair and just world. Of course, that unrealistic expectation often leads to disappointment, but I find it hard to give up my trait.

I still remember staying up many nights before separating from my ex, carefully dividing up china and silverware to make sure that we each got an equal and fair share. (I did this totally alone, my ex refusing to lift a finger toward this endeavor.) I also remember how I expected him to be fair as well and how shocked I was when he told me that he would not share the company stocks and other common assets. I think I was more indignant than hurt by the whole process. Here again, when I realized how your father changed postdivorce and no longer acted like the caring father that he used to be, I was so upset and so shocked. Where was the fairness in all of this, I wondered? How could divorce change a person's behavior to such a degree?

Hard to believe that he used to dote on you when you were young. You were probably his favorite child. The change hurt you deeply, and I hurt for you. I did urge you to forgive him and to visit him in Houston before he died. I did that for your sake as well as his. Thank God you listened and came to Houston to see him. You told me later that you were glad you did and thanked me for my advice.

May 14, 2018

My Dearest Son,

Mother's Day came and went. Thank God! It was painful, but I had anticipated an even worse day. Thanks primarily to my daughter-in-law Olga, it went pretty well. She had organized the day to the max, so the activities would keep me busy.

She picked me up at noon and took me to the Houstonian. That's a very nice hotel in Houston surrounded by beautiful flower gardens and known for fitness training and spa pampering. Olga had made us appointments for almost all of the spa amenities, including a full-body massage and lunch. After the massage, we went to the small indoor pool for a while, and I took a few dips while Olga sat by and read. Not being used to such luxuries, I felt spoiled.

So, despite my grief, it turned out to be a rather nice day, mostly because of Olga's thoughtfulness. I sure hope that the day will come when I can smile at my nice memories of you instead of bursting into tears every time that I have a flashback. The latest example came on Mother's Day.

At one point during the day, while we were at the Houstonian Hotel, Olga and I were separated for a while because of different spa activities. I wandered into the gift shop at the hotel, so that I could look for a gift for Olga to thank her for arranging such a nice day for me. As I was looking around the shop, I absentmindedly looked at my reflection in a mirror hanging in the store and recoiled when I saw the tired, dejected expression on my face. The reflection depressed me. Then I thought of you and how complimentary you used to be.

Whether true or false, I would beam at your compliments and rejoice in your admiration. I thought of all that and started crying, right in the middle of the store. Later, I rejoined Olga and gave her the gift I had selected. I did not tell her about my flashback. I kept that close to my heart, as your gift to me on Mother's Day.

Olga and I left the place around 5 p.m., and we went to her house to change clothes for our evening adventure—a new, trendy restaurant. Spiros, Stuart, and Nicholas joined us there.

Stuart gave me a card and a gift. He had placed a special picture (from the past) inside the card. I took one look at the picture and burst into tears. Stuart looked bewildered, not understanding my reaction. I explained to him what was going on inside me. The picture was one of long ago. There I was, my arms around two very handsome and well-dressed young children (Victoria and Stuart). Victoria had flowers in her hair, and Stuart had a big grin on his face. The picture was taken on the day of your wedding in lovely Northridge, a resort outside Los Angeles.

Stuart—seeing my tears—said, "I'm sorry, Mema. I didn't know where that picture was taken. I have always loved that picture, and I wanted to share it with you." I assured him that it was OK and that he had done nothing wrong. After all, this Mother's Day was full of flashbacks and reminders. I thought to myself, "All holidays are going to be like this from now on. Instead of Jamie's presence, I will have only memories of him."

May 18, 2018

My Dearest Son,

I just read a quote that was very meaningful to me. It said, "Nothing fools you better than the lie you tell yourself."[3] I don't know who the author of the quote is, but it immediately took me back mentally to October 2016, the last time I set eyes on you. Olga and I had come to Los Angeles in a desperate attempt to stage an intervention on your out-of-control drinking and way of life.

At the end of the intervention, as I sat there shaking and crying, you told me that alcohol did not cause your situation. That was the terrible lie that you told yourself, my son. I knew when I heard it that you totally believed that lie. You obviously did not believe or see (or want to see) what the rest of the world was seeing—that alcohol/drugs and your addiction to them had caused the loss of your house, the loss of your career, and the estrangement from your family and friends. What is more important is that it led to the loss of your two boys who left home and refused to visit you or their mother. They had even refused to participate in the intervention, despite my urgent pleas.

As I heard your denial over and over again, my anguish made me unable to speak. It was Olga who asked, "Jaime, what do you think produced the bad situation that you are in?" You looked at her and said, "Well, it's complicated, but mostly it's bad luck!" My heart was squeezed tight at that point, and your words made me lose the last vestige of hope that I was clinging to.

We didn't know it back then, but the worst was yet to come. Your decline was fast and terrible. You had three DWI (or DUI) citations and ended up in jail twice for not following up on your parole conditions and for continuing to drink and drive—among other things. You would lose your license to practice law and end up living under a tent on the streets of LA. Finally, your poor, overworked heart would stop, and you would be found dead, all alone on a park bench. No good-byes, no closure—just shock and tears for the loved ones you left behind.

Yesterday, as I was despairing about all of this, I happened to run across something in an old book—a bookmark from a Los Angeles library. The mark date was 2007. I didn't remember seeing that bookmark for a long time. Maybe another sign from you and the universe to help me with my distress? My memory took me to a different, much happier time. I vividly remembered that particular trip of ours to the Los Angeles Central Library.

During one of my yearly visits to your home, you told me that you had to go downtown on business. You asked if I wanted to come with you and visit your favorite library. "It's a great library," you said, "and I go there often. I know how much you love books, Mom, and I know you are going to like it."

"It has a whole floor dedicated to Greek antiquities," you added. I jumped at the chance to spend some quality time with you with the additional bonus of being in one of my favorite places—a library.

Indeed, it was a great library, and I dearly enjoyed exploring it with you! We spent many hours that day inside that wonderful library. I can still picture in my mind the many floors it covered and our going up and down the elevators, visiting different floors full of treasures of books, and our delighted exclamations every time we discovered unusual and/or interesting collections of books.

Afterward, we went to a unique downtown restaurant that was a favorite of yours. The gimmick there was that customers were encouraged to throw peanut shells on the floor. (You explained to me that it was patterned after a famous New York restaurant.) I remember that I enjoyed my pastrami sandwich and mostly relished your company and our conversations—like I always did.

You were attentive and loving back then. I bought a book that day in the gift store of that library, and I still love to leaf through it at times, especially now, in the middle of the night, when grief about losing you overwhelms me. It's an unusual and unique book. It's titled *The Book Lover's Cookbook*,[4] and it consists of recipes taken from literary works. I was delighted when I found it there because I had never seen anything like it. I cherish the book just like I cherish my memories of you on that particular day.

Maybe, one distant day in the future, I will smile at the happy memories of our times together, instead of choking with crying like I'm doing as I'm writing this letter. I hope so!

May 23, 2018

My Dearest Son,

So many things remind me of you and bring on spontaneous outbursts of grief.

I first read in *TV Guide* that there was a Pink Panther movie marathon coming on TV, and I burst into tears. Oh, how you loved the Pink Panther movies. There were many occasions during my trips to LA when you would play the DVDs of these movies, and you would look for your favorite scenes and say, "Hey, Mom, watch this—this is so funny." Then you would imitate Peter Sellers in his fake French accent as he played bumbling, clueless Inspector Clouseau. Then you would laugh—your loud, booming laugh reverberating in the room—with your boys joining you as well. I didn't care that much about the Pink Panther, but I didn't tell you that. It was such a joy to watch you and your sons relishing the show's humor.

Since I was with you and your family only for ten to twelve days once a year, my time with you was very precious to me. It helped a lot that you and Leslie were always so welcoming to me on my visits. It was always emotionally wrenching to leave you at the end of my visits and come back to Houston.

These visits made me appreciate my mother a lot more. I really understood emotionally how hard it must have been for her to have her only child (me) live so far away from her. History, as they say, often repeats itself. I left Istanbul, my birthplace, when I was twenty-two years old and did not go back, except for some visits when I was much older and had a family of my own. The distance between Istanbul and the United States was certainly a lot farther way than the Houston–Los Angeles commute, and I finally grasped how much love it took on her part to let me leave home. There were complicated factors that precipitated my leaving. My mother encouraged me to come to the United States—especially after the anti-Greek riots of 1955—but it still must have been an agonizing decision for her. I was told in later years that she fainted at the airport as my plane took off. Leaving home was hard for me as well, but like most young people, I was caught up in the exciting adventure of going overseas and having a boyfriend (later, my husband) waiting for me in the United States.

My mother—your grandmother Anastasia—worked hard all her life, despite chronic heart disease, and she used all her savings to come every other year to the States to visit me and you and your brothers. Those were expensive trips—a lot more expensive than my trips to California to see you—and she told me once that one of her friends had jokingly remarked that she could have bought a house in the countryside outside Istanbul with all the money that she spent through the years traveling to and from Istanbul to Baton Rouge, Louisiana; Alexandria, Louisiana; Baltimore, Maryland; and Houston, Texas (all the places where our family lived). Mother told her friend, "I would rather visit my daughter and grandchildren than own a fancy house." Your grandmother lived in an apartment in Istanbul all her life.

I felt the same way as my mother. My trips to California were certainly a lot less expensive than hers, but there were times—especially after my divorce from your dad—when I had to choose between coming to Los Angeles or spending the money on needed essentials for me and/or my house. I never hesitated. Like my mother before me, I would choose to come and see you every time. How I wish I still had that choice. I get into wishful, grief-ridden fantasy thinking, and then the reality of the current situation hits me hard.

As I was thinking about your grandmother, I remembered once more how much she loved you. She loved all her grandchildren, but I have always known that you were her favorite. She observed you once when you were a young child defending your older brother against a bully, and ever since then, she placed you on a pedestal and kept you there.

She often told me that you were so smart that she thought you could be president one day. I reminded you of her belief in you during my unsuccessful but heartfelt intervention. You agreed with me, even in your foggy, substance-altered mental state.

I was sobbing by that time, but I'll never forget that moment—when a remembrance of your grandmother brought you back to your old self for a few minutes, despite your disease. It's just as well that she's not around anymore to see the shattering of her dreams.

May 24, 2018

My Dearest Son,

I pushed myself to go to the YMCA today for my water aerobics class. I'm trying to attend the class on a regular basis, but it's hard to find the energy to do that. Often, my grief takes over and consumes me, and I get too depressed to leave the house. I thought that maybe, if I went regularly, I could sleep better at night instead of staying up until 2 a.m. or 3 a.m., so that thought motivated me to go.

Something totally unexpected happened today during class. I saw one of the participants, somebody I did not know, putting her head down on the side of the pool. She seemed to be crying while trying not to call attention to herself. Another woman approached her and seemed to be trying to console her. I overheard something about being worried about her son, and then I heard the word *addict*. Somehow, I was not surprised when I saw the crying. I suspected something like that. Being consumed by the topic, as I have been, I can quickly pick up the despair of others.

With tears in my own eyes, I approached her at the end of the class. I told her that I had not meant to eavesdrop, but that the few words that I heard her say made me want to reach out to her. She told me that her younger son was struggling a lot, trying not to use alcohol or other drugs, but he was not successful. "He's on a dangerous path," she added. "With heroin being his drug of choice, he has no job or even a place to sleep."

She was at her wits' end wanting to help him without enabling him in his disease: "That's why I was crying," she said. I tried to comfort her, but I too started crying as I told her what had happened to you and how I had lost you forever. I hugged her and told her that I hoped that she would take care of herself and help her son without being codependent. The expression on her face made me realize that she understood exactly what I meant. She thanked me for reaching out to her, and we hugged, both of us in tears.

I kept thinking that you were looking down on us and were glad that I had tried to comfort somebody who had been a stranger to me just a few minutes ago, but she was now a fellow sufferer and a new friend. We bonded by our grief and despair of this terrible disease of substance abuse.

Two mothers in great emotional pain had found each other.

May 28, 2018

My Dearest Son,

In the midst of my agony about your death, I keep trying to find ways to honor your memory and celebrate the person you used to be. A friend told me the other day about an organization that reaches out to the homeless to help their pets. They take them to veterinarians for meds and necessary shots and take care of them if they or their owners are sick or unable to take care of them.

You always loved animals, Jaime. You adored your two cats when you were first married, and later, your beautiful Alaskan Husky dog with the limpid and expressive gray eyes. He was always by your side, even after you lost your house, drifted from one cheap motel to another, and then became totally homeless.

I still remember the distress in your voice when you called me to tell me that the authorities had picked up your dog from the street, while you were in jail, and were holding him. You rarely called me by this time, and you never asked me for money anymore, not after I refused to give you bail money. However, this time around, your love for your dog was strong enough that you asked on his behalf. You knew, I suppose, deep down that I would not refuse this kind of request. A few minutes later you called me back to tell me that the authorities had returned your dog and had waived the fees.

After we hung up the phone, I started crying. I was happy for you that you had found your dog, that you had gotten him back, and that somebody—a stranger—had shown you kindness. You have not had any of that lately. Life has been very difficult for you in the last few years. I cried because it breaks my heart to watch all the suffering that you have endured because of your self-destructive path of addiction.

I also cried because the world has been scorning you and not really seeing the sickness that you are carrying. They just see the self-destruction!

May 31, 2018

My Dearest Son,

I didn't expect to have another crying episode at the water aerobics class, but that's what happened this morning. I ran into Mary, the mother of the young addict that I previously wrote to you about. She told me that a miracle had occurred and that her troubled son had agreed to go to a rehabilitation center. He told her that he didn't want to die and that he wanted to give up heroin and other drugs before they killed him.

I told her that I was happy for her and for her son. I meant what I said, but at the same time, I was filled with such immense sadness, that all I could do was go to a corner of the pool, away from the group, and sob my heart out. I kept thinking the same thing over and over again, "Why, oh, why couldn't it have been you as well that wanted the help?"

I cried and cried, and I'm still crying as I am writing this. Yes, I know what my brain is telling me—just because an addict enters rehab, it doesn't mean that the battle over addiction is won. There's no guarantee that the addict will stay there until the end of treatment or even that the treatment will work and the individual will attain sobriety and keep it, but at least it's a start.

I never heard you say that you wanted to stop using. In fact, I remember your telling me more than once that you couldn't imagine not drinking anymore. The only evidence I have that you even tried to stop and/or shake off your dependence on chemicals was the episode that you described to me (and that Leslie confirmed) that you once went without drinking or drugging for twenty-four hours cold turkey and that you ended up having a severe seizure that night that made you think you were dying. Somebody took you to the emergency room of a nearby hospital.

Did that experience scare you so much that you didn't think you could ever stop using? I told you that after many years of using drugs that you couldn't stop all by yourself and that you needed help from professionals. You nodded and said, "Okay, Mom, I promise that I'll get help. You came all the way from Houston with a bad knee; the least I can do is to get help. I know I drink too much!"

My heart leaped with joy as I heard your words. I had just heard a crack in your state of denial for the first time ever, and that gave me a glimmer of hope. However, I also told myself that promises were easy and that I had to wait and see if you would act on your promise and not brush it off after my visit. And, yet, I wanted so badly to believe your promise to me!

After returning home to Houston, I waited and waited to hear from you. I had a lot of anxiety mixed with some anticipation and a touch of hope. I heard nothing from you for months. I kind of knew what that silence meant: nothing positive was happening. I figured that if you had gone for help that you would certainly have let me know. Your silence spoke volumes.

I was sunk by agony and despair, so I knew I needed some help myself. I went to see my therapist again. I trusted his expertise and judgment, and he had helped me navigate my emotions earlier, before the intervention.

In December there was a phone call from you and Leslie, very late in the evening when I was already in bed. I was happy to hear your voice, even though your words were kind of slurred and not very clear. You talked about being tired of moving from place to place (you were not specific about what these places were) and wanting to rent an apartment. You added that you did not have the money for a deposit and other costs related to moving.

I listened quietly. You did not ask me directly for money, and I didn't offer, even though a part of me wanted to. I told you that if you went to work for a law firm that you could afford to rent and even own another house someday. You wistfully agreed, saying that your wife was suggesting the same thing. Neither of us talked about whether you still had the cognitive ability to practice law. I guess we were both in denial about that.

We also talked some about Nicholas, who by that time was living in Houston in Spiros and Olga's home. I emphasized that your younger son was adjusting well to life in Houston and attending a community college. Neither of us mentioned how traumatized he must have been by homelessness and the disintegration of the family. I tried to lighten up the mood a little by telling you an anecdote about Nicholas. How he had told me that I disrespected my car by not keeping it clean. You laughed with your big-hearted, booming laugh, and I inwardly rejoiced that I had succeeded in making you laugh. I had been missing your humor and laughter for so long!

How terribly sad that I will never hear your wonderful laugh ever again!

June 1, 2018

My Dearest Son,

In September 2017, I received two voicemail texts from you. Your words were once again slurred, and I had a hard time understanding you. After months and months of silence and noncommunication on your part, the messages angered me and frustrated me to the point that I deleted them without fully listening to them.

In March 2018, after your tragic passing, I remembered those two texts. Wanting desperately to hear the sound of your voice one more time, I regretted having deleted them and asked Nicholas (my digital wizard) if he could resurrect those old messages. He said he would try, and to my happy surprise, he succeeded in retrieving them for me.

As I listened a lot more attentively to the context of the voice messages, I heard that you had gone to a few AA meetings (you called them "antidrinking classes") and even had found a sponsor that you liked. I listened to your voice with tears in my eyes and lots of mixed feelings. I was glad that you had at least made an effort toward recovery. Was that a condition of your parole? On the other hand, your slurred words made it clear to me that your efforts had not been successful. At the same time, I felt guilty that I didn't listen to your total message and that I did not encourage you or support you in your attempt of sobriety at that particular time.

I am so sorry, honey, that I deleted those messages without giving them my full attention. I am also sorry that I joined you in your denial about the train wreck rushing into your life instead of using my professional skills to be more observant about the early warning signs of addiction and more objective about my observations.

Looking back, I regret not hiring another professional to do the intervention instead of doing it myself. The rates I was quoted were very expensive, and I didn't have the money needed. Nobody else in the family volunteered to pay for the enterprise and/or even attended the intervention (except for Olga). Your sons (who would have been very important factors toward success) absolutely refused to participate in the intervention. They would not even consider coming to see you and their mother. With no job at stake and a lack of willingness on your wife's part to use any leverage at all, chances for a successful intervention were slim from the start.

Would another professional have succeeded more in altering some of these negative conditions? I'll never know. All I know is that in my desperation, I did not see any alternatives than to do it myself. My therapist told me not to agonize and feel so much guilt about the failed intervention. He said, "Who knows? There's another side to this. Jamie may have listened to you a lot better than he would have listened to a stranger. After all, he would have resented the outsiders, but he does love you!" I would dearly love to believe that he has a good point, but it's hard. The self-doubts continue to gnaw at me, along with the immense grief of having lost you.

I do perceive one positive result that came from my intervention trip beside the fact that I saw you for the last time, even if I didn't know it back then. That positive result had to do with Nicholas. He had refused to participate in the intervention, but he did tell us how to find you in that remote, miserable motel. We spent a lot of time talking with Nicholas, and he even spent the night in our hotel room.

Even in my shocked and distressed emotional state, I realized that my teenage grandson was totally traumatized by his family's situation and quite in need for attention and affection. Olga and I convinced him to come to Houston for an extended visit, and we told him that we would send him an airplane ticket.

Spiros and Olga did send him a ticket, and he came to Houston for the Christmas holidays. He seemed to be shell-shocked, but we were happy to have him here. After the visit, he went back to LA. When his plans for rooming with friends fell through, he decided to come back to Houston and attend school here. I know that as his loving father you would be happy for him, despite the fact that you and Leslie must have been missing your son.

A year and a half after the initial visit, Nicholas is still here and making *A's* at the community college. He's working part-time as well and saving money so he can transfer to the University of Texas as a junior. Spiros, Olga, and Stuart have been treating him as one of their own, and we are all surrounding him with lots of love. You should be proud of your sons, Jaime. You and Leslie raised two fine young men who are succeeding in their life despite the terrible circumstances that fell on their family.

It feels good that my ill-fated visit to LA at least set all this in motion for Nicholas, even though I was not able to alter your path of self-destruction. Unfortunately, your disease proved to be more powerful than a mother's love, even with therapeutic skills at work.

June 5, 2018

My Dearest Son,

There's a lot of ambivalence and mixed feelings in my heart tonight. Victoria, Stuart, and I have been talking about going on an Alaskan cruise this summer. We had discussed the possibility of doing this before your untimely death, and now the kids have brought up the subject again.

I had wanted this trip in the past, but now it feels like a crazy plan. How can I go away on a long trip when I'm grieving so intensely for you? At the same time, I'm also thinking that I need to do this while I still have the opportunity. Two nice young people whom I dearly love are offering to go on a cruise with me to a place I have always wanted to go, and I'm not even paying for their passage. We are thinking of sharing a suite and splitting the cost three ways.

Victoria has been texting me all evening about options for an Alaskan cruise. I am so torn. There's a tiny feeling of excitement about the possibility of the voyage (you remember how your mother has always been addicted to travel) mixed with a lot of apprehension and even disbelief that I'm actually considering the plan.

I wonder if I would even be a good companion to them given my present state of mind and heart. Will I burden them with my grief and frequent crying spells? I discussed some of my concerns with them, and they both reassured me that they would enjoy my company despite my current reality. Would I even enjoy the trip? I don't know. It's really hard right now to enjoy anything at all.

I can almost hear your voice saying, "Go for it, Mom. It will be good for you!" I somehow know that, if you could communicate with me, you would encourage me to go.

June 9, 2018

My Dearest Son,

It looks like I'm going to Alaska in a few weeks. My granddaughter is planning the trip with some of my input. She told me that she had a court case coming up late in the summer, so we need to go soon. Stuart told us that the only time he can get away from the restaurant where he works is in early July. Have I told you that he is now the pastry sous-chef in a local restaurant?

Victoria asked me if I still wanted to go. I said yes while thinking that it was probably too late to make reservations for early July. Well, to my surprise, she found a suite available for the three of us in a relatively new cruise ship. She showed me some videos. It looks nice and has a big balcony (that was one of my few requirements). It is more expensive than I had calculated, and I will have to dip into my small savings account; however, I don't feel like I can back down now, not after Victoria rescheduled her court case and Stuart took some rare time off from work. I still cannot believe that I am going on a ten-day trip with such heartbreak in my heart.

A friend suggested—when I expressed my doubts to her—that I could take you with me! (Symbolically speaking, of course.) The truth is that I take you with me, no matter where I go. You are constantly on my mind and in my heart.

I still occasionally have conversations with you. They are one-sided, but that doesn't stop me. I asked you in my most recent one if I will be able to enjoy any part of the upcoming trip or will I be miserable the whole time and wish I had never gone. We'll see.

I have been on trips before when I was recuperating from romantic breakups (e.g., after my divorce), but those heartbreaks were nothing when compared with my present heartbreak!

June 10, 2018

My Dearest Son,

I went looking for my old digital cameras today for the Alaskan trip. I still can't quite believe that I am making plans to go when I have this huge hole in my heart and all the misery that goes with it. The cameras are for views of the glaciers and other scenic sights. Some say that this type of cruise has the most scenic vistas of all. I thought of that, and then in a flash I had a second thought—that I would gladly give up all the scenic views of the universe for just one glimpse of your beloved face. But that's not to be. You're gone forever from this earth, and I have to console myself, with eyes full of tears, by looking at pictures of you from childhood and adulthood. As I look at the pictures, I ache for you and for the potential in you that never fully materialized. Instead, it was crushed by your disease, which led to your premature death.

In the midst of all the ache, I have a few feelings of relief about your being free from suffering the complications of alcoholism. You don't have to battle the misery of being homeless any more or the feelings of impending doom about another jail term coming into your life. What is more important is that I am glad that you no longer have to struggle with any feelings of self-loathing. I remember the words "hopeless drunk" coming from your mouth. You attributed them to me but I never said them. Is that how you saw yourself? How sad!

You told me once that you would rather die than be locked up. We were talking about rehabilitation scenarios at the time. Of course, we didn't know then that you would end up being locked up twice in a Ventura County jail. How you must have hated that!

Victoria told me earlier in the year that the county's incarceration files showed that you had another court hearing scheduled for the first week in June. Since you had not gone for drug testing (I'm presuming this), did not pay your court fines (most probably), and had not met the terms of your parole, you must have been dreading going back to jail. Well, you escaped that fate and I'm glad for that, even though you paid a heavy price. Your poor, weakened heart stopped beating on March 13 and took you away from all worldly worries. I say amen to that, even as I hate the disease that killed you!

June 11, 2018

My Dearest Son,

Father's Day is coming soon. I think of you and your fatherless boys, and my heart aches for all of you. The fact that they don't exactly know where their mother is increases the intensity of their trauma.

Olga told me of some instances when Nicholas reacted in an angry way when greeted by her friends or when given condolences about your death. I asked him about that gently, wanting him to open up about his feelings. It bothers me both as a loving grandmother and as a lifelong therapist that he generally keeps his feelings locked up, especially the negative ones.

"I don't want them to feel sorry for me," he told me. "I know that my life sucks. I don't need to be reminded of that." I was shocked by his words but tried to reply calmly. I suggested to him that they mean well and that offering sympathy for someone's loss was not the same as feeling sorry for them.

He shrugged his shoulders and left the room. I know that his trauma runs deep. Both Olga and I have tried to talk to him and to convince him to go to some therapy sessions. So far, he has refused. He keeps saying, "I'm OK. I don't need anything." We all know that he's not OK. How could he be, having gone through all that he has? I even talked with Spiros about helping us with this task since Nicholas looks up to your older brother. He said he would try talking with him. I know you'll be glad to hear that Spiros is very fond of your son and thinks that he's a great kid. I urged Spiros to tell Nicholas that he has gone for therapy himself in the past (with some prompting from Olga), and I know that he has benefited from the experience. My hope is that Nicholas will be inspired by his example.

June 15, 2018

My Dearest Son,

Remember when I wrote to you a few days ago about a woman that I met in the water aerobics class? Last two times I saw her, she was terribly worried about her son who is an addict. This time, when I saw her at the class again, I hardly recognized her. What a change in her! She was smiling instead of crying, and she looked about ten years younger.

She came to my side of the pool and thanked me for reaching out to her the week before. She added that she was feeling good, even happy. "He went for treatment," she said, talking about her son, "and he even said that he wanted to go. Can you believe it? I have been worried about him for some time now. Keep your fingers crossed that he finally gets rid of his heroin addiction. I paid the rehabilitation facility for a whole month," she said.

I wished her and her son well and meant it. Later, alone near my locker, I thought of you and cried. How I wish you had gotten help as well, especially in your younger years when cocaine addiction reared its ugly but seductive head (something you kept secret from me all this time) and alcohol and other drugs became such a big, destructive part of your life.

I saw that woman again, this morning at the YMCA. She had a frown on her face instead of a smile and looked somewhat disheveled. She looked at me and said, "He left the treatment center two days ago, and we don't know where he is." I patted her arm and told her how sorry I was about this latest development in her son's addiction journey. She nodded, her eyes brimming with tears. I felt so bad for her. Unfortunately, her pain was very familiar to me. I was reminded one more time of the power of the disease of addiction.

As harsh and painful as your death has been for me and your boys, my one comforting thought is that you are in a peaceful place now, and the addiction monster cannot touch you or make you suffer anymore!

June 20, 2018

My Dearest Son,

My Al-Anon sponsor told me a few days ago that from her point of view your death was a suicide. I cried as she said that. I reluctantly saw her point—that yielding control to the disease and refusing to seek recovery help meant that your death could be considered a suicide. However, I think of you more as a victim of alcoholism and not somebody who intentionally killed himself. It's possible that I'm romanticizing the tragic reality and engaging in some sort of denial again.

I hope and pray that you were asleep when the end came, or too drunk or stoned to realize what was happening to you. You suffered enough while you were alive navigating the journey of addiction. I don't know what the symptoms are of advanced cirrhosis of the liver, but they couldn't have been easy. I believe that a merciful God, having the knowledge that you could not help yourself, decided to end your suffering early.

June 21, 2018

My Dearest Son,

It's 1 a.m., and like every night for the past three months, I'm crying. My days are filled with shopping errands, cooking, and taking care of Skye and myself, and all that is somewhat distracting from my grief. Then, evening starts, and no matter what I'm doing—reading a book, watching TV, or attempting to enjoy other similar activities—eventually by 10 p.m., the blanket of grief starts enveloping me. By midnight, I'm totally covered by it. It always starts the same way—with reminiscing—and then I start sobbing.

Writing these letters to you seems to be the only thing that curtails somewhat the cycle of grieving. It connects me to you in a strange kind of way that I do not totally understand but still welcome. I am very grateful for that.

Good night, Son, wherever you are!

June 24, 2018

My Dearest Son,

Well, the plans are made, and I'm packing to go to Alaska in a few days. I still can't believe that I'm really doing this. I continue to have mixed feelings about the trip. There is a touch of excitement (after all, I have always loved traveling), but the excitement is half-buried under the grief of losing you.

I'm remembering that when you were around fourteen years old, your dad was sent to Alaska by his engineering firm. The company was building a big pipeline in Valdez, a very small town in a remote part of the state. He was supposed to go there for a couple of months, but the two months extended to four. He was even offered a position there for two years, inviting us, his family to go along at three times his regular salary. He came back to Houston to tell us about the offer. I could see that he was seriously tempted. When you and Constantine heard about the job offer, you were enthusiastic about the idea. Spiros, who was in high school at the time, was not at all happy about the offer. I remember that you were so excited about the possibility of going to Valdez that you asked me to take you to the library so you could get some books on Alaska. Eventually we turned down the offer because we found out that there was no high school in Valdez. I certainly would not consider going to Alaska without Spiros.

I had mixed feelings about the offer myself. The timing was not right for me personally. I had just finished graduate school, earning a master's degree in social work while raising three sons almost single-handedly with a semiabsent husband, busy traveling for work many miles away. I was looking forward to starting a professional career for the first time in my life. At age forty-eight, this was no small feat. Beautiful but remote and tiny, Valdez did not offer any professional opportunities for me, yet traveling and living there for a while sounded like an exciting travel adventure, hence the mixed feelings about not going away.

I still remember how crushed you were when you found out that your dad and I had turned down the job offer. You had asked me more than once to take you to the library, and you had been reading all sorts of books about Alaska and showing them to Constantine, who was also disappointed about not going. Spiros seemed relieved. I wonder sometimes if our lives would have taken a different   turn if we had gone to Alaska. Would your dad and I have divorced eight years later? Would you have been exposed to drugs and become addicted to alcohol and chemicals if we had gone to Valdez instead of staying in Houston? Who knows? I know it's foolish to speculate on the what-ifs and regrets, but I do it now anyway. The rational part of my brain tells me that addiction has nothing to do with geography and circumstances, but logic doesn't usually win when competing with my inner self.

What happened to my sweet, adventurous boy who was proud to be in a marching band, an Eagle-ranked Boy Scout, and a National Merit Scholar? Who would have thought that you would die on a park bench, all alone? Certainly not me, your loving mother, who had imagined and hoped for a bright future for you. I did not go in my imagination as far as your grandmother and think that you would be president one day, but even in my worst nightmares, I did not foresee your tragic end.

I am going to carry you with me on this trip. So whenever I see glaciers, whales, flying eagles, and beautiful vistas, I will think of you and remember how eager you were, once upon a time, to go there.

Sending you all my love,

Mom

July 12, 2018

My Dearest Son,

I have not written to you for a while, and it feels like I have abandoned you. My excuse is that I have been on the Alaskan cruise for the last twelve days.

The cruise had beautiful views and crisp and clear weather (temperatures in the sixties). Compared with the 96-degree temperature that we had in Houston on the day we left on the trip, it felt wonderful—even though I froze one evening watching a movie with Victoria. The ship's recreation brochure called it "being under the stars." The film was actually showing on the Promenade Deck, which was on the tenth level of the cruise ship and open to sea winds on every side. Even though we were bundled up in multiple layers of clothing and numerous blankets, it was hard to enjoy the movie (which I had already seen) with temperatures dipping in the forties and even thirties.

I stayed for the whole movie despite the cold because my granddaughter liked the soundtrack. She was wonderful during the trip, helping organize events and outdoor activities, helping me with my luggage (with some assistance from Stuart)—an overall great companion. She didn't even complain about my talking in my sleep or even my snoring, which she didn't deny hearing, despite her fancy ear buds. Stuart who slept on the other end of the suite also mentioned hearing me talking in my sleep as well. Both young people made light of it and were very gracious about our sleeping arrangements.

I kept thinking of you throughout the trip. I somehow knew that you would have loved the small, unpolluted Alaskan towns and all the abundant wildlife. I had never seen majestic eagles flying around before this trip, and it was a sight to marvel at. The kids even went on a whaling expedition, but I didn't go. There was considerable hiking involved, and that was more than I could handle at my age. Besides, I have seen lots of whales frolicking around during my trips to Hawaii when I went to visit my good friend Connie while she lived there. Instead of going to see the whales, I went on a tour by myself in Juneau that involved taking a tram up Mount Roberts to 1,800 feet above sea level.

During the trip, I had my moments of grief, but I tried to keep them private so as not to spoil Victoria's and Stuart's trip experience. I shared my feelings with them only once, during the Fourth of July celebration on the cruise ship, when a lot of free champagne was flowing and Stuart got drunk. I told him that it pained me to see him that way because it vividly reminded me how alcohol and other drugs took your life and how terribly sad that made me. I told Stuart, "Alcohol robbed me of somebody I dearly love. Don't let it happen to you."

Even though I have not written for a while, it doesn't mean that you were not with me on this journey. The truth is that you'll always be with me no matter where I go for as long as I live.

July 15, 2018

My Dearest Son,

Every evening during the trip they placed itinerary brochures in the mailbox outside our suite. I had a big shock the first time I laid eyes on one. The name of our captain was on top. Guess what? It was a name similar to yours, of course. I don't know why I was surprised. Our connection keeps going on.

I'll never forget my first sight of you. A nurse was holding you in her arms, and you had this lopsided little grin that I perceived as a smile (even though I was told it was probably baby gas). I started crying when I saw you. I had been concerned whether I would love you as much as your older brother, Spiros. I knew at that moment that it was a foolish worry and that love of one's children is vast and infinite, but during the time of my pregnancy it seemed like a real worry.

You looked very different from Spiros, who was born with dark brown hair. Looking at your little face, I became fearful that you would look plain and suffer in comparison to your brother—who was truly a beautiful baby. I was wrong to worry about that as well. You grew up to be a very handsome child and young man with big, expressive, deep brown eyes that your father used to call "google" eyes. By the time the years of middle age arrived, the poisons that you had been taking took their toll and ravaged your once handsome features. When I last saw you, you were fifty-six years old, but you looked at least ten years older. How sad it was for me to see you like that.

I love you, my dearest Jaime, and always will.

July 16, 2018

My Dearest Son,

The night I came back from the Alaskan cruise, I had a meltdown at the baggage department of the Houston airport at 1 a.m. The reason for the meltdown? I saw five pages of texts on my cell phone that Nicholas had sent me. He was asking me in the texts what to do with your ashes!

What a painful return to Houston that was! I know your son meant well, but his long texts on the subject totally undid me.

He wrote to me telling me that he was in Los Angeles and that he and Robert had picked up the urn containing your ashes from your longtime friend Reuben. Spiros had asked him to pick them up four months ago and to keep them in safekeeping for your boys.

The texts sounded frantic and rather desperate. Nicholas was asking me over and over again what to do with the ashes. Nicholas and his brother had talked with their mother on the phone, and she sounded angry and seemingly rude. Sadly, she was not helpful at all in guiding them in their task.

Nicholas told me that she kept complaining about having a "shitty" life and blamed it all on you. Your sons got angry about her response to their phone call and told her that she needed help herself. She yelled at them that she was fine and did not need any help, and they hung up on her. Feeling overwhelmed by their gruesome task, they were turning to me for advice.

After seven hours of airplane time and fatigue from the trip, I was so overcome by emotion reading all this that I started sobbing, right there in the airport's baggage department. Passengers, surrounding me while looking for their bags, stopped in their tracks and were openly staring at me. Victoria saw me crying and quickly came to my side asking me what was wrong. I showed her Nicholas's texts, unable to speak. She read them and told me that I didn't have to respond right away or find an immediate solution.

"Just text Nicholas and Robert and tell them that it's 1 a.m. in Houston and that you are exhausted from the trip and cannot think straight," she said. Her words seemed like wise advice and—with considerable relief—I did as she suggested.

The next day, as I reread Nicholas's texts, I realized that he and Robert had found themselves in a painful emotional situation—difficult for anybody, especially for two grieving young men—and had felt panicky. I texted back, telling them that I trusted their judgment and that whatever they decided was fine with me. Nicholas wrote back that they were on their way to your favorite park in Los Angeles and that they were planning to spread some of your ashes there by the water. He was wondering whether to bring back some of the ashes to Houston so as to spread them in the

Galveston area. They remembered how much you loved the ocean—any ocean—and thought it was a fitting final resting place.

I finally realized—feeling a little calmer and more rested—what was being said between the text lines. More than asking me for advice, they were wanting me (and maybe other close members of the family) to participate in the ritual of the ashes, right along with them. I replied back to their text to let them know that their plan sounded like a good one and to follow their gut feelings on this endeavor. So, the drama of the ashes ended on that note.

Since my return from my trip, I have not seen Nicholas yet. He is still in California, but I feel confident that we will act on the plan that the boys want. I'm proud of them for acting in such a mature way about the whole process, and I feel for them. They must be so sad and forlorn about your untimely death. Their frantic texts about the ashes should have given me a clear indication about their anguished feelings, but I was too immersed in my own grief to notice, let alone comfort them. I felt bad about that.

Unfortunately, nothing we do will bring you back, so all we have is a ritual, the hope of some closure, and our shared grief.

July 21, 2018

My Dearest Son,

As I was taking Skye for a walk this morning, a memory came to my mind. I remembered a morning in LA when I saw you from a distance. I was in a rental car with Olga, and we had come for a surprise visit to the cheap motel where you and Leslie were staying during that time. Nicholas had told us how to find you, even though he refused to come along.

We did not tell you we were coming because we were afraid that you would run from us and refuse to see us, not wanting to have us see you in your present alcoholic lifestyle. You had not communicated with me for some months. Now, in addition to the emotional hurt that your silence was imposing on me, I was experiencing a lot of worry and concern about you, especially given the unsavory reports we were getting from your estranged sons and your friends.

I saw you as we approached the motel, and my heart skipped a beat. You were looking thin and raggedy except for a protruding belly. You had a knit cap on your head, but you were barefoot. You had your dog on a leash, so it seemed obvious that you were taking him for a walk in the motel grounds. As we came closer to you, I pointed you out to Olga and then realized how fast my heart was beating. Even with all my concern for you, I started wondering if my heart—suffering from atrial fibrillation—could withstand all this stress of coming face-to-face with your current lifestyle and with the impending intervention that I was planning to unleash on you. In addition to the worry about my heart, I was in a lot of pain every time I walked, because of my impaired left knee. For the first time, I started worrying about my health and the possible consequences of my formidable task of trying to help you.

As we approached your door, I had such mixed feelings. I was full of apprehension and anxiety about our unscheduled meeting, but also felt some gladness for the opportunity to see you again (it was destined to be the last time I was ever going to see you in this life, but of course I didn't know that tragic fact back then).

You looked shocked to see us standing at your door and were speechless for a few minutes. Then you said, "Mom, Olga, what are you doing here?"

Then you shouted, "Leslie, come over here. Mom and Olga came to see us from Houston."

The room smelled bad. Odors of body sweat seemed fused with dirty clothes lying around. There was dog food scattered all around on the floor. The spectacle of the messy room told us some of the story of what was going on in your life.

You know the rest. I read aloud my prepared intervention incidents while you sat there shocked. You initially tried to stop my reading by telling me that you wanted to watch the Michigan football game and that you had been waiting for it for some time. I controlled my trembling voice and told you firmly that you needed to turn off the television and listen. You gave in to me and sat down.

I tried really hard to read in a calm manner, without showing any distress or anger or resort to labeling and name-calling, and you appeared to be attentive and listened to what I was reading. You did not interrupt me or get angry except once—when I read the part that your disease of alcoholism was probably killing your organs, including your brain cells. That's when you yelled at me: "There is nothing wrong with my brain, Mother."

I started crying then. I couldn't help myself. Your angry remark made me realize how deep your denial was about your condition and your situation. We didn't know the future yet. In a relatively short time (one and one-half years from that memorable day), you were going to go to jail twice for thirty days each time, and you were going to beg me for money to post bail before your trials. I would have to refuse your pleas while my heart was breaking. I know in my head that tough love was the healthy way to go, but I still feel terrible about my refusal and about your suffering while in jail.

Later on, your misfortunes multiplied. You lost your beloved law license as a practicing attorney, which you had worked so hard to obtain, and eventually you would lose your life, leaving me bereft with grief that will last as long as I live. I know I should feel grateful for having had you as my beloved son for fifty-plus years and I do, but I will always miss your love, your sense of humor and heartfelt laugh, your appreciation of all kinds of music, and your kind heart.

I will never forget the warm welcome that you would always give me when I visited you. You would meet me at the airport and invariably say, "I am so happy that you are here, Mom." Then you would hug me in a big bear hug, and I would hug you back, so happy to see you.

Even on that dreadful day of the intervention, when I attempted—in a futile and desperate way—to pull you away from the chaos and abyss of your path of addiction, even then, despite everything I told you (a lot of it harsh and hard hitting), I heard love and even some pride in your voice when you introduced me to a fellow motel resident as your mother. I swallowed the tears that were closing up my throat and choking me, and I nodded my head. They are choking me now as I'm writing this, and I need to stop writing.

Sending you all my love,

Mom

July 25, 2018

My Dearest Son,

It doesn't seem possible that four months have gone by since your passing. It seems only yesterday that I heard the terrible news. I hope that with time I will remember mostly the happy memories. I do realize that you must have been suffering a lot while struggling with your addiction and its painful consequences. You had to deal with cirrhosis of the liver and a crippling anxiety that made you wait outside the door of the nearby liquor store at about 6 a.m. in the morning (you told me this). You must have been so desperate at times, being unable to stop it. You almost died from the severe seizure that you suffered when you tried to quit cold turkey.

Looking at your disease from that perspective, you must have seen death as a relief in a way. For that reason alone, I'm grateful that you are in a pain-free, peaceful place. Now it's up to us—the people who loved you—to carry on the suffering. We hope some peace will come to us, too, in time. It's not here yet, at least not for me.

July 26, 2018

My Dearest Son,

I went to see a psychic a couple of days ago. No, I'm not going off the rails. It's just that when I am in deep grief, as I have been lately, I keep an open mind about spirituality and emotional support, no matter where they come from. Previously in my life, I have been to two different psychics in two different situations. The only similarity was that I was going through painful situations, and I was seeking some relief from the pain.

Did those psychics have the ultimate answer for me or provide total emotional comfort? Of course not. I actually relied ultimately on therapy for that. However, each time I went to see a psychic, I heard something in what they said that helped my decision-making and did provide some emotional support.

Does all this seem strange coming from a retired licensed psychotherapist of forty-plus years who believed in teaching clients how to use cognitive reasoning and to live in reality? Perhaps, but as writers and philosophers have noted through the years, death is a total mystery to the living.

I know that there's a lot of scams associated with the psychic world. After all, most of the people seeking answers are very vulnerable, especially those faced with the death of a loved one. So, saying all this, I have to add that I do believe in an afterlife and that one's soul/spirit does

119

live on in an alternate reality. I also believe that there are certain people who are born with a special God-given gift that enables them to communicate with those who have passed on. So, maybe you can see why I don't believe that all psychics are scam artists and why I wanted to hear what a psychic had to say about your passing.

It had been some years since I had been to one, and I let a younger friend who frequents psychics on a regular basis guide me to her special place. This psychic was somebody I had never met before, and I told her as little as possible about my being there, not wanting to give her ready material that she could use.

She started by telling me quite a few things about my particular chakras (psychics seem to like talking about chakras, I noticed). One thing that she said that impressed me was that a strong maternal figure—with the letter *n* in her name had helped you in your transition from earth to afterlife. Immediately I guessed that she was talking about my late mother, the grandmother who adored you and whose name Anastasia definitely has an *n* in it in any language.

I cried when she told me that. I may be naive and gullible about this, but I do believe that my mother's spirit would do everything in her power to help you and welcome you to the other world. After all, you were her favorite grandchild (even though she kept insisting that she had no favorites and that she loved all her grandchildren equally). But then she would add, "Jaime is special and has such a kind heart!"

August 1, 2018

My Dearest Son,

Nicholas just left my house. We had lunch together earlier (his idea) to talk about the disposal of your ashes. He told me how he and Robert went to your favorite park—Will Rogers State Historic Park—when they were both in LA a month ago. They had been invited to their friend's summer rental house on Balboa Island for a week. They had gone there in previous summers and loved it.

It was after their stay there that they had texted me about your ashes. They did not think about the particular time difference between

California and Houston and how it was 1:15 a.m. when I read their messages. Nicholas told me that they had texted me earlier. Given that Victoria, Stuart, and I were busy disembarking from the cruise in Seattle and getting on a plane to come to Houston, I had not looked at my cell phone for a few hours.

I explained all this to Nicholas and also told him about my emotional meltdown at the baggage department of the Houston airport. He said he had no idea that this was the day of our return from the cruise. The bad timing of the texts was totally unintentional, so I don't blame the boys at all.

I cannot believe that I'm discussing your ashes, as if they were some commodity that we needed to dispose of. They are a vital part of you, of what remains of your precious body. Even though I deeply believe that the soul/spirit of the person is the most essential part and that it leaves the earth when the body dies, it's still painful for me to talk about your ashes and strategize about dispersing them.

I admire your sons for trying very hard to be respectful and meaningful about all this. Poor things, they lost a father at a young age (relatively speaking) that they loved dearly, and on top of that they have to be responsible and make mature decisions about painful situations without much guidance from adults.

How I wish you were still alive and able (instead of your ashes) to come with us to Galveston. It would be so nice to have a loving, breathing person with us instead of some ashes in an urn or box. I still remember when you came to the island many years ago one weekend, surprising the family. You were hurting emotionally in the aftermath of a broken relationship when your live-in girlfriend had left you suddenly for somebody new. The timing of her departure was especially bad. You had just been hired by a big law firm in LA for your first professional job since law school. You had wisely realized that emotionally you were too heartbroken and depressed to plunge into training for the job, and so you decided to get on a plane and come home.

You looked at me when you arrived and said, "I told my new bosses that my grandmother had just died and that I had to come home to Houston. I sure hope that Grandmother Anastasia up in heaven forgives me for lying and using her as an excuse to take a few days off." You added, "I just had to leave and get myself together before I go back and start the new job!"

121

"Don't worry about that," I said. "It's a harmless white lie, and knowing your grandmother well, I'm sure she totally understands why you said what you said. I firmly believe that she's probably happy to help you in any way she can. After all, she loved you dearly!"

August 11, 2018

My Dearest Son,

I had a very unusual event happen a couple of nights ago. Something startled me out of deep sleep, and I suddenly sat up in my bed. To my extreme shock and disbelief, I saw the slight figure of a boy standing by the side of my bed. The room was dark as usual, but the figure was brightly lit from the rear and clearly visible.

I was not scared by the sight. Somehow, I knew that the figure was not going to hurt me. It was dressed in a weird costume, with a cloak and a small hat (perhaps like Ottoman Empire attire from the past) and stood there for a while—silently and without moving. Then it disappeared from sight. The apparition did not look like you or even like the typical ghost figure that we see in movies, but I had the distinct impression that it was a manifestation of your spirit.

Could I have dreamed the whole thing? Possibly, but I do believe that I was totally awake when the vision occurred. It was over in a few minutes and not a word was spoken, but it left me awake for a long time while I tried to make some sense of what had happened. Can I logically explain the vision? No, of course not. The truth is that I am not in the habit of seeing visions or apparitions. In my eighty-four years of living, I have never seen or experienced anything like it. I had numerous dreams of my mother after she died and at times definitely felt her presence, but I never saw an apparition or manifestation of her. The experience left me mystified and even awed.

I don't dare to tell people about this. They will probably think that I'm totally nuts. Well, maybe I'll tell Connie. She has been my closest friend through the years (even when we lived at great distances from each other), and she has a lot of spirituality in her and an open mind.

I am definitely not telling your brothers. Constantine became very upset last week when I confided in him about going to see a psychic. He called her "a devil's tool," so I can only imagine what his reaction would be if I were to tell him what I experienced. I'm guessing that he thinks that five months of grieving are enough and that I should move on.

"After all," he said, "Jaime was a grown man when he died and not a child," as if that makes any difference in how I grieve for you.

August 18, 2018

My Dearest Son,

I was alone in the house all day because of a stomachache. Thoughts of you inundated my mind throughout the day and often left me in tears. The grief seems to be worse when I'm alone with no distractions except for my little dog.

It comforts me some when I talk about you, but I get the feeling that most family members and friends don't really want me to talk about you. Maybe I'm wrong and maybe I'm not being totally fair, but I believe that they have the mistaken idea that talking about you will upset me.

I remember that in the few occasions when I started crying in their presence, they seemed very uncomfortable. In fact, about a month ago, when I burst into tears at the sight of *keftedes* in a restaurant, remembering that they were a big favorite of yours, Constantine got visibly upset and told me that I probably needed some antidepressants! Yes, I know that a Greek restaurant—or any restaurant for that matter—is not an appropriate place for displays of grief, but my emotions were still very raw at the time. I couldn't refrain from showing them.

My therapist has suggested that when your brothers ask me how I am doing that I shouldn't cover up my truth and say, "OK, I guess" (my standard response). He asked me to consider telling them some of what's going on and how I'm struggling emotionally with your loss. In other words, I should confess the truth that I'm not OK.

I'm going to try to follow the advice, but on some level, I do believe that people who have not lost a child do not really understand the extent of the grief involved. That's why I try not to miss the monthly meetings of the Compassionate Friends group. Most group members are bereaved parents who have lost a child. They may have lost a child (of any age) years ago, and yet they still come to the meetings. They still cry when they talk about their children.

There was a young couple there last week, and it was their first time in the group. Their fourteen-year-old son died a few weeks ago by falling from a tree. This happened at a Boy Scout meeting, and the parents were not even there when the fatal accident happened. I thought about all the Boy Scout camps that you went to and how you loved them.

The poor mother of the deceased child kept crying throughout the meeting and had a dazed look in her eyes. I knew that look. I saw it in my mirror in the early days after your death. It's the look that says, "I don't really know what just happened. Surely this is a bad dream, a nightmare. Can I go back to the time before this terrible thing cropped up? And why are people chitchatting and even laughing? Don't they understand that the world is upside down and nothing is the same anymore? How dare they laugh when I'm dying inside!" My guess was that's what she was thinking (or something similar) because those were my own thoughts during the first group meeting that I attended.

Jaime, honey, remember the eulogy I wrote for you last month as an assignment from Robert, my therapist? I wrote about the special child and young man that you used to be and all your accomplishments. Also, I wrote about the potential for success that you had, both public and inner, before your substance abuse became toxic. Mainly, I wrote about how you loved the special people in your life (especially your children), animals, and nature. I decided to send that eulogy to my grief group's newsletter. They always ask for contributions about our departed children, so I thought I would comply. I hope you approve.

In my bedroom I have a picture of you taken in 2016 at Nicholas's high school graduation. You have a proud and happy look on your face. It's the last picture that I have of you. I look at that picture and smile and cry at the same time.

I miss you so!

Love,
Mom

August 24, 2018

My Dearest Son,

I don't know whether to call this a "God moment" or not, but it was certainly a personal experience that felt deep and almost spiritual. I was recently at an elegant restaurant with the family, celebrating the birthday of your niece Victoria. I looked around at the well-dressed crowd, laughing and chatting in an animated way, as if they didn't have a care in the world, and I felt a stabbing of sudden envy. I know that appearances can be deceiving, but they all looked like successful, wealthy people having a great time. This was a trendy new restaurant, and the menu was expensive for Houston. The place was packed.

I couldn't help but think again of you in that lousy Los Angeles motel, and then I imagined you living in a broken-down tent under a bridge or something similar in the last year of your life. The contrast of that image with tonight's restaurant scene was very painful. I felt such immense sadness! I looked at your son, Nicholas, sitting at our table with nonsmiling, sad eyes, and that increased my sadness.

I got up from the table, with the pretense of going to the ladies' room, because I did not want to burst into tears at the birthday celebration. After all, it was supposed to be a festive occasion for my granddaughter whom I dearly love. As I closed the door, a song suddenly came on in the loudspeaker (away from the noise of the restaurant crowd, I could hear the loudspeaker very clearly). It was Van Morrison singing "[My Mama Told Me There Would Be] Days Like This."

I gasped. I knew that song well because you had texted it to me in one of your last communications to me. You had not added any comments to the song, but I interpreted it then as a message from you that you were thinking of me and still loved me, despite the state of estrangement of our relationship at the time.

As I heard the song loud and clear in the ladies' room, I started sobbing. Thankfully, I was alone. I couldn't believe the so-called coincidence of what just happened, and I marveled at it. I immediately thought of it as a message from you. A comforting message, for sure, and I smiled amid the tears.

After a while I composed myself and went back to join my family at the dining room, a different person from the one who left the table a few minutes ago. Victoria, perceptive and thoughtful as usual, asked me if I was OK. "Yes," I said, "I am perfectly OK!" This time I meant it.

I remembered that you often told me that there was a deep connection between us. Last time you said that, your exact words were, "Mom, I don't know how you do this, but you always seem to know when I'm in trouble or when I have a problem, even when we are far away from each other. I am amazed!"

This time around, you were the one who reached out from the other side to comfort me when I was in a lot of pain and distress. Thank you, my darling boy.

August 29, 2018

My Dearest Son,

So many things remind me of you. Today as I was driving to the YMCA, a guy on a motorcycle passed me by, and I immediately thought of you. You loved your old motorcycle so much! Even after you had a horrific accident on it that almost took your life and even after it was broken beyond repair, you longed for it and lamented its loss for many years after.

The accident happened during the big California earthquake of 1992. You were on your beloved motorcycle on your way to work, and as the highway buckled, the car in front of you made a sudden stop. You were not able to do the same; therefore, you and your motorcycle flew over the stopped car, and you landed on the concrete highway flat on your back.

You almost died that day. A miracle happened and you survived the terrible accident. According to the doctor who treated you later, your helmet saved your life. The irony of that is that you absolutely hated wearing a helmet and often complained, like the Libertarian that you were, that it restrained your freedom and individual rights.

Thank God you wore a helmet on that fateful day. It was a present from your bride (you were a newlywed), and you wore it because she insisted. The accident left you with a broken hip and several fractured ribs, but compared with dying, that was small stuff. At the time, I was very shaken by your accident. I desperately wanted to get on a plane and go to LA to see you and take care of you, but everybody told me not to go because of possible aftereffects of the earthquake. When you and Leslie joined the chorus of people telling me not to, I gave up and stayed home.

Later on that year when I did come to visit you, you told me more details about your accident. As you lay on the concrete of the highway, you were unable to move, and you told me how scared you were. You thought of my mother, your grandmother, and you asked her to help you from the other side. You then tried to make the sign of the Greek cross (the way she taught you when you were a child), and you were not able to lift your arms to do that. That panicked you, you said. Thinking of being paralyzed for life scared you more than the prospect of dying. As you were telling me all this, imagining what could have happened brought tears to your eyes (and mine as well).

You had to spend a month in bed after the accident, and you spent that month at the home of a very nice friend and his wife. You spent the time reading; watching television; and chatting with the couple's young daughter, who would visit you often, along with your wife, who was working full-time and could not take time off from work to take care of you. I will always be grateful to your friends who took care of you at a crucial time of your life. You were in your thirties at the time of the accident. You lived another twenty-five years and raised two sons, and your only complaint from the accident was about chronic hip pain. I believe that the universe was trying to give you a message about taking better care of yourself, but unfortunately you did not pay much attention.

You never replaced your broken motorcycle. You definitely wanted to do it, but your wife and friends talked you out of it. You bought a small truck, instead. It was a rational decision, but you always longed for your lost motorcycle. You often told me that.

I wish that the rest of your life would have been full of rainbows, beautiful sunsets, and lots of joy, but it wasn't meant to be. I'm glad that you had some happy moments in your life, such as the birth of your two boys and some success in the practice of law. You never forgot the sense of freedom and delight that your beloved motorcycle used to give you. I dearly wish that the disease of alcoholism had not brought such a dark tragic shadow over your life and led you to an untimely death.

The heartbreak continues for those who love you, but you are finally free of the shackles of addiction and of the suffering. Rest in peace, my son. I will always love you.

September 1, 2018

My Dearest Son,

Today was tough. No particular reason except for my ongoing grief journey. I felt very sad all day. Sometimes my grief is subdued and almost bearable, and other times it hits me like a tsunami.

The grief surge was especially surprising because I had some nice moments yesterday when the September newsletter of Compassionate Friends arrived in the mail. There, on the second page, was the eulogy about you that I had sent them. I was happy to see the eulogy printed, so I don't understand why I woke up so depressed.

I thought of distracting myself by going to see a movie, but I just didn't have the energy—physical or emotional—to do it. I decided instead to tackle a project that I had been putting off for a while. My fear behind the procrastination was that it would plunge me into more emotional pain and distress. Then I thought, I'm feeling lousy anyway, so instead of distracting myself, why don't I immerse myself right into the grief instead of trying to avoid it?

So that's what I did the rest of the day. I went through all my photo albums of your and your brothers' childhood and selected a collection of photos that I liked that represented your childhood and adolescent years. I had been wanting to do this for a while now. My plan is to have two copies made of each picture and assemble then into an album or disk for your boys for Christmas. My hope is that Nicholas and Robert will appreciate having mementos of your growing-up years. I braced myself for some emotionally painful hours while putting my plan in action, but I believed that the result would be worth it.

My endeavor had rather surprising results. Assembling your pictures did bring me some emotional moments and even some tears, but to my surprise, I realized when I finished that my immense sadness had lifted some. It felt good to accomplish the task.

I try to honor your memory any way I can, and the picture project was part of my resolve.
Sending you all my love, as always,
Mom

September 8, 2018

My Dearest Son,

I just saw a movie on TV that I had seen some years earlier. It's called *Crazy Heart,* and I remembered it was a good movie. I also remembered that the basic theme of the movie was alcoholism, so I had some trepidation about watching it right now. It was a good movie and the antagonist was a fifty-seven–year–old alcoholic singer (your age when you died), going downhill because of the disease.

Yes, it was painful to watch at times, especially when the guy tries to get sober after a traumatic experience. That's when I cried, and once again I lamented the fact that you wouldn't or couldn't do it. Your words of denial reverberated in my brain: "Alcohol and drugs did not cause this situation, Mom. You are wrong about that!"

Even so, despite your words and despite my inner despair, I still held on to a thread of hope until the bitter end that you were going to drop your denial one day and finally get sober. I did not know then the terrible truth: you were already running out of time, and your poor, weakened heart was going to stop before its natural time.

I left LA at the end of 2016 heartbroken and without knowing the full truth or the tragic future coming soon upon us. My body felt the truth as well. By the time our plane reached Houston on the way back from my desperate attempt at an intervention, I literally was unable to walk.

Even so, the news of your death shocked and shattered me. I told myself, in between sobbing fits, that you were at peace now and no longer suffering from your addiction and its consequences. No more jail sentences or worrying about your next meal. I tell myself that all the time, but I still agonize about no longer having any hope (not even a slim thread) and about having lost you forever.

Unlike the movie, there was no happy ending for you, my dear son, nor for me either, because when you left this earth, you took a part of me with you. I will grieve for you and miss you for as long as I live.

One of these days, I am going to join you or at least your spirit.

I hope it doesn't take too long. The pain seems unbearable right now.

September 13, 2018

My Dearest Son,

What a sad day this is for me. It's the six-month anniversary of your passing. People say that time heals and that after a while, the sadness of losing a loved one is replaced by recollecting happy memories. I have a hard time believing that. Of course, the people whom I am now quoting are usually not parents mourning their children.

Some of the grieving parents whom I met at the grief group tell me that their grief has never gone away. Perhaps the intensity of the emotions alters, but not the grief itself. And there are plenty of self-doubts relating to the deaths and plenty of agonizing regrets!

As I'm writing this letter to you, I'm looking outside the window. It's a dreary, rainy day, almost stormy. A big storm and/or hurricane is expected momentarily to hit the East Coast, mostly the Carolinas. The dreary day outside is matching my insides.

Jaime, remember when we used to spend summer vacations in North Carolina's Cape Hatteras and Nags Head to be exact? That was during the years when we lived in Baltimore, Maryland. For six years, we went to Nags Head every summer for a couple of weeks or so.

You were six years old when we started going, and you used to love our going to a rented summer cottage there. The water was rather cool (especially compared with that of Pensacola, Florida, where we used to vacation during our years in Louisiana). You and your brothers didn't care about the water temperature. You loved it there. Even Chum, our dog at the time, would jump in the ocean and join you all there.

I still have a picture of all of us in the family car, on the way there. You and Spiros and Constantine are laughing as you are looking at Chum. One of you had placed some sunglasses on our dog, and you all thought that he was a riot! I love to look at that old picture, because it was a rare event in our family to see you guys united and laughing together. Ordinarily, it would be a case of you and Spiros fighting and somebody— mostly you—crying and complaining that your older brother was hitting you. Then, Constantine, feeling the tension, would also start crying. Later, Spiros would be the one crying or angry because your dad would usually blame him for the fighting and yell at him or punish him.

Our annual seaside vacations provided some respite and relief from all the family tension. You all loved them, and even your dad's usual gloomy mood would lighten up. So, of course, I loved the vacations as well.

Spiros who (as we later found out) suffered from severe attention-deficit disorder with hyperactivity was not an easy child to raise for sure. However, as a psychologist was to point out in counseling years later, you would provoke him at times and get his goat. Your father's habit of constantly comparing you with your brother to your advantage worsened the situation. So, to my dismay and occasional despair, our home was a constant battleground with lots of conflict. It did not help that your dad and I had totally different parenting styles. For the sake of fairness, I have to point out that your father was raised, as was I, as an only child, and we had no clue about how to handle sibling rivalry.

It hurts a lot to realize that I am never going to see all three of my sons together anymore. When Olga and I came to California one last time, about two years ago, at one point during the intervention you called Spiros "Satan." I knew you were under the influence of alcohol (and who knows what else), but I was still shocked and pained to hear you talk of your brother in that way. He had refused to come with us on the trip, even though I asked him more than once. He told me that he was so angry about your alcoholism and about "abandoning your children" (as he put it), that for him to come to the intervention would do more harm than good. He reminded me that he had sent you money on lots of occasions and that he was fed up with your refusal to stop drinking and drugging and get help. I reminded him that you were suffering from a terrible disease and didn't intentionally abandon your boys, but he just shook his head and walked away. I was disappointed about his decision not to come with us and to partake in the intervention, but I had to accept his decision. As for Constantine, who told me that he also sent you some money at times (under pretense that it was a loan) and never saw it returned, he also refused to come along on our fateful trip; however, he did tell me that if Olga backed out of going, that he would come with me instead.

I kept trying to explain to your brothers that you would not behave the way you did if your brain had not been altered by chemicals. They would just look at me in a certain way and sometimes even articulate the words that they were thinking: "Here you go again, Mom, finding excuses for your son and trying to be a therapist instead of facing the facts!"

Was I making excuses for you? Perhaps a little, but what is most important is that I deeply believed, both as a therapist and as your mother, that you were a victim of your addiction. That's why I refused to get angry about your behavior and your downfall. I also know that we are all responsible for the paths we take in life, victims or not!

As I navigated my role during your ill-fated journey of addiction, my profession as a psychotherapist and knowledge of therapy were both a blessing and a curse. I knew too much about what ailed you and about the power of the disease, and I was in despair about the inevitable outcome. At the same time, as your loving mother, I always had a shred of hope in my heart that you would eventually defeat your inner demons.

On March thirteenth of this year, my hope died right along with you, and so did a piece of my heart!

September 18, 2018

My Dearest Son,

I have been reluctant to write in this journal lately, and I didn't know why. I always want to know what motivates me. Like the ancient Greek philosopher Socrates, I believe that "the unexamined life is not worth living." That motto and "Know thyself"[5] have been my guiding mantras. It bothered me to not know why I didn't want to write to you anymore.

After all, these letters have been a great source of comfort for me since your untimely death. I was truly perplexed. Well, today, my therapist helped me figure out the reason behind my sudden reluctance. I realized for the first time in the six months since your heart stopped that I have been struggling with feelings of anger toward you. I have not wanted to acknowledge them.

The truth is that I have been angry with quite a few people since your death, including myself, but I have refused to direct my anger toward you. How could I be angry with you, the person I dearly love and have lost forever? And yet, I am getting in touch with some feelings that are disturbing and real.

First and foremost, you did not get any help for your addiction and illness, despite the fact that you promised me that you would do so. I spent hours and hours researching resources in LA and gave you a long list of names and addresses, but I bet you never even looked at it. Instead, you tried to do it your way and go cold turkey, and you had a severe seizure and almost died. I am pretty sure that they told you in the emergency room how dangerous and ill-conceived your actions were. Did you listen to the expert, professional advice? Of course not.

I am angry with you about that. You were so damn stubborn that you thought that you could fix your problem all alone without anybody's help. I know (or can guess) that the vast amount of alcohol and drugs that you consumed messed up your thinking, but why wouldn't you listen to anybody, including me, the mother who loved you so deeply and had helped so many others in the past?

Above all, I'm angry that you threw your potential and your future out of the window and allowed your body and soul, as well as your vast intelligence, to be consumed by and ruined by the stupid drugs that you took. Children are not supposed to die before their parents. I'm angry that you died before I did and left me in pain and despair to mourn your needless death daily.

Deep inside, I know that you always loved me. Our estrangement of the last couple of years was another bad consequence of your addiction. You would not answer the phone or even any of my texts. I don't know if you were too drunk or stoned to communicate or still angry with me for not bailing you out of jail. Whatever the reason, you were not available to me (or to anybody else in the family, either, including your sons).

I am angry about that, too. How sad that we lost precious time while you were still alive by not communicating! How sad that we were still estranged when you died and there were no goodbyes. In your final moments, did you cry out for me or your grandmother? Did you remember that I loved you more than life itself? I hope so!

Oh, honey, what happened to your own functioning in life? How did you end up homeless and in the streets of Los Angeles? You had a law degree and a bright future, but you allowed alcohol (and, possibly, other drugs) to ravage your life and eventually kill you.

I was never an ambitious mother with lofty goals for you. I didn't dream of your being a judge and certainly not a member of the U.S. Supreme Court. I just wanted you to be healthy and happy, raising your boys and enjoying the practice of law. I hoped that you would have a normal life. Was that too much to ask?

October 2, 2018

My Dearest Son,

My grief about your death takes me to some strange emotional places. For example, Skye (my little dog, remember?) was running after a roach in the family room (you remember, don't you, that in Texas, roaches are a way of life, especially in hot weather). Even though it's October, it's still hot in Houston. Anyway, Skye kept barking and running after the roach, trying to catch it. I finally got tired of his barking and game, so I joined the hunt. I finally saw the roach behind a chair. I didn't have time to go for my bug spray, so I impulsively threw one of my slippers at the big insect who had invaded my space. It hit the target, so I picked up the lifeless body and flushed it away.

Then a strange thing happened. I burst into tears. I cried and cried over that dead roach, and I didn't think I could ever stop. The truth is that I don't like killing anything, even insects, but I have never cried like that over an insect's death. Obviously, I was crying for a lot more than one roach!

In the last six months my emotionality has been extreme, and my reaction tonight is a good example of that.

October 3, 2018

My Dearest Son,

Today is your older brother's birthday. I hope that by now that you are at peace about Spiros. You two were close in age (seventeen months apart) and fought a lot as youngsters. You used to complain frequently to your father and me that Spiros kept beating you up.

Despite your negative feelings about the past, you asked Spiros to be best man at your wedding. Then a big problem arose. A best man's function at a Greek Orthodox wedding is different from the traditional American function. A Greek best man is called a *koumbaros,* and among other things his role during the marriage ceremony is that of uniting the new couple by placing *stefana* (wreaths of flowers) on the heads of the bride and groom. What is most important is that the *koumbaros* has to be of the same faith, that is, Greek Orthodox.

At first glance, that was no problem. You and your brothers were all baptized as babies by a visiting Greek Orthodox priest (there was no Greek Orthodox Church in Alexandria, Louisiana, where we lived at the time). However, Spiros and his wife, Olga, were married in a Methodist church (Olga's choice). So, their marriage had not taken place in a Greek Orthodox church. That fact made Spiros ineligible to be the best man at your wedding!

Well, honey, remember what happened next? Your brother was so determined to be your *koumbaros* that he and Olga had a second wedding in Houston's only Greek church at the time—the Annunciation—ten years after their first wedding. Not only that, but they had to undergo numerous sessions of counseling by the Greek priest before the wedding ceremony. I was the sole guest and witness at this wedding. I was proud and honored to be invited to this special ceremony and very proud of your brother who went to such lengths to be your best man!

Now, I ask you, is that not proof of his love for you?

Don't forget that he is currently raising Nicholas as his own son, with plenty of goodwill and affection. Not exactly a Satan, right?

Today is his birthday (as I wrote earlier and addressed). For many years now, I have cooked him *keftedes* for his birthday. Of all the Greek dishes that I cook, both you and he have always liked my Greek meatballs

135

best (your father's choice as well). You and he used to get up in the middle of the night whenever I cooked the dish and compete to be the one who would finish the leftovers.

Well, this year I will not be able to cook his favorite dish. Nowadays, I can't even eat meatballs in a Greek restaurant without crying. They remind me too much of losing you. I will have to explain to Spiros why I have to skip the yearly ritual, and I hope that he understands and forgives me for the omission. In order to make it up to him some, I baked him some *koulurakia*. That's his second favorite dish of mine.

Unlike your brothers, you never had much of a sweet tooth, Jamie, but you did like my special Greek cookies. I would make them during my annual visits to LA (along with the Greek meatballs), and you always seemed to enjoy them. I made them today for Spiros and didn't even cry during the lengthy shaping (they have to be manually hand rolled and twirled). I hope he won't mind too much that I am skipping his beloved *keftedes!*

How I wish you were alive so I could make them for you as well!

All my love,

Mom!

October 15, 2018

My Dearest Son,

The other evening, Nicholas and I went on an emotional adventure that involved you. I had asked him to go to a ceremony sponsored by my grief group, Compassionate Friends. I am pretty sure that I have already mentioned this group to you. They have helped me a lot during my grief journey after losing you.

I wanted Nicholas to come with me for two reasons. I needed him to drive me there because the special ceremony was more than an hour away from my house and at night.. (I have a hard time driving currently at night because of my eyesight.) What is more important is that I also wanted him to come with me so that we could have a bonding experience about your passing. He and I have gotten a lot closer since he has been in Houston, and that has been a big solace and comfort to me.

I was honest with him about my reasons for inviting him along, but I did omit a third reason for asking him. I had hoped that it would help him open up about his own feelings of grief about you. He had been open and vulnerable with me earlier on, especially after your passing, but lately it seems to me that he is bottling up his feelings. He keeps telling me he is "fine," but somehow I doubt it. How can he be fine? His personality is like yours in so many ways. You didn't like talking about feelings either (especially as a child and young adult).

When I stayed with Spiros and Olga for a few days after they told me the terrible news about your death, Nicholas and I had some lengthy talks about you. We shared stories as well as feelings and memories. They were sad yet very healing talks, I believe, for both of us. He would see me crying alone on the patio, and he would join me and try to comfort me (and probably himself as well).

On one of those occasions, he played a George Strait song from his cell phone and told me how you used to play your guitar and sing it for him when he was young. There was one song particularly (something about land in Arizona?) that you sang to him regularly at bedtime. It was so touching to me to hear this story about you as a father! I didn't even know that you loved country music and George Strait, even though I always knew that all genres of music appealed to you. We listened to the song together, and we cried together. It was a bittersweet moment!

Getting back to the night of the grief group meeting—he came to pick me up as he had promised, and he was sweet and attentive, even though he was suffering from a bad cold. During the evening, I remembered at one point that Leslie had told me that Nicholas was your favorite, and I asked him about that. He explained that he had been your frequent companion and would willingly go with you on many errands, while his older brother preferred to stay home and play computer games with his friends.

It felt good to hear him reminisce about his childhood, and I was glad that I had asked him to come with me. When we went to the park where the grief ceremony was to take place, we launched paper lanterns filled with love notes on a lake. Some lanterns got caught along with us in a violent rainstorm. Your resourceful son got immediately on his cell phone, checked the reports, and informed me that the weather was going to get worse later on in the evening. We were already getting drenched (despite two umbrellas), so we cast some regretful looks (mostly mine) upon our semiupright floating lanterns and left the ceremony before it ended. I felt bad about the weather and also worried that Nicholas's cold was going to get worse because of our outdoor adventure, but I was still glad that he and I had gone together to an event that honored your memory and that of others' departed and beloved children.

It is clear to me that he loves you a lot, just like I do.

November 5, 2018

My Dearest Son,

I have not written for a few days, but please don't think that I have forgotten you. How can I ever forget you? You will always be in my heart, a part of me, forever.

I remember when you were born so clearly. I have to confess that I had some mixed feelings when I found out that I was expecting you. Not because I didn't want any more children. To the contrary, I had always wanted to be a mother. Other girls dream of a perfect wedding and a glamorous wedding gown, but that wasn't me. It is just as well, since I married your father twice, first in a white suit in front of a judge and the second time in a gray suit in a Greek church in New Orleans. As a teenager and a young woman, my dreams and fantasies about my future consisted of me as a wise and loving mother, surrounded by a flock of happy children, preferably boys.

Well, I got my wish—three boys to be exact. The only reason that I had any ambivalence about my second pregnancy was because your older brother was still very young, a baby of eight months and a handful at that, with severe colic and sleeping problems. Add to that my inexperience in taking care of children. I was an only child with no babysitting experience whatsoever. You can see why babies were still a mystery to me. So, the idea of having two young children so close in age scared the daylights out of me.

In addition to the above, there was no family nearby to help and support me in child-rearing. My family (small but loving) was back in Turkey. My mother had arrived for Spiros's birth and ended up staying for a few months, but there was no guarantee that she would be able to come back for your birth. At the time of your arrival, there were no conveniences like Pampers and Huggies. We had to use cloth diapers, so that meant daily washing and drying of diapers. Since back then we didn't own a dryer, I had to hang diapers outside to dry.

I can still remember the image of me, constantly going outside with a bulging belly (with you inside me), hanging diapers on a backyard line, while prisoners from a Louisiana penitentiary were working in the fields behind our house and were whistling at me. That was kind of creepy, and it made me very uncomfortable. Then one day, I went to the hospital with labor pains, only to find out that my doctor, a specialist in obstetrics and gynecology, was in Bermuda on vacation, and you were a breech baby whose position in my body needed to be reversed before birth.

A superstitious person might say that was not a good beginning, but at the time all I could think of and feel was fear about your safety. That's when my ambivalence flew out of the window, and I realized how important you were to me.

Later, I foolishly worried that you would get compared with Spiros unfavorably because he was such a beautiful baby with a head full of dark thick hair. You, on the other hand, looked like a tiny version of a bald, wrinkled old man. Your odd little face tugged at my heartstrings. You looked so vulnerable and helpless. I felt a strong urge to hold you tight and protect you from the world and its challenges. Unfortunately, the day would come when I could not protect you at all, you ceased to exist, and my life changed forever.

November 9, 2018

My Dearest Son,

We had midterm elections a few days ago and the results are mixed. The Democrats did gain back the House of Representatives, and some female politicians won their races. That was the good news (for me, anyway). The not-so-good result was that the Republicans held on to the Senate majority. I know you are beyond caring for such worldly matters, but I did want you to know that we still have a very divided country. Add to that a combative, immature president, and that's quite upsetting.

Oh, I don't want to forget to mention that there was yet another massacre in our country, and twelve innocent people were gunned down—all because of a sick, disturbed individual and our lousy gun laws. Or, to be more precise, because of the inept U.S. Congress, which is too cowardly to upset the National Rifle Association or other lobbyists and thus unwilling to try to prevent such tragedies from happening.

Jaime, I know that there are no massacres in heaven, so these matters are not your concerns anymore; however, I do believe that you probably still care about what happens to your loved ones here on earth. That's why I'm telling you all this. Maybe you already know. How I wish you were still here alive to share your views with me, even though we would probably disagree about certain political matters. By your own admission, you always voted Libertarian, so you would probably want the government to take a hands-off position. Has being on the other side changed your view on this?

I do know for a fact that you and I would agree on certain societal issues involved. You were always a big advocate of social justice, civil rights, conservation of the environment, and humane treatment of animals. You were happy that your boys were growing up in California. You told me proudly that they didn't understand why some people had been against President Obama because of the color of his skin.

The newest massacre happened at Thousand Oaks, California. I felt so sad and even outraged about all the grieving families and all the lost individuals, young and old. The site of the tragedy brought back personal, painful memoires as well. Thousand Oaks is where that infamous motel is situated and where Olga and I came to see you unannounced and tried to intervene on your destructive path of addiction exactly two years ago.

I can see your image etched on my mind as I first spotted you upon entering the grounds of the motel. You had a knit cap on your head, even though the weather was mild, and you were in the process of taking your dog for a walk. Your face was turned away from us. From the car, we saw only your back, but I instantly recognized you. Dreading what was to come, I felt my stomach lurch.

I had spent countless hours preparing the script of the intervention, pondering and agonizing about every word that I wrote in the incidents, and wondering how to address the problem of your alcoholism and engage you in the process without antagonizing or angering you. My efforts were somewhat successful, in the sense that most of the time you seemed to take in what I was saying without getting defensive or angry. The only time you showed any anger was when I mentioned that I was afraid that your brain cells were dying because of the excess amounts of alcohol and/or other drugs.

"Please don't say that again, Mother," you said. "My brain cells are just fine. I am still a damn good lawyer."

That's when my eyes filled up with tears, and I felt my body tremble. I heard your denial loud and clear, and I ached for you. How I wished that what you were saying was true, but unfortunately, I knew better. Then some months later, you lost your law license (it was probably revoked because of your DUI convictions), and your decline progressed rapidly. I didn't even know at the time that you had cirrhosis of the liver. That must have already begun poisoning your body. Two short and eventful jail terms followed, and the family and I stopped hearing from you.

When I was in Los Angeles with Olga, in that smelly, grimy motel room, begging you to get some help for your illness, you told me that since I came all the way from Texas (and with a painful, debilitated knee) that you would be sure to get help. I almost believed you. I should have known better. It was another false promise, added to all the other broken promises along the way. Maybe a small part of you wanted to believe that you were sincere in your promise to me. I hope so. Unfortunately, your addiction won this contest.

My Al-Anon meetings kept reminding me that we are all powerless over alcohol and other drugs, but I stubbornly refused to totally believe that! I kept hoping with desperate love that a mother who was a therapist could succeed where others failed. Alas, it was not to be.

November 17, 2018 (a.m.)

My Dearest Son,

I just heard your voice say, "Mom!" The sound was so clear and strong as a bell, and your voice felt so real that I jumped up! I had just finished taking my blood pressure. I don't usually check it at this time, but it was really high last night, forcing me to take some extra medicine. It was high last week as well, and I did not feel well. The weather was unusually cold for Houston (temperatures in the thirties and forties), and I had to take in the patio plants to protect them from the cold. All that must have placed a strain on my heart. At least that's my theory.

A couple of weeks ago, I ended up in the emergency room of a hospital because of high blood pressure. The staff did all sorts of tests and did not see any worsening of my chronic condition. Maybe you remember that I was diagnosed with atrial fibrillation and congestive heart failure ten years ago. Since then, I have been diligent about taking my medicines and taking care of myself, even though my family finds my endeavor obsessive at times. They seem to ignore the fact that at times my blood pressure gets too high or too low (a new problem). I feel that I have worsened physically in the last year. That's no surprise, given my broken heart about losing you.

The total truth is that I have mixed feelings about my heart nowadays. Right after I learned of your passing on, I didn't really care if I lived or died. I was not exactly suicidal, but there was a big part of me that wanted to join you in the afterlife. Currently, my feelings about this have been altered some, and I have moved toward wanting to live a little longer, if possible. When Constantine sees that I am in a depressed mood or discouraged about my health challenges, he says, half joking, "Mom, you have to go on living, at least until you reach ninety!"

I don't care about longevity numbers, but it would be nice to see how my grandchildren evolve and maybe even see the face of a great-grandchild. I would certainly like to live long enough to attend my oldest granddaughter's wedding. (She has a steady boyfriend of a few years, and they have discussed future wedding plans.) It would be also very nice to be able to call Stacy (Constantine's oldest) "Dr. Sendukas!" (She is finishing medical school and will begin her postgraduate residency next year.) How about that? For the first time ever, we'll have a real doctor in the family (and a female at that). İnşallah (God willing), as they would say in Turkey, the country of my birth.

You were the first lawyer of our family, and now Victoria has taken over that title. Who knows what the rest of them are going to achieve? I do want to witness some of that. But as your younger son, Nicholas, is fond of saying, "It is what it is!" So, we'll see what the universe has in store for me. I do believe in the idea of karma or kismet or whatever else one's fate is called, but I also believe that we shape and control at least some of that.

Your karma used to look good for some time, at least to me. You were able to heal from a big romantic heartbreak in your late twenties. I still have a couple of pictures of you and your ex-girlfriend. She was so pretty! She looked like a model. She was also a very bright and sensitive girl, but with some emotional baggage (having grown up in an alcoholic home).

She was such a big part of your life, both in law school and during the early years in Los Angeles. She and I had grown close during my regular visits to California. I cried when you told me that you two went your separate ways and that she had left LA. I never told you this, but she sent me a letter from overseas a year later, telling me how much she cared for me and how much she missed me. I kept that letter for a long time.

I'll never forget the beauty of the setting of your first apartment in LA in Marina del Rey. Even the name of the place sounded romantic to me. I'll never forget the sight of those lovely white and blue sailboats marooned around the apartment complex with the lovely tinkling sound of the sails and all the shimmering water surrounding the place. You and I always shared a love of the sea. After I visited you there a few times, I could certainly see the appeal of the place and could certainly understand why you preferred LA to Houston—much to my chagrin of having you live such a far distance away.

I remembered my own departure from my hometown of Istanbul when I was twenty-two years old to come to the United States of America and how my mother fainted at the airport after my plane left. (I was told that later, and I would understand that history was being repeated.) I wished you well with your move. I loved you enough not to nag you about living away from your family, even though Spiros kept trying to coax you to come back to Houston. I would try to put a positive spin on your decision to live in California and look forward to my yearly visits to see you as a wonderful vacation for me.

Our reunions were great as well. You always seemed so happy to see me when I arrived at the LA airport. I would always remember your booming voice across the airport passenger terminal, shouting, "Mom, I'm so glad you're here!" And I would look at your smiling handsome face, hug you tight, and beam with joy.

December 18, 2018

My Dearest Son,

It has been about twelve days since I last wrote to you. I have had some turbulent weeks. My blood pressure has been out of control, and it has been a scary time. I ended up in the emergency room again and then at a hospital for two nights. A cardiologist did a catheterization procedure on me last week to determine what's going on and why I have been feeling so bad in the last couple of months. The reason why I went to the emergency room again was because of chest pressure and painful discomfort. I was scared, but I didn't even tell the rest of the family before going (they don't like for me to go to the ER).

After the hospital stay, I made the big decision to change doctors and switched to the consultant cardiologist. This was a very hard decision because I liked my ex-doctor a lot as a person. He used to give me a lot of information about my heart condition and seemed to care about me, but in the last few months he seemed to change. I felt that I had not gotten much help from him. He kept telling me not to worry, but that advice was not very helpful when I felt bad so often and saw high numbers for blood pressure on my monitor. The new doctor is suspecting pulmonary problems, so that's another worry. He referred me to a specialist, so we'll see what happens.

In the meantime, I celebrated an important birthday. On December first, I turned eighty-five years old. How about that? I went to Spiros and Olga's house for a small celebration, even though I still didn't feel very well. I asked them for a ride, and guess who turned up to pick me up? Your son, Nicholas. He's such a sweetheart. He does favors for me, without any complaints and with a smile on his face. I wish you could see how he looks now. He is such a handsome, personable young man!

The family dinner was very nice, and I tried to put on a happy face. It looks like I'm getting a new cell phone for a present. Olga gave me some special food items that she picked up in a Turkish food store in New York recently. Victoria, who is still recovering from a recent pneumonia scare that she had while she was overseas on a business trip, gave me a big dark chocolate bar in the shape of the famous Cologne Cathedral in Germany.

The night of my birthday, I had a strange but welcome dream. There was a big fire in the house I was in, but neither I nor the other people who were in my dream seemed concerned about the fire. Nobody made any attempt to stop it, to extinguish it, or even to leave and get out of the burning house. Then you appeared in the dream. This time your eyes were open (the only other two times I dreamed of you since your passing, your eyes were closed shut). You were in adult form, and even though your back was turned to me part of the time, you seemed to accept my hugs and kisses with some pleasure. I don't know what happened to the fire. Once you appeared in my dream, I was oblivious to my surroundings.

I wonder what it all meant. Was the fire in my dream a symbol of your illness of alcoholism?

It could have been. After all, we (the family) were oblivious to it for a long time, until it got too bad to ignore. Regardless of the meaning, it felt wonderful to see you again and to hug you again, even if it was only in a dream. It was my nicest birthday present!

December 28, 2018

My Dearest Son,

I have not written to you for a while. I have not been feeling well, honey. I went to the emergency room again, this time for severe chest palpitations and a high heart rate. This time, I did not even call 911 but asked my neighbor to take me at 4 a.m. (She does not sleep well and is often awake in the middle of the night.) This happened two days before Christmas. Usually this time of the year, I'm busy baking some of my specialties for the Christmas Day celebration, not going to the emergency room. Unfortunately, my physical body doesn't know about holidays, and health challenges do not respect the calendar.

The truth is that I have not been feeling like celebrating anyway. This is my first Christmas since your death, and it certainly is not a happy time for me. I had already figured out that holiday time would be hard, but I certainly did not expect to spend Christmas Eve in the hospital in the Cardiac Intensive Care Unit. Yes, they hospitalized me "for observation." I wonder what the medical diagnosis is for a broken heart?

The palpitations were real, of course, and so was the intense chest pressure, but I believe the causes behind my symptoms were complicated, not all of them physical. My family is not happy at all about the recent ER visits and hospital stays, and they keep telling me that I worry too much (the implication being that I am responsible for not being well). I have no doubt that my grief about losing you played a big role in my worsened health situation, but I don't agree with my family that I should not have gone to the ER.

I left the hospital on Christmas Day. I did not even call anybody—took Uber instead—and went home. I was determined to salvage at least part of the holiday and go to Spiros's house for the annual family celebration. I had no presents to give anybody, but figured I would be forgiven, given the circumstances.

Well, the above is not totally true. I did have a present, of sorts, for your boys. A month ago, I finished putting together and preparing photo albums for Robert and Nicholas. Each was a special album that was made up of pictures of your childhood and young adulthood. I had decided to do this project months ago, but preparing it turned out to be more emotional and difficult than I had anticipated. I had to stop myself from crying every time I saw your sweet face in the pictures, because I knew if I gave myself to the grief, I would never finish my project.

Congratulate me! I did finish and sent one of the albums to Robert a couple of weeks ago. Christmas Day I looked at Nicholas as he opened up his album, and the expression on his face was worth all the emotional stress of putting it together.

Your brother Constantine helped me with the digital aspect behind the albums. He copied the pictures with his cell phone and placed them on a disk. I took the disk to Walgreen's and had the pictures printed. Robert also must have appreciated my present because he thanked me twice, both by text and in a phone call.

Both of your sons are so wonderful. They are young men of few words, but they are men of merit. You would be so proud of them. They both go to college as well as work part-time. Last time we met, you and I, for the intervention, I said to you at one point, "How can you stand this situation of yours? You are estranged from your sons, and they are struggling to make it in the world without your help." You looked at me with a stern look and said, "Keep them out of this, Mom. They are good kids. They'll be fine."

Well, you were right about that. That doesn't mean that they haven't been traumatized by your alcoholism. Of course, they have, but they are both working hard to overcome their difficulties. They both miss you terribly. I see the sadness in Nicholas's eyes every time I see him. I don't see Robert often, since he lives in San Francisco, but he does sometimes come on holidays.

Nicholas has been living with Spiros and Olga for two years now. Yes, the same Spiros whom you called "Satan" when you were under the influence of God-knows-what is raising your son with not just a sense of obligation but also a lot of affection. When I thanked him one day, when we happened to be alone, for everything that he and Olga have done for Nicholas, he looked at me and said, "Mom, having Nicholas here has been a joy!"

As you know, that's high praise coming from your older brother. He gives compliments very sparingly. He loves Nicholas and so does Olga, and so do we all. It doesn't hurt that Spiros has finally discovered a family member who loves football almost as much as he does. Olga tells me that he and Nicholas watch football on TV for hours on end.

Nicholas is making straight A's at community college, and he has done so well as a valet attendant at restaurants that he was promoted to shift supervisor at age twenty. He's shy (like you were at his age) and rarely talks about his feelings, but I know how much he misses you and the rest of his family. I try to get him to open up about his feelings as much as I can. I have asked him to come with me to some grief group meetings, and he never has refused me when I have.

Last time we went to a meeting, he had a bad cold, but he still volunteered to drive me to the park where that special meeting took place. It was about an hour away and it rained cats and dogs that night. Despite the rain and the chill in the air, your son never complained. (His cold did get worse the next day, and I felt guilty.)

His actions reminded me of when you were a Boy Scout and had gone on a field trip with your troop. It rained that whole weekend. When your father and I came to pick you up from the camping trip, your scoutmaster came to our side to tell us that even though the weather was terrible and camping conditions were rough, you were the only scout in the group who never complained. We were so proud of you! After the grief group ceremony, I looked at Nicholas and thought, "Like father, like son!"

January 1, 2019

My Dearest Son,

This is the first day of the New Year, another time landmark that you are missing. I am glad that 2018 is over. It was the worst year of my life. How could it not have been? After all, it was the year of your death. During this fateful year, in addition to the immense grief I was feeling, my health problems got a lot worse.

I ended up in the emergency room a few times and even was hospitalized for a couple of days for high blood pressure and heart problems. Seeking help at the hospital was nothing that I relished, but it felt necessary at the time to get extra medical care.

I have always been an optimist, one who saw the proverbial glass half full instead of half empty (to use the apt cliché), but it was really hard to maintain my optimism in 2018. My hope is that the new year will bring a diagnosis and/or understanding about why I have been feeling so badly.

My family keeps reminding me (as if I didn't know) that my grief over your passing has a lot to do with the state of my health. The problem for me is that they make the above statement sound almost like an accusation of sorts, as if I could control the quantity of my bereavement over losing you. I could not control that any more than I could control my breathing!

In addition to hoping for some improvement in my health, my other, even more important goal is finally to find some solace in your passing and truly believe that you are finally at peace. Another angel in the afterlife. They do have middle-aged angels out there—wherever out there is—don't they? I know that if I totally believed what I just wrote, I would let you go and not lament your passing so much. All that makes sense in my head, but my heart tells a different story. It misses you terribly, despite the reality of the last few years that were full of chaos and despair.

Oh, sweetheart, how I wish that your life could have taken a different path! I used to fantasize a lot that you would stop drinking and drugging, that you would fight your addiction to chemicals, and that you would claim victory over their power on you. I used to rehearse in my mind over and over again the exact words that I needed to tell you to propel you toward sobriety. I know that you tried to do it your way by going cold turkey once, but all that act produced was a severe seizure that must have scared you enough so as not to try such shenanigans again.

I told you more than once—as a mother and a therapist—that you needed help from professionals, your fellow addicts, or both at AA. I emphasized that the problem was too big and too hard to tackle alone, but you were too stubborn to listen and follow my advice.

Jaime, you paid dearly for that stubbornness or defiance. Being homeless, hiding from authorities because of a stolen U-Haul truck, and enduring two jail terms were part of that price. Who knows what you suffered internally while dealing with the ravages and demons of addiction! I still remember the anguish in your voice when you called me after my knee-replacement surgery and said, "Mom, they took away my law license." I didn't know if you knew exactly how to get it back and earn a living.

It broke my heart to hear how badly things were going for you. It didn't help that I was in a lot of physical pain after surgery (knee-replacement surgeries are notorious for being painful), and I didn't have the emotional capacity to hear any more of your distress. All I remember telling you was, "Honey, I am really sorry about your license. I hope you get it back one day. I can't talk anymore because the doctor just came into my room."

The last part of my reply was a lie. I couldn't bear to hear any more about your misfortunes. My physical pain lowered my emotional resources a lot, so I hung up the phone. Looking back, I feel some guilt that I wasn't able to comfort you at a very low point in your life. Your law license was very important to you. I have always known that, but I couldn't rise to the occasion.

Tough love notwithstanding, I am glad that at least I didn't give you any judgmental lectures about your path in life and the bad choices you were making. You were hurting too much, and I didn't want to sound self-righteous or unfeeling. I do wish that I had told you, in a more emphatic manner, that I hurt for you about your loss and misery and that I loved you, no matter what!

January 14, 2019

My Dearest Son,

I have missed writing to you. Lately, my blood pressure and atrial fibrillation kept getting in the way. I have a new cardiologist who keeps prescribing potent medications that give me a lot of side effects, some of them severe. Unfortunately, I seem to be a kind of pariah to him and his medical assistant. Even though I keep complaining about the disturbing side effects—like a raised heart rate, a flushed face, and palpitations— what I hear back is that his other patients do not have them. As if that fact erases my own experiences. I get the impression from them that they see me as a difficult old woman who complains too much. As a result of this, I have not been feeling well lately, and I have sort of isolated myself. Maybe it's time to change cardiologists again. I have been thinking about it, but I don't want to appear flaky to the medical community. After all, I just changed doctors a little while ago.

I have also had some concerns about the emotions associated with writing these letters to you. This idea may have been fueled by a girlfriend who thinks that this kind of writing may aggravate my health situation. She told me that she is worried about me, and that's why she's telling me all this. I am sure that she means well and has my best interests at heart, but I am certainly not giving up writing to you. These letters provided emotional solace when nothing else worked for me and still do.

A few days ago, I went for a sleep study, courtesy of my new pulmonary specialist, who thinks that I have sleep apnea (rather than pulmonary hypertension). He believes that it's apnea that's causing some of the high numbers of blood pressure and unpleasant symptoms. I was dreading this all-night study, fantasizing about all sorts of horrors happening to me during the study. As a consequence of those fantasies, I was superanxious before the 6:30 p.m. appointment, almost to the point of having a panic attack.

Miraculously, your brother Constantine arrived at my house with his girlfriend, just I was considering canceling the appointment. His visit was totally unexpected. I had texted him earlier about some of my fears about the appointment, but he had not responded. I was very happy to see them at the doorstep. I felt as if they had been sent by heavenly angels. They reassured me about the appointment and drove me there. I was still kind of shaken, but became a little more resolute that I had to go through with it.

The experience was both better and worse that I had imagined. They placed twenty-two (no kidding, I counted them) electrodes on my head and body. These electrodes had dangling wires of many colors on them, and when I looked at myself in the bathroom mirror, I practically screamed. I looked like a zombie monster in a vampire movie! A thought occurred to me then: if you were still around, I would have taken a selfie and texted it to you. How you would have laughed, with that wonderful, booming laugh of yours. I couldn't even cry when I had that thought, even though I felt like it. I was afraid that my tears would mess up the sleep study and the electrodes all over my head and body.

I was convinced that I would not be able to sleep a wink, given all the crazy apparatus on me, but amazingly, I slept enough to give them the data that they needed. At 6 a.m. (the designated time), I asked the technician, who was in the room next to mine, to remove my electrodes so I could go home. I took Uber (not wanting to wake up my family at that early hour) and went home.

Oh, Jaime, I miss you so much! So many things remind me of you. Yesterday, I saw a blues guitarist on TV, and I immediately thought, "Jaime would have loved this. He loved music and playing his guitar." Instantly a memory flashed through my mind. You were a lot younger (we were both a lot younger), and you had recently graduated from law school. You were staying with me in Houston for a couple of months while studying for your bar exam.

I told you one day that a famous blues guitarist, B. B. King was coming to Houston. I asked you if you wanted to come with me to his concert. I added that I loved his music and thought you might enjoy him as well. I was tentative about the invite, wondering if it would embarrass you to go to a concert with your mother.

You didn't hesitate at all. You quickly said, "Sure, I'd love to, Mom." So we went. B. B. King was great, even exceeding my expectations. Before the concert, I had been a little apprehensive about your reaction, wondering if you would like him as well. To my relief and joy, you seemed to really enjoy the concert. You turned to me at one point and said, "He's great, Mom. I can see why you like him so much." Then you placed your arm around my shoulders and hugged me—in public no less! That gesture meant a lot to me.

When you were little, you used to be a sweet, lovely child, but not very physically affectionate (unlike your two brothers). It used to bother me that you didn't care for a lot of hugging and cuddling. You certainly made up for that when you grew up. You turned out to be the most affectionate and demonstrative of all your brothers. Then, once you settled in California, I saw you only once a year, but I loved those annual trips. I looked forward to the trips with great anticipation and joy, partly because you were so loving and attentive to me when I did visit.

It was a sore subject for you that—unlike me—your father did not visit you. I tried to explain to you that I knew he loved you, but because of his old-fashioned beliefs and values, he probably thought that adult children should be the ones to visit their parents, not the other way around. Having been divorced from him since you were twenty years old, I felt bad that I no longer had any influence on him and could not urge him to visit you. Deep inside, I felt angry with him for neglecting you and your family, but my hands were tied. All I could do was to do my part: come to see you as often as I could and relish the time spent with you and the kids.

Maybe one day I will only smile when I think of my special memories of you—like the B. B. King concert—but now I cry instead and wish I had done more to show you my love.

January 19, 2019

My Dearest Son,

I went out this cold morning (unusually cold for Houston) to take out Skye for her morning walk and to pick up my daily newspaper. (Your brother Spiros tells me that I am one of the last few diehard subscribers of the local paper.) Well, I couldn't pick it up because the delivery person had thrown it into the ditch instead of the front yard. As I was looking around, trying to figure out how to retrieve the paper, I had a flashback memory involving you and me during one of our times together, and tears came to my eyes.

This is what I remembered: I was visiting you in LA as usual. You were still a bachelor then and working for a big law firm. You were living in a very nice apartment set in a lovely setting, Marina del Rey. I used to call it your resort apartment because it had all these fancy amenities—a pool, a sauna, and a hot tub—all facing the marina. One could lie in the pool or hot tub and watch all the pretty white boats with the blue sails, while the sails would sway in the gentle breeze and make a lovely tinkling sound. I would have visited you anywhere in the world, but I used to love that place and relish visiting you there!

During one of those visits, you picked me up from the airport, greeted me in your usual warm way, and took me to your apartment. When we arrived there, you turned to me and said, "Here, Mom, I thought you might like this. It will keep you busy while I'm at work," and you handed me a big bundle of what looked like newspaper pages. Looking at the bundle more closely, I realized that it was a year's collection of the dining section of the *Los Angeles Times*. I looked at you dumbfounded. You grinned and said, "I know that you love reading newspapers, Mom, and I noticed when you visited me that you especially enjoyed reading the recipes in the dining section of the paper on Wednesdays. So, during the year when you were not here, I collected those sections for you."

I hugged you and thanked you for your gift. I was so touched that you took notice of what I liked and that you took the time and went to the trouble to save all these sections of the newspaper for a whole year, just to please me. You couldn't have given me a better gift. What a thoughtful, affectionate son you were, and what a lovely gesture that was! No store-bought present would have meant as much as your sweet surprise.

In later years, when addiction changed your personality and led you to another reality, how I missed the wonderful son that you had been in the past.

You used to say, "You and I have this uncommon connection, Mom. You always seem to sense when I'm in trouble or when I need help. It's uncanny how you do that!"

Unfortunately, I wasn't able to use that connection when it came to your disease of alcoholism. By the time I figured out what was going on and tried to intervene, it was too late to save you. Now all that is gone, and you are gone along with it. I'm left with the regrets and the terrible ache of what I have lost forever.

January 22, 2019

My Dearest Son,

Have I told you that I have to wear a heart monitor for a few weeks? Yes, that's the latest diagnostic tool that I have to deal with. It's almost like a do-it-yourself health project. I carry a medical smart phone with me 24/7, and I have to make sure that both the heart monitors (I have two) and the smart phone are charged at all times. Given my technological phobia, I panicked at first when I realized all I had to do to make a success of the project. In addition to keeping the devices charged, I also had to attach a strip to my chest in a strategic position and snap the heart monitor to the strip.

After reading the complicated instructions, in desperation, I took the whole package to my cardiologist's office and asked one of the nurses to show me how to do it. After she recovered from her surprise, she reminded me that I had to remove the monitor and reposition everything each time I showered or when the battery was too low. I may have congratulated myself too soon on my idea to be shown how to do the darn thing. I may never shower again! (Just kidding.)

Next thing I have to look forward to (yes, I'm being sarcastic) is having to use and take care of a CPAP (continuous positive airway pressure) machine on a nightly basis. It seems that I do have sleep apnea and that might be one of the big reasons why I have been feeling so bad lately. At least, that's what my new pulmonary specialist is saying. He is from India and I do like him, even as I'm dreading the use of a CPAP machine. It looks so weird! I can't imagine how I'm going to get used to putting on a mask every night. Ah, the joys of old age! The older I get, the more health challenges seem to crop up, and they get more and more serious each time. Well, at least you will never have to deal with that stage of life, given that you left earth and your loved ones at fifty-seven! As I'm writing this, I am starting to tear up because I realize that I'm being flip about the tragedy of your premature death. I'm sorry, Jaime. I know that you will miss seeing your boys fully grown into adults, marrying, and probably having children of their own. I am so sorry that you will not be able to enjoy grandparenting. It is really nice to have grandchildren. I derive a lot of joy from mine, and I wish you could have had that pleasure.

It's exciting to see my seven grandkids evolve into their creative careers and lives: Stacy is currently enjoying her postgraduate residency in a big hospital in Dallas; Victoria is a lawyer for a big firm in Houston; Sotiris is a graphic artist who is loving living in New York; Celeste is testing cosmetics so as to make them more healthful; and Stuart is a sous-chef. Their career paths are diverse and exciting. Your boys are still in school, but I'm sure they will have interesting futures, as well. Who knows what adventures they will have? I hope that I live long enough to see them succeed in the careers they choose. I will hug them for you when they do and will wish that you were still with us and could rejoice with them yourself.

I remember how proud you always were of them and how you called them "the light of your life" when they were born. I hope they always remember the loving father that you used to be in their younger years and not get stuck in the negative memories of their traumatic later years, when their family life got all messed up, torn into pieces of alcoholic debris.

January 24, 2019

My Dearest Son,

Nicholas texted me today and said he was close to my house, attending a community college nearby. He asked me if I wanted to join him for lunch. I wasn't really hungry. I had eaten a late breakfast, but I wasn't about to turn down an opportunity to spend time with your son. I said yes to the invite.

Your younger son is getting more and more independent and confident in himself. He applied to three top-notch universities for his last two years of college. He wants to get a business/finance degree. He is worried that he doesn't have the means and/or the right family connections to get accepted at a good school, but I told him not to worry. I believe that his excellent grades and his determination to overcome the trauma of the last few years would make him welcome at any school. My advice to him was to be truthful with school administrators and let them know how far he has come from his adversities. He looked at me with a doubtful expression on his face, so I reminded him that as a therapist with forty years of experience that I knew a little something about human nature and how to achieve goals.

You would be so proud of him. He doesn't look like you a lot—he looks more like his mother's Swedish roots—but his personality reminds me a lot of how you used to be when you were his age. He's shy like you were, and he takes his responsibilities very seriously. That impresses your older brother a lot.

He's a handsome young man—again like you were—and personable as well as eager to help. That impresses Olga, who asks him to help run errands for her antique business. She pays him for his help, and he saves that money for college. He is not dating at present. He tells me, when I ask, that he is too shy to approach girls. I seem to remember that you also were a late bloomer in the romance department.

I feel honored that he trusts me enough to confide in me about his life. Olga tells me that they often have long conversations in the evenings about things that bother him or confuse him. I know that we cannot replace you and his mother, but we do our best to be there for him. He has been in Houston for two years now, and it's evident to everyone by now that Spiros and Olga love having him live with them in their home. They recently told me that they are making plans to take him to Las Vegas for his upcoming twenty-first birthday. They invited me to go along, but I doubt that my health situation will allow it. Robert was also invited to join his brother's birthday celebration.

I have to confess that I have mixed feelings about the plan and the trip. I am grateful to Spiros and Olga for wanting to celebrate Nicholas's first adult birthday in a big way, but after what alcohol and addiction did to your life, I am scared about your boys and the idea of drinking. There is bound to be a lot of drinking in Vegas. After all, a twenty-first birthday—when drinking alcohol becomes legal—usually involves a lot of that (at least in the United States), right?

I don't remember anybody mentioning alcohol or drinking when I turned twenty-one in Istanbul, Turkey, so I may be a little biased around the whole subject. The truth is that I'm terrified about any other member of the family developing an addiction to alcohol or other drugs. You may remember that I made your younger brother, Constantine, go to treatment when he was nineteen years old. I had leverage then because of his age and dependency on me, and even though he was very angry with me at the time, my tough love approach changed the trajectory of his life. Unfortunately, your problem did not show itself to me until you were in your fifties and in another state, faraway from Texas. I could not take you by the hand and place you in a hospital, much as I wanted to.

When I came to LA in October 2016 and saw the sad situation that your life had become, all I could do was attempt an intervention—without teeth—and then watch helplessly from afar as your life went more and more into decline and then tragically came to its sudden, shocking end, leaving me forever in grief and despair. I can no longer look at homeless people on the street corners without a painful skip in my heart. I remember your walking barefoot on the grounds of the dingy motel in Los Angeles. I never saw you in a tent or on the streets, but the pitiful sight of you, shoeless and crestfallen, has stayed with me ever since. Now, every time I see a homeless person on the streets of Houston, my eyes immediately go to the feet of the person to see if they are wearing shoes. I see you in every homeless person I see, and my heart aches.

I would dearly love to find a charity one day that would provide socks and shoes for homeless people and/or help them in their journey back to civilization. That would be, I believe, a nice tribute to your memory.

Good night, sweetheart. I am going to place my new sleep headgear on and try to go to sleep.

January 31, 2019

My Dearest Son,

I apologize for neglecting my letter writing lately. I have been so engrossed with health matters, like wearing a heart monitor and trying to get used to wearing a sleep apnea mask at night, that I have not kept up my writing. As a result, I have missed the frequent contact with you, in my head anyway. I know in my rational mind that our contact is one-sided, but in some strange way, it helps with the unrelenting grief of losing you.

Who knows really what happens after we die? Maybe in some mysterious fashion, your soul/spirit knows that I am reaching out to you through these letters. Wouldn't that be wonderful? I would like to believe that somehow you know that I'm talking to you and rejoice that I love you

157

so much that I want to stay connected to you even after death. By now you may be saying, "Come on, Mom, enough sentimental stuff. Let's move on." So, I shall.

Yesterday was your grandmother Anastasia's birthday. I hope you two celebrated it together in heaven or wherever spirits reside. Your own birthday is coming up in two months, and I don't know how I'm going to bear it. Last year I was in such agony on your birthday. After all, it was only seventeen days after your heart stopped that I thought my own heart was going to stop as well (and that was not such an unwelcome thought). In the last months, I have moved some from that emotional state. I still miss you terribly and ache for your loss every single day, but I have some earthly goals that I would like to accomplish before my own departure from earth. I don't know if I'll get that chance, but at least I would like to try.

Please remember that I will always love you and will try to honor your life and memory as long as I live.

February 5, 2019

My Dearest Son,

I had another happy memory flashback tonight. Those are rare, so I treasure them when they come. I was watching one of my favorite shows on television, the PBS show "Austin City Limits," which features alternative music, mostly to my liking. Willie Nelson was on. He has been a favorite of mine for a long time. I am amazed that he can still stand up and play the guitar and sing (he is close to my age).

He is all white now—white hair, white beard, and even white eyebrows—but, boy, he can still perform. His voice may not be as strong and melodic as it used to be, but it still has the unique cadence and style that made him famous and special to his many fans, like me. Some of his old magic may be gone, but his unique voice can still hold the attention of an audience. If you close your eyes and just listen to the strumming of his guitar, he can still cut the mustard (as the old saying goes).

I am digressing here. I started this letter talking about a memory, so here goes. It was New Year's Eve and you were spending the holidays with me. You were young then and still single. You were in a long-distance relationship with your first serious girlfriend who was still in Michigan finishing law school. You had graduated the previous spring. I met her when I came to your law school graduation. I was struck by how pretty she was and how smart and personable as well. I liked her right away.

It was so nice to have you stay with me for a while, especially during the holidays. After my divorce from your Dad and your days in college and law school, your visits to Houston were rare and short, so it was a special treat to have you spend a week with me.

New Year's Eve morning, I read in the local paper that Willie Nelson was performing in Houston for only one night. I told you about it, saying that if I had known earlier that he was coming, I would have tried to get tickets. You turned to me and said, "You like him a lot, don't you, Mom?"

"Yes," I replied, "I do like him."

"Why don't you call and see if there are any tickets left for tonight?" you said.

I laughed, "You've got to be kidding, Jaime. It's New Year's Eve tonight. I'm sure the concert is sold out."

"Call," you insisted. "You never know."

I thought it was a crazy idea, but I did as you suggested. I called the ticket office. To my great surprise, they told me that they had a few tickets left in the balcony of the theater. I hesitated. The tickets were rather expensive, and I don't like theater balconies. In addition to all that, who would I find at the last minute to come with me? I certainly didn't want to go alone, especially on New Year's Eve. Again, you were the voice of optimism.

"Mom," you said, "just get the tickets and stop worrying. If your friends are busy or have other plans, I'll come with you." I was shocked by your response.

"Do you even like Willie Nelson?" I asked.

"I am not very familiar with his voice," you replied, "but it doesn't matter. You know me. I like all kinds of music, and if you like him that much, I bet he's good. I can always appreciate a good guitar!"

So, off we went to the concert. I was so happy and excited that night. Not only was I going to see my favorite performer in a live concert, but I would be going in your company. What a rare treat that was.

I marveled that you were willing to go with your mother to a public event, a concert, but for once, I didn't analyze it too much. I just took you at your word that you truly wanted to go with me.

I had a great time that evening. Willie was marvelous, and you were so attentive and nice to me. I still remember his entrance on stage. He came on with a headband on his hair and his guitar strapped on, and he started singing his big hit "Whiskey River." No introduction, no fanfare, no chit-chat—just his music.

I sneaked a look at you, and you looked pleased. He had your total attention—like he had that of the rest of the crowd. I stopped worrying about whether you were going to like him or not and just lost myself in the music.

We did not spend the whole evening in the balcony. At the first break, you whispered, "Come with me, Mom," and started walking. I asked you where we were going. "Don't ask questions," you said, "Just follow me."

I followed you. Somehow, we worked our way downstairs and despite the fact that the concert venue was packed with people, you found us some empty seats on the main floor, close to the stage. I looked around me in amazement. I had never done anything like this before.

You were grinning. "Didn't I tell you to follow me, Mom?" you said. "Would I steer you wrong?"

I placed my arm around your shoulders and whispered, "Thank you, honey, for finding us these great seats, and thank you for coming with me to see my favorite performer."

"My pleasure!" you said. "I am enjoying this concert, too, Mom. He is really good—great guitar playing."

I hope that you meant what you said and that you were truly enjoying yourself. I do know that you gave me the gift of an unforgettable evening, and a lovely memory. Thank you, baby.

February 18, 2019

My Dearest Son,

I woke up this morning crying. I had just seen you in a dream. I did not want the dream to end but it did, and that's why I woke up crying. I have seen you three times in my dreams in the eleven months since you left Earth, which is not a lot, considering that you are always in my thoughts and in my aching heart. The other two times I saw you, you just stood there. I hugged you and hugged you, but you never responded. The first such dream was a few months after you were gone. Your eyes were closed and you were very still. The second time I dreamt of you, your eyes were open and you didn't resist my embrace, but again you didn't move at all.

The big difference about this morning's dream was that you were animated and talking for the first time. A door opened in the scene, and you appeared holding a boxed TV set. This time you were an adult, not a child as in my previous dreams. You said, "I made a great bargain on this buy, Mom." You were animated and smiling, and I was so happy to see you. Before I had a chance to react, I woke up, and that's why I started crying. The dream was so short! There I was back in my bedroom in Houston, an old woman with empty, aching arms. I cried and cried for a long time.

My darling boy, I miss you so much! It doesn't feel like eleven months have passed since you died. Sometimes the grief is so fresh that it feels like your death happened only yesterday. There are other times when the time that has passed feels endless, like an eternity!

"They" keep saying that time heals. I just don't believe that old saying anymore. Not when you lose a child—even if that child is fifty-seven years old.

You were my baby and will always be my lost baby.
All my love, Mom

February 25, 2019

My Dearest Son,

I wish I could hear your voice, telling me you are okay, wherever you are. I know that your spirit came to me one night, some months ago. No, it wasn't a dream. It was very real. Was that vision meant to reassure me that you were fine? Maybe some part of our "incredible" (as you called it) connection exists beyond death. I would surely like to believe that, even if it sounds crazy.

You know I never told your brothers or even Nicholas about that spiritual vision. I'm not sure exactly why I didn't tell them. I suspect it's because I don't think that they'll believe me and that they will dismiss the idea of the vision, telling me that it was probably a vivid dream. I did tell a couple of close friends, because I knew that they wouldn't laugh at me or dismiss it.

Jaime, I want to thank you and your spirit for coming to visit me. I don't know how you managed to pull it off. It can't be easy to produce a vision. Maybe God in his/her mercy and the universe had pity on me for losing you and decided to help you come up with a miracle. That's how I perceive that vision—a glorious, incredible miracle! Thank you, sweetie.

March 1, 2019

My Dearest Son,

This is your birthday month as well as the month of the first-year anniversary of your leaving our earthly family to join the celestial one. I don't know how I am going to survive this month. The grief I'm feeling today feels as new and painful as it did in the early days and weeks after your death.

In the Greek Orthodox church calendar, there is a one-year memorial for the departed members of the church. Through the years I have attended quite a few of those memorials because they take place at the conclusion of the weekly Sunday service. I never understood their deep significance until now. Since you were cremated and did not have a proper Greek funeral (only a small prayer service that I arranged for the family and me), sadly, there is no one-year church anniversary that I can attend to honor your memory. The closest I can come to that vigil is to go to a special meeting of the grief group that I attend monthly.

The evening of March 12, the night before your actual anniversary as it happens to be, I will get up in the group and talk a little about who you were as a person and pass around the group a few of your pictures. The last picture I have of you was taken at Nicholas's high school graduation. You have a proud, smiling expression on your face, and I'm glad to see that.

I am happy that you seemed to enjoy the occasion despite the fact that you were on the verge of disaster in your life (only I didn't know it back then). Soon after that graduation, your home was repossessed and then you, Leslie, and Nicholas started the painful path of going to cheap motels, eventually ending up homeless. Robert was lucky enough to have escaped that painful family path. He had gone to San Francisco two years earlier to attend college.

So, I'm glad that at least you had those happy moments of graduation day before your world started caving in.

March 5, 2019

My Dearest Son,

Today I went to see Robert, my therapist. I had not seen him for over a month, and my grief is spilling over and making it hard to function or sleep. I suspect that I'm probably having anticipatory anxiety, in addition to my ongoing depression, because the one-year anniversary of your passing is coming up on the thirteenth of the month. March is also your birthday month, so it's a double whammy! I'm trying to help myself through this very difficult month. In addition to seeing Robert for therapy, I'm also planning to go to the grief group next week. I asked Nicholas to come with me to the group meeting. I told him that I needed his emotional support. Very true, but the part that I did not tell him (but thought of) is my belief that this special meeting will be healing for him as well.

He immediately agreed to come. I am so fond of Nicholas. One upside from the terrible tragedy of your death is that your younger son and I have gotten a lot closer since he's been living in Houston with Spiros and Olga. As I've told you before, they are also very fond of Nicholas, and they are even planning to take him to Las Vegas for his twenty-first birthday in April. I never liked Vegas. I went twice and both times I was not impressed: too many gambling machines, too much noise, too much drinking, and all that goes with that. The vibes there are those of an escapist destination. They actually advertise Vegas that way, and the notion makes me rather uneasy.

Don't misunderstand me. I am happy that Spiros and Olga want to please Nicholas and give him a special trip. Stuart and Victoria and Robert are going as well. My only concern is about the drinking. I have never seen Nicholas drink alcohol, but now that he will be legally able to drink, it worries me some. I know, I know, my fears are probably excessive, but I also know from my history as a therapist and alcoholism counselor that children of alcoholics have a much higher hereditary tendency to be addicts themselves; therefore, the thought mixed with your history and their mother's history scares me.

I want to tell your boys about the odds, but I hesitate. I don't want them to view me as a lecturing old nag of a grandmother! Can you help me guide them from above or wherever you are in our cosmos/universe? Can you also see how I struggle daily with your loss, eleven and a half months after your passing?

I know the grief will never go away, but I need help in learning how to live with it, instead of drowning in it. Please, help me.

March 13, 2019

My Dearest Son,

It's 2:30 a.m., and of course I cannot sleep. It's the one-year anniversary of your death. How on earth am I supposed to sleep? This was the worst day of my life, bar none.

I did go to the grief group with Nicholas, and it was a comforting event, despite the emotional pain. I read your eulogy to the group, and I was able to finish it without sobbing. My voice cracked a few times, but that's all.

Knowing that Nicholas was there, listening to the eulogy, provided a cushion of emotional support that went above and beyond what the grief group gave me. I told the group how much you loved animals and how you used to place your cat's food on your wedding china to the dismay of your wife, and they laughed.

Knowing you, I know that you would have appreciated the humor in the middle of the grief. I can even hear your voice telling me, "Good work, Mom. All that drama and gloom needed some lift. You did good. By the way, there was nothing wrong with my feeding the cats on china plates. They were part of my family, after all."

As for Nicholas, he has been a big source of support for me all year long. He is a rather quiet and shy young man, but he does share some of his feelings with me. Olga tells me that he confides in her also, and I'm very glad to hear that. He is and always will be a part of you, and I cherish his company for that as well.

I miss you so much, Son. Not the addicted Jamie of the last years of your life. (I still loved you, of course, but didn't like your behavior or who you had become.)

I miss the son with the wry grin and the booming and affectionate laugh, who would always tell me how happy he was to see me.

I miss the son who stayed by my bedside at an emergency room in LA, when I arrived with a raging stomach virus. You stayed with me from 5 a.m. to 10 p.m., and then you begged the attending doctor to let me leave the hospital. You promised him that you would bring me back if I fell sick again at your place. I didn't and we didn't have to go back, but I have never forgotten how solicitous you were and how worried.

I miss the son who planted five kinds of lettuce in his backyard (I didn't even know that there were that many varieties of lettuce) and would paint a discarded old bench over and over again until it looked nice.

I miss the lover of all music, who on a trip to Tijuana, Mexico, fell in love with an old guitar that he saw in the window of a pawn shop and bought it without haggling about the price, saying that one shouldn't haggle over the price of a musical instrument—it was too sacred!

I miss the son who surprised me by arranging for a train trip during one of my visits because he remembered how much I loved trains.

Jaime, you were a wonderful son for many years, and I should be grateful for those years, instead of lamenting the ones I lost; but it's hard to let go. I am glad that you are not suffering anymore from your addiction, but now the rest of us—the ones who loved you—are suffering instead.

I keep thinking lately of the old Irish ballad called "Danny Boy." In my younger days, I remember being somewhat annoyed by the sentimentality of the song. It's only now that I have lost you that I understand the depth of feeling that inspired the song and can appreciate it better. It had to be a grieving parent who wrote that song. Now I cry whenever I hear it, instead of being annoyed.

Rest in peace, my boy. Your disease cannot hurt you anymore.

Your spirit is free to fly!

March 18, 2019

My Dearest Son,

I had an unexpected meltdown this morning. Usually, my emotional meltdowns involving you happen late in the evening or in the middle of the night. This one came bright and early. Upon waking up, as I washed my face, for some reason I looked at my hands, and instantly an image popped into my head. The image was of your hands as I saw them during one of our last encounters. They were dark red in color, almost purple, especially your fingers.

I was instantly alarmed by the unusual dark color, and I asked you about it. "Oh, that's nothing, Mom," you said. "No need to worry. My hands have always been kind of rough and reddish in color." I tried to believe you—that this was nothing to be concerned about—but I wasn't totally convinced.

I told you to please go to your doctor and check that out. I still didn't like the look of your hands. I thought it might signify something important about your overall health. You kind of nodded, but I did not believe that you totally agreed with me. After we parted, I googled the color of your hands. The response was "possibly a circulation problem." That made me worry even more. I hoped that you would follow my advice and go see a doctor. I was naive enough back then to think that you had a family doctor to consult. I had no idea at that time that you had a serious addiction problem.

Looking back now, I realize that the weird color of your hands was a warning about your general health, but my denial and codependency were too strong to allow me to perceive the danger totally.

PART III
CONTINUING GRIEF, SOME
HEALING, AND A TOUCH OF CLOSURE

Letters of March 27, 2019, through August 5, 2019

March 27, 2019

My Dearest Son,

Happy Birthday, sweetheart! This day may not mean anything to you anymore, but it means a lot to me. Fifty-eight years ago, you looked at me, and I instantly fell in love. All my earlier concerns about your being too close in age to your brother, Spiros, were erased from my mind.

It had been a rather difficult birth. Second-baby births are not supposed to be very long or very difficult, but your birth had two strikes against it. My regular ob-gyn doctor was on vacation in the Bahamas, and I had never met his partner, the doctor who delivered you. Not an ideal situation by any means. In addition to the above, yours was a breach birth, and because it took longer than usual, they had to give me gas so as not to give me another epidural injection.

I fought the idea of gas and told them I didn't want it. I had hated the stuff since a traumatic experience when I was ten years old and had been given gas for a tonsillectomy at a physician's office in Istanbul. The technician who administered it was not very competent or experienced, and it had not been a swift or easy procedure. I finally agreed to the gas after I was told by the doctor that it would be dangerous for me to get a second epidural shot. So, all of the above contributed to a more difficult than usual birth. In retrospect, a superstitious person like my mother (and me, a little) would say that the problematic way you were born could have been a sign that your life would be troubled as well!

The truth is that life went smoothly for you for some time. You were my golden boy during your childhood and young adulthood. You were smart, kind, and handsome. You were an excellent student who never needed any prompting to study. You always did your homework by yourself, with no help from me or your dad. You adored music and loved being in the school marching band. You were liked by your teachers as well as other students. You seemed to have it all.

You were shy, when young, and not very comfortable with girls, even though I could tell that you liked them. You did not date during your high school years. You waited until college for that.

The college that you chose—you were a National Merit finalist and so had quite a few acceptances from prestigious colleges—was Washington University in St. Louis. I wasn't thrilled about your choosing a college so far away from us, but you earned a full scholarship and you seemed happy about it.

You did not come home a lot during your college years, but I attributed that the fact that your dad and I were going through a divorce at the time. On one of your trips home, you told me that you were dating, and I was pleased to hear that, assuming that your social anxiety must have gotten better. My therapeutic guess now is that you probably discovered that alcohol diminished your anxiety and that realization probably started you on an unfortunate path of addiction. You hid your addiction and functioned well, despite it, for some time. You became a lawyer, a husband, and a father.

I keep guilt-tripping myself about the fact that, despite all my years and knowledge as an addiction specialist and a psychologist, for many years I didn't catch or understand the clues and signs that I was seeing. In my defense, I saw you only once a year, for ten days to two weeks when I would visit you in California, but that's a flimsy excuse. However, I didn't see anything suspicious during my visits. You were always attentive and affectionate toward me and went out of your way to make my visits pleasurable, including planning special trips and visits to the Getty Museum and other sites of interest.

It was only during my last visit before the intervention—when I came for Robert's high school graduation—that I became concerned.

You talked with me then for the first time about your severe anxiety and not being able to sleep at night. I also realized you had serious marital problems and that your wife was quite depressed. Both you and Leslie came to me separately to complain about each other. I tried not to take sides and instead urged both of you to go see a doctor and ask for referrals to marriage counseling experts.

I hated to see you both so unhappy and didn't know what to do to fix your problems. I did not realize, even then, that alcoholism was at the root of the problem.

My regrets about not going deeper go on and on like a sea of regrets. There is a passage in a novel I read recently, *Lincoln in the Bardo* by George Saunders,[6] that spoke to me:

> When a child is lost there is no end to the self-torment a parent may inflict. When we love, and the object of our love is small, weak, and vulnerable, and has looked to us and us alone for protection; and when such protection, for whatever reason, has failed, what consolation (what justification, what defense) may there possibly be?
>
> None.
>
> Doubt will fester as long as we live.
>
> And when one occasion of doubt has been addressed, another and then another will arise in its place.

March 28, 2019

My Dearest Son,

I survived your birthday, sweetheart! A friend volunteered to go to a nursery with me so I could select some pots of flowers to honor your special day. The venture sounded much more positive than sitting at home and crying all day, so I agreed to the idea.

I picked up some pots with nice-smelling flowers that I was not familiar with. The little tag on the pots told me that they were called "Sweet William." Somehow, they seemed appropriate for the occasion. When you were young, your grandmother Anastasia used to call you "Sweet Jaime," and always added, *"Ti kalo pethi!"* ("What a good child!").

I went to see a medical specialist the day before your birthday and found out that I had a serious problem related to my bladder. He did a scan and a pelvic exam and told me that I needed more intensive testing. He is referring me to another doctor for that. Now that I am in my eighties, the medical problems keep multiplying. Maybe I'll join you in afterlife sooner than I thought. OK, I know I'm being melodramatic now.

You may get a kick out of this. The same doctor that I saw for the bladder problem told me that he was very impressed by my cognitive abilities.

"You are sharper than 90 percent of my older patients," he told me. "How do you do it?" I didn't exactly know how to reply to that. I thought of saying, "I knit a lot," but I didn't think he would appreciate the humor. I told him that the only explanation I could think of was that I read a lot. Later in the session, I blurted out how difficult emotionally the last year had been and told him of your passing.

"I'm sure that the stress and grief have affected my health," I said. He nodded and told me how his father's death when he was fourteen years old had affected him: "Sixty years later," he added, "I still get teary-eyed when I think about it."

I was surprised and pleased by the empathetic response. Most doctors do not reveal personal information to me or their other patients. The most I get when I tell them of your death is a quick "I'm sorry to hear that!" After the visit, I thought to myself that I should keep a closer eye on your boys. I don't think it has hit them yet that your untimely death will affect them the rest of their lives.

The conversation with the empathetic doctor also inspired me to call Nicholas and ask him to have lunch with me this week. He takes a class at the community college near my house, so lately we often lunch together. Unfortunately, Robert lives far from here in San Francisco, so I can't have lunch with him except when he comes to Houston to visit; however, I make sure to text him or call him for special occasions or just to chat at times.

When Nicholas and I went to lunch (he almost never refuses my invites), I made it a point to ask him how he felt on the one-year anniversary of your death. I know that he does not like to talk about his feelings, but it still shocked me to hear that he didn't have any particularly sad feelings on your birthday. "It was just another ordinary day," he said.

I looked at him, dumbfounded. "How can it be just an ordinary day?" I said. "I know how much you love your dad and miss him!" He just shrugged his shoulders and didn't respond. His response baffles and concerns me. I saw how heartbroken and traumatized he was after you died. Now, a year later, he acts as if he's fine. With you gone and his mother kind of lost to him, there's no way he can be fine. As a loving grandmother, as well as a therapist of many years, I strongly believe that feelings need to be felt and acknowledged or they are going to spring up years later and mess up important relationships, especially intimate ones. I do wish that he would see a therapist or go to an Al-Anon group, but so far, he is resisting the idea. Spiros and Olga have even offered to pay for his therapy, but he refused their offer.

I tried to convey some of my reasoning to him. "The last two weeks have been especially hard for me," I said (referring to the dual sad anniversaries of your passing and your birth). His response was quick and curt: "I accept reality, Mema," he said. "It is what it is!"

"Hey, honey," I retorted, "Remember you are talking not only with your grandmother, but also with a retired psychotherapist with forty years of experience in dealing with emotions! I believe that you are burying your negative feelings, and that concerns me. Accepting reality does not mean that you try to erase your feelings of sadness or anger or grief." I wanted to tell him a lot more, but I did not want to sound like I was lecturing him, so I stopped. At that moment, the buzzer beeped on the restaurant's mobile device so he got up (probably with some relief) to go retrieve our food. It was a nice lunch, nonetheless.

Later after lunch, he helped me with a writing project. He typed it for me and sent it, digitally, to a magazine. He spent a lot of effort on my project, and I paid him a small sum for his efforts. I was impressed with how diligent he was to get it done—and to get it done well.

How I wish that you were still on earth to see how well your boys are doing. Who knows? Maybe you are aware of that fact, wherever you are! I surely hope so.

Good night, sweetheart. I am going to bed.

April 10, 2019

My Dearest Son,

I did something today that I don't think that you would like, and for that, I'm sorry. I told a total stranger at Starbucks that you died from alcoholism. It's true that he opened the door to the admission by asking me if I had any children and how many. I told him that I had three sons and that I lost one of them. Then I went on to tell him how you died.

I didn't have to tell him that last part, and I regretted my act the moment I did it. I felt that I had betrayed you somehow. I could have just told him the partial truth—that your heart stopped. I'm so angry at the disease that killed you, that caused your heart to stop, that I have a hard time keeping it a secret. I want to shout it from the rooftops.

I also know that it's your life that I'm talking about, and you may not want me to share it with people (especially strangers at Starbucks). You knew you were an alcoholic. You admitted it to me in October 2016 on my last trip to Los Angeles during the intervention. However, you made it a point to tell me that your greatly dysfunctional lifestyle back then was *not* caused by alcohol and other drugs.

I detected great embarrassment—even shame—in your tone when you called yourself "an alcoholic." Unfortunately, you took on our society's general attitude about alcoholism—that people can make rational, healthy choices when they are addicts and that they are weak individuals who would stop using chemicals if they first had more strength of character. The concept of addicts suffering from a powerful, deadly disease totally escapes them. That certainly was your father's belief, despite everything I tried to teach him.

During the intervention, you also told me how you walked every morning at 6 a.m. to the nearest liquor store to buy the cheapest alcohol you could find. "I have to go, Mom," you said. "The anxiety builds up in me during the night, and it's a terrible feeling." As I heard your words, my heart bled for you, but I held back the tears and tried to explain to you, in the calmest, most professional voice I could muster, how anxiety worked.

"There is a vicious cycle going on with the anxiety process," I said. "The alcohol lessens it all in the moment, but it's only temporary relief. The alcohol makes the anxiety much worse in the long run. It's only a Band-Aid." You looked at me with some sadness in your eyes and listened to what I said, but I don't think that you believed what I was telling you. Or maybe you did but did not want to admit it.

How I wished at that moment to hug you tight and make the anxiety go away. I knew then—more than I knew before—that you were suffering a lot. I didn't even know back then about your cirrhosis of the liver diagnosis. Nicholas told me that the autopsy conducted after your death showed "severe cirrhosis of the liver along with heart disease."

Well, my darling, at least you are not suffering anymore. No more physical pain or diseased body and mind full of anxiety and distress. I hope your spirit is soaring free in the new place where you are. We, the ones who loved you, are left here on earth to feel the pain and sadness of the end of your journey.

Tomorrow, I'm planning to attend my grief group. They have their annual balloon ceremony in honor of the members' departed children. From what I remember from last year's ceremony, it is a meaningful, touching event. I'll let you know how it goes. You made your presence known to me last year by the way your balloon kept gently hitting my face nonstop.

Of course, you may not need me to tell you what transpires. You may be watching the whole thing. We, the living, have no idea what happens after death. I would like to believe that there is life after death—only different. I get a lot of comfort from that belief.

I know you are somewhere in our vast universe. I just don't know the particular details!
Sending you a lot of love,
Your Mom

April 11, 2019 (1:30 a.m.)

My Dearest Son,

I'm so sorry that I wasn't able to attend the grief group today. I missed the balloon ceremony that I had been looking forward to for some time. The occasion would also have been the one-year anniversary of my attending this particular grief group, Compassionate Friends. This group has been such a comfort to me in my terrible year of grief.

I remember last year's ceremony as if it were yesterday. I was crying almost nonstop. You had just died the month before, and the grief was very fresh and palpable. At the same time, I could not help but be intrigued and almost amused by the movement of the balloon I was holding that was representing you. There was a light breeze at the time, but I noticed that my balloon was the only one in the group that kept hitting and covering my face. Everyone else's balloon was standing still. At one point, I thought to myself, "Cut it out, Jaime!" I definitely thought that it had to be your spirit showing your presence and trying to comfort me. Later, as we released the balloons, the balloon with your name did not soar into space, but clung to a nearby tree, hanging close. Was all this the work of the wind or just a coincidence? That's what skeptics and cynics would say, but I refuse to say it or believe it.

All in all, I was so disappointed that I felt poorly today and ached all over. Certainly not in any shape to drive forty-five minutes or so to go to the group meeting place. I wanted so badly to see what your balloon would have done this year. I cried out of disappointment and total inconsolable sadness!

April 12, 2019

My Dearest Son,

I'm still feeling sorry for myself and lamenting the fact that I was not feeling well yesterday and could not attend the grief group. I felt kind of tired and out of sorts all day. I went to bed around midnight—my regular time—yawning all the way. Once in bed, though, I felt totally awake and started tossing and turning, as usual. Here I am at 1:30 a.m. again at my letter-writing rendezvous with you.

A year and a month have passed since you left us bereft on this earth of ours. One would think that now my grief would have lessened or at least been more subdued. Maybe I'm not crying all day and half the night (like I did earlier in the year), but the memories and awareness of my tragic reality come often—both during the day and in the middle of the night. When they come, the intense grief and the pain still grip me, and then I wonder how can I go on living when I hurt so much.

The health issues that I am experiencing lately do not make my life any easier—they intensify all the emotional pain that I am feeling. Is there a connection? Do these health problems have something to do with my ongoing grief? Of course, they do—they must. In my practice of therapy, I saw and heard first-hand how stress and grief affected my clients' health and well-being. Unfortunately, most doctors still do not give credence to the concept and ignore the emotional component. I say bullshit to that. (You didn't know that I occasionally cursed, did you?) The ancient Greek philosophers had it right when they were proclaiming that "mind and body are one!"

Oh, my eyes are closing a little, honey, so I'm going to go back to bed and try to get some sleep. Hope my body and mind can mingle in a good way and allow my heart to stop hurting for a few hours.

Goodnight, sweetheart!

April 17, 2019

My Dearest Son,

I asked your younger brother to help me send an email letter to the monthly newsletter of Compassionate Friends concerning my disappointment about missing the group's annual balloon ceremony. I added some thoughts about my appreciation of the group and the support that I receive every time I attend. I asked him to email it himself, but he insisted that I do it. This is part of Constantine's ongoing crusade to get me to improve my digital skills. I was apprehensive about the task, but I was determined to send my contribution. To my surprise, I was able to do it on my first try.

I hope you don't mind that sometimes I make my grief about you public. The group consists mostly of grieving parents, and they understand my pain a lot more than society at large or even our family. Some people I know who are not in the group have pointed out at times that you lived fifty-seven years and were not that young when you died. I deeply resent those kinds of remarks. As if your age makes any difference to me! You were and are my precious baby, no matter how old you were when your heart stopped. My own heart almost stopped when I heard the news.

177

The bereaved parents of the group get it. They come to the group years after the death of their children, still grieving, no matter what age their children were when they died. I talked to one of those parents recently. This was a mother who has been coming to the group for the last ten years. She still had tears in her eyes when she talked about the daughter who died so many years ago. I may not have ten years left; after all, I'm in my eighties with a heart condition. However, I have no doubt I will grieve for you until the day I die!

I used to be somewhat fearful about dying. Not anymore. That was your last gift to me. You made dying seem not so bad, not if it meant seeing you again at least in spirit. It comforts me that I have always believed that the spirit or soul of a person lives on, even after departing this earth. And if I needed any proof, the vision I had of you in my bedroom some months ago clinched it. Thank you, honey, for visiting me. It meant a lot, and it did not frighten me in the slightest!

I will always wish that you had lived longer so as to see your sons become men and accomplish worthwhile things. Maybe you could have been able to hold a grandchild or two in your arms. Regretfully, it wasn't meant to be. The truth is that in the last years of your life, you were estranged from your children and me, and you were lost in the abyss of the disease of alcoholism. You—a lawyer with so much potential earlier on—were living on the streets of Los Angeles and going in and out of jail for DWI's, a stolen U-Haul, and violation of parole. That situation must have been a torment, even in a brain foggy with chemicals.

The only time I remember your getting angry with me and raising your voice was when I told you during the intervention that your brain cells were probably dying right along with your liver and other organs. (I didn't even know at the time that you had been diagnosed with cirrhosis of the liver.)

You told me a few things during that last visit that did not make a lot of sense, and I felt so sad that my intelligent son, who had been an outstanding student, was spouting nonsense! Seeing you like that was agonizing for me. In a way, death was merciful. You no longer had to decline physically and mentally, and it ended your earthly sufferings. I am grateful for that fact, even though it dashed my hopes about the potential of any recovery and increased my own suffering. I love you enough to be glad you are at peace, even though I lost you.

Good night, sweetheart. I'm ending this letter and going to bed. I am hopeful I will sleep some and maybe—just maybe—I will dream of you.

April 21, 2019 (2 a.m.)

My Dearest Son,

It's very late again, and I'm still awake. Tomorrow is Easter for most Christians in the world, but not for me and the other Greek Orthodox ones. We are a week behind because we follow the Gregorian calendar, remember? Don't ask me why. All I know is that the Greek liturgical calendar follows an authentic historical sequence of the last supper and the subsequent events.

In other words, we cannot celebrate Easter until after the Jewish people celebrate their Passover. Somehow, that feels logical to me. After all, Jesus was born Jewish, and that's what happened in his lifetime.

My friend Betty called me earlier in the week to tell me that she had attended a seder ceremonial dinner. We have been friends for a long time—more than thirty years—and she always used to invite me to her annual seder dinners. I used to love going and joining her and her family for the joyous celebration. Nowadays she lives in an assisted living situation and is unable to host any seders anymore. I do miss them!

I have been planning to go to the Palm Sunday services in the Greek church tomorrow, but unfortunately the service is at 10 a.m. I don't think I can get up on time and take care of Skye and other early morning duties and still make it to church. I used never to miss any of the Easter services in the past, but in the last few years, I have missed some because of health and grief issues.

Last year when Easter came soon after your passing, I was in a state of shock and stupor and fighting consistently high blood pressure. I resigned myself to the idea that I would not be able to go even to my favorite service of the year—the midnight Easter service of the Greek church.

Then my darling grandsons Stuart and Nicholas surprised the heck out of me by showing up at my door—all dressed up and holding tall candles—and insisting that I go with them to church. It was a very sweet gesture on their part, and so I gathered all my strength (physical and emotional), and off we went to see the wizard, or rather the midnight ritual of *Christos Anesti!* (Christ has risen!).

I have not heard from my family about tomorrow. We usually get together and celebrate American (as I call it) Easter at Spiros and Olga's house. I felt rather sad, thinking that they had forgotten me, but your brother Spiros texted me today that they are planning a big dinner next Sunday on Greek Easter and that Olga was going to cook traditional Greek dishes. I guess they haven't forgotten me after all.

I wish I could make my annual Greek Easter bread that I have made for fifty-plus years, but I don't know if I'll be able to do all the kneading that it requires. Remember how I used to send you one of my loaves to Los Angeles every Easter? This was my annual Easter gift to you. How I wish I could still send you a loaf. I would happily spend hundreds of dollars just to have you enjoy something that I had created. Now that you're gone, the project doesn't have the same appeal, even if I could physically do it. Nevertheless, it makes me feel old and rather useless not to be able to contribute any of my cooking specialties to the holiday table. I will try to make a least one. We will see.

This has been another tough grief cycle lately. The health problems have worsened my mood, and I'm struggling with feelings of depression. Just as one health problem gets resolved, another one pops up. My right knee has been hurting a lot lately, and the thought of a possible second knee-replacement surgery is too daunting to contemplate. I certainly hope that I don't need another operation.

At times, it seems kind of hopeless. I still refuse to take any antidepressants. I don't think that one should take them for the normal grief journey that I'm on, but I have agreed to take an antianxiety pill daily before bedtime. I still have problems sleeping—hence all my letters to you in the middle of the night—but I believe that the problems would be worse without the medication.

I may be wrong about this, but I feel at times that I am close to the end of life or—God forbid—close to a nursing home. That would be like a nightmare come to life. My forays into rehab facilities after surgeries gave me a glimpse of what a nursing home is all about, and the idea makes me shudder. In addition to all the indignities that are part of the lifestyle, there is also the matter of diet. I am a big advocate of Mediterranean cooking. Studies have proven time and time again how healthy and nutritious it is, yet I found that hospitals and nursing centers have never heard of it or never think to apply it to the residents' diets. I'd rather stay at home for as long as I am able, somehow manage to take care of myself (even with all my health challenges), and continue cooking my familiar Greek dishes (even if only the easy ones).

OK, honey, I don't think you want to hear any more complaints or ruminations from me tonight, so I'll stop. I do hope that you are in a peaceful, lovely place. Don't worry about me or your kids. We'll be fine. You might be pleased to know that your wife (or widow, I suppose) is no longer struggling in LA. Nicholas told me that she lives in Minnesota now at his grandmother's assisted living apartment. He is still estranged from her, even though she is trying to reestablish contact. He tells me that he still doesn't know if she is trustworthy.

She has not contacted me since the week of your passing. I am still holding some resentment toward her because of her lack of effort to help steer you away from your path of destruction. I know I should forgive her. After all, she was in the midst of her own disease of codependency, surely, but I am not there yet. Sorry about that, Jaime.

While we are talking about forgiving, I have to admit that I haven't totally forgiven myself, either, for my inability to rescue you. There remains a part of me that, regardless of all the Al-Anon slogans, still believes that there could have been a way to save you. Somehow, I blew it and missed the way. It certainly wasn't for lack of wanting or even trying. I would gladly have sacrificed an arm or a leg or much more if only I had been able to save you from the abyss!

April 24, 2019

My Dearest Son,

I don't know why, but for the first time since you left us, I feel a surge of anger toward you. I feel so guilty for feeling this anger! I know as a therapist that anger after death is one of the five stages of grief as described so eloquently by Elisabeth Kübler-Ross, but I swear to you that in the year or so since you died, I never once felt angry with you, not until now.

I have been very angry with your disease of alcoholism, angry with your life, even angry with your brothers, and certainly angry with myself, but not with you. I was even angry with Al-Anon and my sponsor for teaching me tough love principles and thus keeping me from sending you bail money. Even though my therapist-trained brain agreed with them that I should not rescue you from the consequences of actions related to your addiction, my motherly heart bled for you, and I wished that I could have spared you some of the suffering that I'm sure you endured in jail.

I remember somebody (can't remember who) asking me last year soon after your passing if I was angry with you. I was utterly shocked by the question. "Why, on earth," I thought, "would I be angry with my precious son?" Well, tonight, I am angry. I am angry that you allowed yourself to be caught in the terrible path of addiction. I am angry that when you realized you were caught in a devilish trap (at some point you must have realized this), you closed your eyes, stayed in denial, and did not get any help.

I am angry that even when you tried to help yourself, you stubbornly did it on your own, went cold turkey, and almost died as a result. Your effort "to just stop using" and the subsequent seizure was a big mistake that you should have anticipated, even with your chemically muddled brain. Your ill-fated action (that you must have taken without consulting anybody who knew better) must have surely discouraged you from trying to stop yourself from proceeding on the path of addiction you were on.

I am also angry that you lied to me, time and time again, by telling me that you were fine, even when you, Leslie, and Nicholas were wandering from one cheap motel to another and even when you were homeless.

I am angry that even when your denial was pierced, by my intervention as well as other means, and you admitted to me that you were an alcoholic and would get help, you never did. You told Leslie (after I left) that you would rather go to jail than rehab. You were so stubborn! I spent months doing research, finding resources that were hard to come by, in Houston and LA. I gave you concise information based on that search. You never even tried to contact them.

I feel drained by the immense anger that I'm feeling tonight and the belief that you did not consider your loved ones at all (including me). You left us to suffer in your absence and just went away. I feel too desolate about all this.

April 29, 2019

My Dearest Son,

Here I am again, at 1:30 a.m., unable to sleep one more time. Writing you seems to be the only thing that calms me down some and later allows me to fall asleep. It is kind of strange, but it's only when I write to you that I still feel the connection between us, the connection that you used to call "incredible"! My mind tells me that you are gone and that you are never going to read these letters, so why do I feel some healing comfort from the act? I don't have a logical answer to that. All I know is that death is a mystery, and we the living don't really know what happens after death; therefore, who is to say that your spirit is not beside me or reading these letters over my shoulder? Anything is possible.

I have to confess something to you. After I wrote the last letter about feeling anger toward you, I felt so guilty! Part of me felt that I didn't have the right to be angry with you for dying. After all, you lived your life the way you wanted to, even if that meant an early death at fifty-seven years. Who am I to tell you that you didn't have that right? Yes, I know. Dying alone on a park bench is not a nice way to die (if there is such a thing), and your addiction and disease had consequences for you and your loved ones; however, it was your life to live as you saw fit. I just wish I wasn't feeling so desolate about it all.

Nicholas came by today and we went to lunch. It was a belated birthday meal. I asked him about your ashes that he still keeps in his room. His wish is eventually to go with your brothers and me to Galveston and spread the ashes in the Gulf of Mexico to honor your lifelong love of the sea and all the years that you spent in the Houston area. He asked me if I would help organize a family outing there after my health issues improve. I promised him that I would.

What came to me, while hearing Nicholas outline his plan, was what I wrote in my will some time ago. I wrote that I wanted to be cremated and my ashes spread in the gulf in Galveston, close to the house that Spiros and Olga used to own, of which I had so many nice memories. I cherished my time there with my two grandchildren when they were much younger. I would take them with me on long walks on the beach, collecting the best shells we could find. I always loved the sunsets in Galveston as well. As I thought of my will, I teared up, thinking that at least your ashes and mine would land in the same place and be kind of united at the end. Too bad that the Greek church does not approve of cremation and will deny me a proper funeral. I believe the church's position is archaic and wrong, and my views differ greatly from those of the church about that.

As I'm writing this, I realize that I am in a morbid state of mind. Lately, I have been battling depression. I refuse to take antidepressants. This may be a strange attitude coming from a retired psychotherapist, but I believe that my grief over you is normal. I don't want it dulled or minimized. I listened to a doctor's advice some months ago, and I started taking an antianxiety pill at night; however, judging from my sleepless nights, it isn't helping a whole lot right now.

Skye, my small terrier, is lying on my bed right now. I'm pretty sure that she would like me to join her. If I stay away too long, she gets up and leaves the bed. So I'm going to stop writing and try to go to sleep, if nothing else, for Skye's sake. It's nice to have somebody wanting me close, even if it's only a small animal. I do miss some intelligent conversation in bed at night, though. Skye is not big on conversing. Are you laughing, honey? How I miss your booming laugh! What I would give to hear it one more time!

May 2, 2019

My Dearest Son,

Here we are again, conversing at 1:30 a.m. Yes, I know that this is a one-way conversation—a monologue really—but it still feels like a connection. I can just imagine you, laughing with your wonderful laugh and telling me, "You know I'm dead, right, Mom? You know I can't talk back. But that's OK. If it comforts you to write to me, keep writing!"

I spent some time with your Nicholas today. He came to see me after school. I may have already told you this. He takes a couple of community college classes five minutes from my house. These are in addition to the classes he takes on the downtown college campus.

You would be so proud of him. He has a 4.0 grade average, and he wants to go to a good school with a big campus to finish the last two years of college. We talk about you a lot. I tell him stories of your childhood (he calls them "funky" stories) and about the trips you and I and Leslie took before he was born.

Today I told him about our trip to Tijuana, Mexico, where you bought an old guitar you saw in a shop window right after you declared that you had no intention of buying anything during this border town trip. Nicholas told me that he remembers your playing that guitar, especially when he was little boy and you were putting him to sleep.

I also told him the tale of the raspberry liqueur that I bought in Tijuana and how the bottle broke inside my suitcase and colored all my clothes a weird flamingo pink color, including my underwear. Nicholas burst out laughing, and I teared up remembering how you tried to hide your own laughter when we opened up my suitcase and saw all my tinted clothes and the shattered bottle. You told me at the time, "I'm sorry I'm laughing, Mom, but I was afraid of this debacle when you bought that darn liqueur!"

I'm going to miss my frequent meetings with your younger son when his community college days are over. It will be hard to see him go out of town to school. He has been in Houston for two years now, living with Spiros and Olga, and I know that they are going to miss him as well. I see how fond they are of him. Spiros has finally somebody in his immediate family who loves watching football games on TV almost as much as he does.

As for Olga, she takes him to the movies with her, and they have a weekly dinner date when Spiros attends a bowling league. Stuart teases Nicholas but treats him as a younger brother and has procrastinated about leaving home because Nicholas is there now (at least that's my assumption). The truth is that we are all going to miss him.

He told me that he loved the trip to Las Vegas, where Spiros and Olga took him for his twenty-first birthday. The whole family went along, except for me.

Nicholas kind of wishfully added that you all didn't travel as a family when he was young and that he wished you had. (You brought him to Houston when he was little, but he doesn't remember that.) I refrained from mentioning your addiction/illness, because I didn't want to seem as if I were defending you or looking for excuses to explain why you didn't take the family on trips. I kept quiet about that. I did mention my own travel addiction and added that I always wanted my kids to enjoy traveling as well.

You loved going to Turkey and Greece with your father and me, didn't you, honey? You were about ten years old, and you never forgot it. I planned that trip for a long time before we took it. I wanted so badly to show you and your brothers where your dad and I were born and teach you about our roots and about your cultural heritage.

You, of all three, seemed to really immerse yourself in the trip. You were especially awed by the Hagia Sophia Cathedral in Istanbul. This Byzantine architectural wonder still stands after thousands of years and a multitude of natural disasters, including multiple severe earthquakes, and impressed you in a profound way. However, it wasn't the architecture of the place that mostly stayed in your memory. There is a large mural of Christ in the second floor of the cathedral (now a museum) that is perpetually being restored. Many years later, you still remembered that mural and talked with me about it. On our visit there, you said you were fascinated by noticing that no matter where you moved in the vast church, the eyes of Jesus would follow you.

I was astonished by what you told me. I visited the Hagia Sophia many times in my life, but never noticed that phenomenon. I never read about it either or saw it on any of the numerous documentaries I have watched through the years about this iconic monument that has always been so important to me and my fellow Greeks. You were only ten years old at the time of your visit there. It's so amazing to me that a child would notice and remember something like that. I am so proud of you for having had such precious skills of observation, Jaime.

During our Baltimore years, you also used to love going to Nags Head, a seaside resort in North Carolina, for family vacations. You always loved the sea, so of course you loved it there. I enjoyed those family vacations as well. There would be less tension and conflict in the family during those times, and even you and Spiros got along better.

The ocean temperature seemed a little on the cold side to me, even in the middle of summer, but you boys didn't seem to mind. Even our old dog Chum would join you and frolic in the waves. You and your brothers loved to climb endlessly up and down the sand dunes by the seashore.

I don't know if you remember this, but it was during one of those summer trips that Neil Armstrong walked on the moon. We watched that historic event at the Wright Brothers National Memorial and Visitor Center near Nags Head. There you were fascinated by the feat and by the museum itself. You always had such a thirst for knowledge. Many years later you would take me to visit the Los Angeles Public Library in downtown LA and tell me that it was your favorite place in the city. You also took me to both Getty museums: the old (The Getty Villa) and the new (The Getty Center). It was so sad for me to observe that, along with other traits, your intellectual curiosity and love of knowledge became less and less important in later years. I believe that as your addiction and disease rose in prominence in your life, they stole the better part of you.

May 6, 2019

My Dearest Son,

It's 4 a.m., later than my usual writing time, but I still can't sleep. I'm going to the dentist tomorrow to replace a broken crown, and I guess I'm worried about it. It's probably going to be a painful procedure. Of course, it's going to be an expensive one. I know that worrying about it doesn't help, but anticipatory anxiety has always been my downfall. You had a lot of anxiety yourself. You probably inherited my tendency. You often talked to me about your anxiety. I urged you to get help, citing successful therapy results of my clients as well as my own.

I do not think that you ever took my advice about getting help for your anxiety. Judging by what you told me, I'm guessing that you tried to self-medicate, using alcohol and other drugs. I told you more than once that alcohol acted like a Band-Aid. It seemed to help at the onset, but in the long run, it *increased* your anxiety. You looked like you were listening, but I don't' think that you ever totally believed me (or maybe you didn't want to believe me).

Jaime, sweetheart, I feel so sad every time I think of the suffering and inner turmoil that you must have endured. I know from personal as well as professional experience how terrible it is to have anxiety. In the last years of your life, you also had cirrhosis of the liver added to your severe anxiety. You never told anybody in the family about having the dreadful liver disease. Did your wife, Leslie, or anyone else know?

Nicholas found out about it from reading your autopsy report. Poor child, it must have been so devastating for him to read the report and find out about your illness as well as the details of how your heart

187

stopped. He told me that he had no idea about your suffering from the cirrhosis until he read the pathologist's findings. You kept it a secret from all of us. Were you embarrassed by the diagnosis? I know you must have known because you spent a week in a jail hospital. You told me that.

I, in turn, hearing that, was so stunned and overwhelmed with emotions that I didn't even dare ask about the reasons behind the hospital stay. Now, I feel a lot of guilt about my lack of empathy then. That's what alcoholism does. Not only does it damage addicts, but it also damages their families. Ordinarily, I would have been full of questions. It's hard to function well when one is overwhelmed with emotional pain. How sad that our relationship disintegrated in the last two years of your life, right along with your bright potential. You seemed so happy when your boys were born. I am so glad that at least you had some happy years when the kids were young and you were able to function as a husband, as a father, and as a successful lawyer. How I loved seeing you that way!

May 9, 2019

My Dearest Son,

It's kind of weird how I feel your presence at certain times. I'll be watching TV or listening to the radio, and I'll hear an Americana type of song (the kind we both like). I'll start moving my arms or feet in rhythm, but whenever I do that, I hear your voice in my head (clear as a bell) saying, "Way to go, Mom!" That's when I stop moving or semidancing and start crying. I immediately think that you must then be disappointed in me for stopping my dancing around and cry even harder. It sounds a little crazy, but that's how the grief pattern often works. One of these days, I hope that your voice in my head will bring me only joy instead of sadness and that it will spur me on to continue dancing, even at my age.

This grief journey of mine has brought me such unusual—even weird—experiences of mind and heart. I never would have thought in a hundred years that I would have a vision of a dead person's spirit, yet I did have a vision of you some months ago with a background flash of bright light. No white ghostly sheets around, but I will swear until the day I die that the vision was real and not a hallucination or a dream!

Are my experiences since your death part of the spirituality of my grief journey or hocus-pocus fantasies? Who is to say? All I know is that I believe in them, which kind of surprises me because I had always thought of myself as a rational human being, albeit one with deeply felt emotions.

I read somewhere that grief is a never-ending river that is always moving. That saying speaks to me in an eloquent way. I have been moving and evolving in this grief journey of mine in ways that in the past I never thought were possible. It's like those before and after photos. The tragedy of your death has changed me in fundamental ways, both inside and outside. I see the difference every time I look in the mirror. There are crease lines and crevices in my face that were not there before, and time alone is not the responsible factor. At the same time, my emotionality and empathy have increased tenfold.

I'll be watching the news, I'll hear that something significant happened somewhere in the world, and I'll immediately think, "I wish I could discuss this event with Jaime." Or, say, somebody in the family is doing something significant or having an important moment in their lives. Even though I feel happy for the person involved, at the same time I feel some sadness that I cannot share the news with you. I remember when I told you that your niece Stacy was entering medical school. You said, "Good for her." Well, she is graduating in ten days, and all I can do is write to you about it.

You are always in my mind and in my heart, and that will never change. I will love you forever, Son. I hope you know that, wherever you are.

May 10, 2019

My Dearest Son,

How are you? What a silly question, right? How is it in the spirit world? Are there good days and bad days, like it is here on earth, or is every day wonderfully the same? I hope it's the second scenario. I would like that for you. To be calm and peaceful would be a nice change from the chaos and turmoil of your life in your last years.

I would think that it certainly beats going to the liquor store at 6 a.m. every morning so you could buy some cheap booze to try to soothe the terrible cravings and severe anxiety pains that built up during the night. You told me of those desperate early morning forays in October of 2016 when I saw you for the last time. I told you then what I had told you at other times—that alcohol is only a short-term solution. I tried to explain the vicious cycle that alcohol and drugs produced.

"There are some effective medications for anxiety," I said. "Please, Jaime, get some professional help," I pleaded. You looked at me with a blank face and did not reply. I gave you the list of resources that I had prepared back in Houston. It had taken months and months to prepare the list. I was almost numb by then from emotion, but I did notice that my hands were shaking as I handed the list to you.

"For only fifty dollars," I added, "you can get help from the State of California for detoxing and family counseling. The only condition is you have to go and apply in person. I cannot apply for you. If you don't have the fifty dollars available, all you have to do is call me, and I will gladly send the money." As I finished giving my speech about getting help, I started crying.

"Don't cry, Mom," you said, "please don't cry. I promise you I'll get help. You came all this way to see me and talk to me—the least I can do is get help!"

My heart leaped with joy as I heard your words, even though my brain was reminding me that addicts lie and lie, and you probably wouldn't keep your promise. And yet, I wanted to believe you so badly!

I looked at you: you looked so different from the way you used to look. You were barefoot and looked sickly and bloated. I dearly wanted to put some shoes on your feet and place a jacket on top of your faded T-shirt (it was an unusually cool day in LA). I longed to put my arms around you, hold you close, and take care of you. I even yearned to put some money in your pockets.

Unfortunately, I couldn't do any of those things. You are not a child anymore (even though you will always be my child). I could not do what I used to do—run to the bus stop on cold school mornings, place a coat around your shoulders, or hug you and try to comfort you when you were upset about something. You were a middle-aged man and the father of two young men. All I could do was look at what you had become and feel my heart break into hundreds of pieces. What a sad day that was! The crazy truth was that—despite everything I saw and experienced—a part of me was still happy to see you, even in despair. When you later introduced me to another motel resident with affection in your voice, I could feel my eyes fill up with tears.

Mother's Day is coming in two days, Jaime, and I don't know how I am going to bear it. It's the second Mother's Day since you left this earth, and if it's anything like last year, it's going to be pretty bad. I am learning from experience that when one is in grief, holidays are the worst of times.

All I remember from last year's occasion is that I kept going to the bathroom of the restaurant we were in so as to have some privacy to cry. My family pretended not to notice what was going on, but, surely, they must have seen my moist eyes every time I returned to the table. Nobody said anything about that or about the sad fact that you were gone and could not say "Happy Mother's Day, Mom," to me anymore.

My grief group talks a lot about our families' (and society's) resistance to talking about our departed loved ones. The group and I believe that they have the misguided notion that it would upset us to talk about the dead. To the contrary, the truth is that it would be comforting to hear your name and talk about you.

I saw a wonderful, animated movie last week called *Coco*. The movie's main message was all about how important it is to remember those who are gone from our lives but not from our hearts. The people of Mexico do it right. They have a special day during the year dedicated to honoring the dead, visiting their tombs and/or altar, and celebrating their lives by special decorations and special meals. They call it *Día de los Muertos* (Day of the Dead).

My mother was Greek, not Mexican, but she would definitely have liked this idea. She would often tell me to light a special candle in church after she was gone for the Day of the Souls in the Greek Orthodox calendar. I feel guilty that I have not fulfilled that request of hers for many years now. The last one and one half years, I have sometimes had the excuse of illness. The truth is that even before that I lost track of that religious occasion and on which day of the year it fell. Too bad we don't make a big deal about it in the United States, unlike our geographic neighbors. I think that we can certainly learn from other people and other cultures.

Anyway, I digressed from Mother's Day. (It seems that the older I get, the more I digress.) I will probably go to a restaurant again with your older brother and his family and pretend to be OK. If I feel super gutsy, I will mention your name and lack of presence. I will put on a fake smile and not tell them there is a hole in my heart that only you can fill!

May 12, 2019 (1:45 a.m.)

My Dearest Son,

I'm writing this in the early hours of Mother's Day. Of course, I couldn't sleep today unless I wrote to you. First of all, I want you to know that I will always be your mother—just like I will always be Spiros's and Constantine's mother—no matter how much time has passed since your death. This is my second Mother's Day without you walking on this earth, and even though I know that you are at peace now and no longer in physical pain, I still miss you like crazy. I go to bed every night hoping that I will dream of you. Alas, I only had two dreams of you this whole past year. When I woke up from those dreams, I cried and cried. I don't care. I'll gladly pay the emotional price. I just want to see your sweet face and hug you, even if it's only in a dream. Maybe tonight will be the night. I can hope.

I know that our thoughts and feelings, both conscious and unconscious, produce our dreams—at least that's what Freud said—so I don't understand why I don't dream of you more often. After all, you are constantly in my thoughts and certainly a big part of my feelings. The bottom line is that I don't care about a scientific explanation of the process, I just long to look at you and hear you say, "Mom, Mom, I'm here!"

I found out yesterday that I have a staph infection. I have been in some physical pain the last two weeks, and it was kind of a relief to find out that there was a reason behind the pain. The past year has been so intensely painful in more ways than one. I seem to tolerate pain more than I should. That's what the doctor told me when she announced that I had an infection going on and needed a form of antibiotics.

I keep thinking that maybe I'm reaching the end of my earthly time. I have mixed feelings about that idea. I am not in a big hurry to rush to my demise, but on the other hand, the thought of seeing you on the other side is a joyful one.

Surely the compassionate God in whom I believe will let us see our loved ones, in spirit, after we die. I would like to believe that he/she knows our special pain and will at least let bereaved parents see once again the children who left earth before they did.

Good night, sweetheart. I love you and always will.

May 13, 2019

My Dearest Son,

You may be glad to know that I survived Mother's Day. I was sad, of course, but I put a smile on my face for the sake of the family. Nicholas, your sweet boy, surprised me with a present for the occasion. He also gave Olga a present. She's been his substitute mom for the last two years. She is very fond of him (we all are), and she tells me that he often confides in her. I'm very glad.

I didn't feel very well physically, but I didn't want to stay at home on Mother's Day. I asked Constantine to pick me up and drive me to the restaurant, and he did, even though his home is a long way from mine.

He is a lot more attentive and affectionate with me nowadays. I don't know why. Maybe he realizes that I'm in the winter of my life. Or maybe it's because his father died a few years ago, and he realizes that I'm the only parent that he has left. I'm speculating that maybe he has some empathy about my grief journey. He doesn't talk about your death unless I bring up the subject, but I do believe that he grieves for you in his way.

Minh, his Vietnamese American girlfriend, has been a very positive influence on him. She is calm and sweet with an easygoing personality, and she clearly loves him. I used to worry about his lack of patience and short temper, but he seems to have made some improvements about both.

How are you, honey? I surely hope that you are calm and happy where you are. Do spirits have feelings? I wish I knew. I never used to wonder about the afterlife and the quality of spirit existence, but your death changed all that. I understand now a lot better what drives people to go to psychics, especially after they lose loved ones. Some psychics may be scam artists, but I do believe that there are some special people who have a unique gift that they are born with, a "special sight," if you will.

I know personally somebody who fits that definition. I have known her for many years, and she has often told me that her so-called gift feels more like a curse at times. She says that she wishes she didn't have it. She calls it a burden and then recounts some personal experiences when she knows that she has been in the presence of spirits of dead family members or friends. The spirit of her dead ex-husband especially annoys her, and she keeps telling him to go away. She never uses her gift to make money, and I respect that. Shortly after your passing, I went to see a professional psychic. I previously wrote to you about that adventure.

It turned out to be an interesting experience, despite my ambivalence about going. I never went back, though. I did not want to make a habit of going to a psychic. I would rather deal with my grief by going to my therapist and by attending my grief group. Unlike the rest of society (even family and friends), the parents who attend the group really understand on a deeper level what I'm going through and are a big comfort to me.

Another important way I deal with your loss is by writing these letters to you. The ongoing ache inside me feels a little less painful after each writing session, and I get to feel closer to you. You always told me that we had a deep connection. I believed it then, and I believe it now. Just because you are gone does not mean that our relationship is over. As long as I'm alive, I'll carry it inside me.

I'm sending you hugs and kisses and all my love,
Mom

May 19, 2019

My Dearest Son,

I'm sorry I have not been writing much lately. I have been feeling pretty lousy, fighting a staph infection. After a week on antibiotics, I'm finally feeling better.

The physical pain is mostly gone, but the emotional pain of losing you goes on and on. I'm nowadays accepting the idea that it will always be there in some form or other. Going to the grief group reinforces that idea. I see parents there who lost their children many years ago, and they are still grieving. Nobody else seems to understand the intensity of this particular grief—only other parents. It saddens me and sometimes angers me that nobody in our family talks about you nowadays unless I initiate the conversation. Even then, they seem uneasy and awkward about doing it. I suspected this before, but now I know for sure that our society as a whole doesn't know how to deal with grief or death.

I make it a point to often talk with Nicholas about you. He is the only one in the family who seems to welcome my reminiscing. I tell him stories about your childhood, and he listens intensely. That pleases me a lot. After all, he is a part of you. He is still estranged from his mother. Your widow (seems strange to call her that) currently lives in Minnesota in her mother's apartment for assisted living. (This is Nicholas's other grandmother.) We hope that she is doing well, but we don't really know. She does not communicate with our family.

I still have a hard time forgiving her for not helping you overcome your addiction. Nicholas tells me that she is blaming you for all her problems and for the dismal turn that her life took in the last years of your life. Unfortunately, she does not seem to accept any responsibility for her own problems and actions. For your children's sake I hope she realizes one day that alcoholism is a family disease and repairs her relationship with them.

Your boys are doing well despite all the trauma and challenges that came their way. I know that you are proud of them, wherever you are. Robert is graduating from college in San Francisco soon, and he did it almost totally on his own. He had to work two jobs as well as attend school, so it took him six years instead of the usual four to graduate, but he made it happen. He is nice looking and a very personable young man. I get a lump in my throat every time I see him because he looks so much like your younger self and because he is so gentle and sweet in demeanor (like you used to be).

Nicholas recently turned twenty-one and is now legally an adult. He is a responsible and serious young man, and everybody seems to like him. He has been working hard as a valet attendant as well as attending community college and is saving his money so as to finish his last two years of college in a good school. He bought Olga and I presents on Mother's Day with his own money. Wasn't that sweet?

He wanted a guitar for his birthday, and Spiros and Olga got it for him. He is teaching himself to play it, just like you did. I told him the story of how we went to the border town of Tijuana, Mexico. Remember how you told Leslie and me that you were determined just to look at stuff and not buy anything and how you bought a guitar that you saw in a pawn shop window the very first day we were there? Nicholas laughed when he heard the story of the guitar and told me how you always loved that guitar and played it often, at least until the unfortunate homeless days of your last years.

We don't know what happened to that guitar. Nicholas and I speculated that you probably sold it for a few bucks to buy the stuff you needed to fuel your addiction. I should be a little more charitable and say that maybe you sold it along with other possessions to alleviate some of that crippling anxiety that you complained about. Of course, the anxiety was part and parcel of the addiction process, but your denial wouldn't let you believe that.

Oh, my darling son, I'm so sorry about how your life evolved and prematurely ended. You should be alive and well. A successful lawyer and father, enjoying your children's coming into maturing and becoming wonderful young men. You should be enjoying the middle years of your life with good health, happiness, and laughter—the laughter that is gone forever and that will be missed until the end of my days.

May 20, 2019

My Dearest Son,

Did you see me tonight by any chance having dinner with Nicholas? That was his belated birthday dinner. Between the family trip to Vegas and my staph infection, we had not been able to celebrate his birthday before tonight. I splurged some and took him to a nice restaurant. He deserved it. He has a 4.0 average in college, and he hopes to be accepted either at the University of Texas or the University of Southern California.

Do you remember giving me a tour of the USC campus during one of my early visits to LA? We almost got a jaywalking ticket that day for crossing the street between signals. You told the policeman that we were both visiting from Houston and didn't know any better. He let us go without a ticket. We later laughed about your half lie.

You always made me feel so welcome every time I came to visit. There was only one time when you clearly did not want me to come.

196

You were, it seems, in the middle of a romantic crisis with your first serous girlfriend, and you asked me to postpone my visit. I was in the middle of my own romantic crisis. I had just broken up with my first postdivorce boyfriend, and I was heartbroken. I told you that I couldn't postpone my visit, that I had to come and see you because of a personal crisis. I knew that I was acting in a rather selfish way, but I did it anyway. Looking back, I'm not thrilled about my actions. Not like me to go somewhere where I'm not wanted, but my excuse is that people in love can do crazy things when things end badly.

You and Sally were polite and even gracious during my visit, despite your earlier concerns, but I could definitely feel some tension between the two of you that made me worry about you. I knew how much your girlfriend meant to you. There was a little tension between the two of us, as well, and that was unfamiliar and very uncomfortable to me. Despite all that, my visit still had a good effect on me and gave me some relief from my sadness. It was always so wonderful to see you and be with you.

Except perhaps for that one time, you always seemed so happy to see me, even on my last visit to your home before you lost it to foreclosure. The clouds of doom must have started to gather back then, but you pretended that everything was fine. I had timed my visit to come for Robert's graduation from high school, and as always I loved being with you and your family.

There were a few signs that things were not great. You told me one day that you were worried about your wife because she was depressed. You never said anything about excessive drinking (yours or hers), just that she was depressed and would nap for a long time, burning food on occasion. The irony was that Leslie took me aside and told me that she was worried about you and that something wasn't right. When I pressed her for more details, she would not give me any. Both of you tried to convince me of each other's need to see a doctor. When I suggested that maybe both of you needed medical help—together and separately—you two shrugged your shoulders and changed the subject.

Jaime, you also told me privately that you had a big insomnia problem. You woke up at 2 a.m. every night, you said, and then you couldn't get back to sleep. You also told me that your anxiety had gotten worse.

I gently suggested that maybe alcohol at night was the culprit behind the insomnia. I added that maybe you could try giving it up for a while to see if that made a difference to your impaired sleeping patterns. I had no idea, as I said all of that, of the immensity and gravity of the problem you were facing. I never saw you drunk and/or belligerent, and I never saw Leslie drinking, except for an occasional glass of wine. Little did I know what was coming and how your life was going to explode.

I now blame myself for my own denial. I should have looked more closely at the signs of trouble in your world, instead of minimizing the problem. The truth is that you kept a lot of important secrets from me. You didn't tell me of the DUI or of a cocaine phase earlier in your life that Leslie knew about. You must have been behind in your mortgage payments already or you wouldn't have lost your house some months later. The cirrhosis of your liver might have already started, since it was at an advanced stage when you died.

You would be homeless two years after my visit, but I didn't know that. Worst of all, your addiction would end your life, and, thankfully, I didn't know that either. By the time I put the pieces of the puzzle together, it would be too late. Of course, the fact that we were living so far apart contributed to my ignorance of the real situation, but I have to face the fact that I was in denial of your disease—just like any other family member that I had treated throughout my career as a family therapist!

Alarm bells started ringing for me only when you told me not to come for Nicholas's high school graduation. I told you that I had gone to all of my grandchildren's graduations and that now was Nicholas's turn. "Hold your horses, Mother," you said, "that may not be a good idea." When I persisted, you reluctantly confessed that your house had been foreclosed. I cried when I heard that. I loved your house and had many wonderful memories of my annual visits there. I also cried because I finally realized that there were some very serious problems in your life that were coming to the surface.

After that phone call, the bad news from LA accelerated at an alarming rate. Every week or so, Spiros and Olga were getting calls from longtime friends of yours, telling us that your life was going downhill. One shock followed another. We heard that you, Leslie, and Nicholas were going from one dingy motel to another, and/or living in a U-Haul truck. The specter of homelessness started showing its ugly head. I was terrified for you and your family and did not know what to do or how to help you. In the meantime, Nicholas was taking three buses each way to finish his last year at high school.

It must have been a miserable year for all of you, and all I could do was cry and go to Al-Anon meetings; meanwhile, my health problems increased by tenfold. By this time, you seemed to only call when you needed money. I gave in to a few of those requests, such as paying your cell phone bill and covering the rental of a tuxedo so Nicholas could go to the prom, but most of the time, I turned down your requests (as I suffered anguish about my behavior), explaining to you that giving you money relating to consequences of your addictive behavior would be against my Al-Anon beliefs. You called me less and less after each refusal of mine. That was a very sad time for me. Practicing tough love and turning down your requests for money were the hardest things I ever did. It killed me emotionally to think of your ending up in the streets of LA (your beloved town), homeless and penniless.

I still remember how your voice broke when you called me the day after my knee-replacement surgery to tell me that your law license had been taken away. "Mom, I am glad you are OK after surgery," you said, "but I have some bad news. They took my license away. I can't work as a lawyer anymore. Maybe I can get it back one day. I think it costs $300 to try and get it reinstated. What do you think, Mom?"

I was still kind of foggy from anesthesia and only understood half of what you said. The news that you had lost your license was like the last domino falling in your path of decline. I was in a lot of physical pain, despite the pain pills, and I could hardly speak, let alone respond to your latest misfortune. I knew how much your law license and your career meant to you, though, and I heard your heartbreak in the tone of your voice. I hung up and burst into tears. I didn't know then that this would be the last time that I would hear your voice.

May 21, 2019

My Dearest Son,

Nicholas went to San Francisco this morning to be with Robert on his graduation day. Did I tell you that your oldest son is graduating from college this weekend? Maybe you already know. I hope so. No guilt trip intended here, but Robert accomplished this all by himself. He worked at Safeway part-time to earn the money to go to school. It took him longer than four years, but he got his degree. I am very proud of him. I know you are too.

Nicholas told me recently that his brother, Robert, wants to be a policeman or a fireman. I didn't like hearing that. Both are community-minded but dangerous occupations. I don't know if you are aware, but California has been plagued in recent years by frequent wildfires that place firemen in constant danger. Robert is such a sweet, gentle young man that I have a hard time envisioning him as a member of the police force. Nicholas doesn't approve of his choices either. He thinks that they are both crazy ideas. I hope Robert doesn't follow up on those plans. I would constantly worry about his safety.

Nicholas, on the other hand, wants to go into the financial field (maybe inspired by Spiros?). He is excited about securing an internship with an investment firm in Houston. It seems that Nicholas had been thinking about working on an offshore oil rig this summer to earn money for his last two years of college. I asked him, "Why an oil rig?" "Well," he replied, "Spiros did it and Dad did it, so I thought I could do it also." I had forgotten about that. It has been sort of a rite of passage for men of our family, I guess. I remembered then that I had not been pleased with either one of you working on a rig (too many safety hazards), so I was happy to hear that Spiros steered Nicholas into a safer alternative.

I am proud of both your boys. Instead of wallowing in self-pity and despair, they turned the disintegration of their family and the tragedy of your untimely death into something positive for themselves. I sure hope that they stay in that path and have a healthy and happy life. That does not mean that I am dismissing the specter of addiction and its hereditary tendencies. I keep trying to talk Nicholas into going for some therapy sessions and/or twelve-step meetings like Al-Anon. I am afraid that if he doesn't address the trauma of the last few years that it will affect him in the future in a negative way.

He keeps telling me, "It is what it is!" whenever I bring up the issue of his having been traumatized and needing therapeutic work. I believe that he does believe that he is perfectly OK. He is a proud young man (like you were early on) and has a great fear of being pitied. He tells me—trying to prove to me that he's OK—that he doesn't care if he ever talks to or sees his mother ever again; however, I know that the estrangement has been hurtful to him, just as I know that your passing has affected him deeply.

Anyway, keep a watchful eye on him. I'll keep trying to convince him to get some professional help.

May 22, 2019 (1:30 a.m.)

My Dearest Son,

I couldn't sleep again. I try to go to bed around midnight, with the thought that I will be tired by then and thus fall asleep, but the strategy doesn't work very often. I used to be asleep by 11 p.m., but that was before your troubles started (or at least before I knew of them).

My little dog, Skye, usually goes to my bed before me and waits for me, but it's raining tonight. Rain prompts her to go to her usual hiding place in the bathroom. In her little doggy mind, she must think that if she's half hidden from view that she's also hidden from danger.

I've never seen anything like her phobia of rain. I've had dogs before and they were scared of thunder and lightning, but Skye is scared of plain rain. She's my weather barometer. I know when rain is coming based on Skye's behavior. She will look anxiously outside and then run to the bathroom.

The irony here is that, after specializing in anxiety disorders (for humans) for forty-plus years, I ended up with a phobic dog! (I hope you are reading the above and laughing with your special, wonderful laugh.)

I wish you could tell me how to bear this misery and immense sadness about your loss. My grief takes such weird twists and turns. From time to time, I still obsess about having missed the early signs of your disease and how I was not able to save you from your addiction.

In my rational mind I know that ultimately only you had the power to save yourself, but there are still times when I get into guilt and regrets, blaming my own denial and my inability to help you. After all, I helped many individuals and families through the years, why the hell couldn't I save my own beloved son? I know what Al-Anon members would say: "You didn't cause it, you can't control it, and you can't cure it." But it's very hard to remember that wise saying when I get into my moments of despair.

You had many wonderful opportunities, Jaime, but you also had your father's stubbornness. I know you probably believed that you could overcome your dependence on alcohol and drugs all by yourself. By the time you realized that you were not able to do that—maybe when you quit cold turkey and then had a violent seizure—you probably gave up on the effort. You did not even want to ask for help with your problems (your father taught that, as well).

I know that I am partially blaming him here for the tragic turn your life took, but I have some grounds for that. It used to drive me crazy to hear him say that he didn't believe in therapy and psychology all the while he was married to a licensed therapist—me. In addition to what he taught you by his words, we also have the evidence of his abandonment of you after you moved to California. He never visited you, not even once, after your boys were born. You were so sad about that! I know that his behavior was very hurtful to you. You told me that numerous times. I was so angry with him about that.

I have to admit that I also feel some guilt regarding his nonvisits. I can't help but think that things in that regard would have been different if I had not divorced him. I would have insisted that he come with me to visit you. His foolish pride probably kept him away as well. He believed in the old-fashioned, silly idea that grown children needed to visit their parents, not the other way around. I'm sorry, sweetheart.

I'm also so sorry about the cirrhosis of the liver and all the suffering you went through, both physical and emotional (especially in the last years of your life). Your addiction and its consequences must have been so overwhelming for you. I know that they have been overwhelming and terrible for me as well. That's part of the tragedy of alcoholism and addiction-related diseases. Not only do they ruin the addict's life, they also deeply hurt those who love them.

I cried and cried when you told me that you had spent a week in the jail hospital. The news was so upsetting to me that I didn't even ask you why they took you to the hospital. I guess I didn't have the emotional strength to even find out what the doctors told you.

I am glad that you are at peace now. I hope that one day I may be at peace also about our joint journey, but I am not there yet.

May 25, 2019

My Dearest Son,

I was lying in bed, trying to go to sleep tonight and an image flashed into my head. I saw myself sitting in your backyard in LA, enjoying the nice local weather and admiring the view of your tall poplar trees on top of your hill. Remember how I loved those trees? They reminded me of a trip to Italy, the Siena region in particular. I was enjoying the weather in the 70s (versus the 101-degree weather in Houston) and reading a book, my favorite pastime. Life was good, I thought, and I was very happy to be visiting you one more time.

You approached me and pointed out an old bench in the middle of your backyard hill. You excitedly told me that you had found the bench in a neighbor's trash. "Leslie was appalled that I picked up something from a trash bin, but I couldn't resist," you told me. "Here in LA people throw away all sorts of useful things. Doesn't it look like a nice antique bench?" Not wanting to offend you or insult your tastes, I diplomatically said that it looked fine, even though I wouldn't go as far as to call it an antique.

"As you can see, I painted it black" you said, "but Leslie doesn't like it." "Maybe you can repaint it dark green," I suggested. "It may blend in better in your backyard."

"That's a good idea, Mom," you said. "I'll do it."

You sure did. When I woke up the next morning, I saw that you had done as I had suggested, and I smiled. The green paint made the bench look much nicer and now it even had some vintage flair. I told you that the bench looked really nice and you beamed with satisfaction and pleasure.

"Thanks for the advice, Mom," you said. "Even Leslie likes the bench now!"

I can see the bench vividly in front of my eyes. The image is clear and shiny, despite the tears in my eyes. I can also see you standing tall and beaming at me with your big, brown expressive eyes. You seemed so proud of the fact that you rescued an old abandoned bench from a trash bin and gave it new life.

I wonder what happened to that bench. Was it thrown away when your house was foreclosed and then sold? Did it find its way back in the trash bin, with nobody caring about all the time you put into it trying to revitalize it? Probably so. I know it's a very small thing compared with everything you lost toward the end, but it still saddens me now to think about it.

I also miss the sunsets I watched while sitting in your backyard. I never tired of seeing the glorious colors of sunset silhouetting your majestic poplar trees and captivating me with their beauty. I have always been a sucker for sunsets. Tell me of a beautiful sunset, and I'll follow you anywhere (or did before age took its toll). I still remember when my best friend, Connie, bought her beautiful house on Lake Travis in Austin. She lured me to visit her the right away by calling me and telling me that I had to come and see the amazing sunsets above the lake, as viewed from her renovated deck. I did go and she was right. The daily sunsets provided a show like no other; they were mesmerizing.

For about ten years, the Galveston house of your oldest brother and his wife also provided me with wonderful views of sunsets. They eventually sold the house, but I was a frequent visitor while they had it. Like you, I loved being close to water. I would sit on their balcony, enveloped by a light breeze from the gulf, and stare at the sunsets. Sometimes, especially after a rain shower, there would be a lovely rainbow along with the daily sunset.

You shared a few of those sunsets with me. The one that stuck in my mind was when you came to Houston from Los Angeles, right after your breakup from your first serious girlfriend. You were so devastated about the breakup. It was hard for me to see you hurting so deeply.

We sat on the balcony of the beach house for a long time as you told me of your heartbreak. I listened and tried to comfort you as much as I could. You told me also that you had to give your new law firm a good reason for leaving your training, so you fabricated the story that your grandmother had died.

You felt guilty about the lie. After all, your grandmother Anastasia, the only grandparent you knew, had died five years before. You earnestly asked me if I thought your grandmother would be angry with you for using her as an excuse.

"Of course, she wouldn't mind," I said. "She is probably happy to help you with your crises in your life, in any way she can. She always said that you were special and had a big heart. She would forgive you everything and anything. You were always her favorite grandchild!" You smiled, and I was happy to see a smile on your face, even if it was a feeble one.

It was always such a great joy for me to make you smile or laugh. You seemed to understand and appreciate my sense of humor more than your brothers or even my friends. You even liked my writing. You often asked me if I had written anything new.

During my annual visits to LA, I loved reading to you and Leslie parts of my book about growing up in Turkey (*Bridging the Aegean: Growing Up Greek in Turkey*), even before it was published. You always listened intently and even commented favorably about the essays related to my childhood and adolescence.

The only time you ever had a negative reaction—almost alarm—to something I wrote was when I read you a story that my Mother used to tell me when I was young. It's an old folktale about a son who kills his mother and cuts out her heart so as to prove to his beloved that he loves her above all others. The tale followed the son's journey as he transports the heart to show his girlfriend that he indeed did the evil deed. He trips and falls while on the way, and his mother's heart speaks up from inside the container where it lies and says, "Did you hurt yourself, my son? Are you all right? "

When you heard the story, Jamie, you jumped up from your chair and exclaimed, "Mom, that's such a creepy, scary story. Don't ever read that to my boys. They will freak out!"

Well, you were right, honey. The old folktale is gory and creepy. I used to cringe as a child when I would hear my mother tell it. However, its message is powerful and very real: a mother loves her children always and forgives them whatever they do, no matter what. As I'm writing this, the irony of what I'm saying is also pretty clear. I, too, am a loving mother who loves you and forgives you for giving me the most emotional blow of my life—the unimaginable grief of your death.

June 1, 2019

My Dearest Son,

I never told you about this when you were alive, but a month or so after you unexpectedly showed up in Houston, I received a letter from your newly departed girlfriend, telling me some of her reasons for leaving you and the relationship. She was also telling me goodbye. She added that she had always liked me a lot, but that was not a good reason to stay in a romantic relationship. She asked me not to tell you that she wrote to me. I respected her wishes and never did tell you. What is important to note here is that she told me that parts of your personality reminded her of her alcoholic father and that had alarmed her.

Of course, I ignored that part of the letter. I told myself that it didn't mean anything significant, that she was just trying to rationalize her decision to leave you. Looking back, I'm embarrassed by my denial and of ignoring her warning about your impending disease.

I never replied to your ex-girlfriend's letter. I had liked her a lot as well and was torn by my feelings of sadness about losing her from our lives as well as some anger about her leaving you and hurting you so deeply. I regret that I didn't pay more attention to her intuition and experience as an adult child of an alcoholic parent. The end of that relationship was a turning point in your life. My guess is that you never totally got over losing her.

Goodnight, sweetheart. I'm glad that you are at peace now, with no more earthly sorrows.

June 7, 2019

My Dearest Son,

I haven't written for a few days because I have been emotionally in a bad place. I was shocked last week to discover that my Cologuard test came back positive for colon cancer. I had some stomach and abdominal pain off and on and my family doctor suggested that I take the test. The word *cancer* had never been mentioned. She had said that a peptic ulcer was a possibility.

I never expected a positive result. Of course, I know that a lot of people get diagnosed with cancer, and I had my own bout with the dreaded disease years ago (thyroid cancer). I never thought there would be a repeat performance. Colon cancer was something dark and prevalent in your father's family. Both your paternal grandparents, whom you never met, had it. With that hereditary influence, I had always been concerned that you or your brothers might get it.

I thought I was safe. After all, nobody in my family ever had it. I had two colonoscopies in my life, and they were both clear of any malignancy. I was so miserable preparing for them (I turned out to be allergic to the liquids that you have to take as preparation) that I hoped never to have another one. Guess what? I bet that the new gastroenterologist whom I'm going to see next week will make me get another one, even though they are not recommended after seventy-five years of age unless absolutely necessary.

I cling to a small hope that maybe the Cologuard test result is a false positive. If I do have it, I'm heading straight to MD Anderson Cancer Center. Physicians there treated me for thyroid cancer, and I couldn't have asked for better care. They are not in my Medicare network, but I don't care. It's a very caring institution. They even have a nap room so patients can rest between treatments. Who does that? Another thought that popped into my head was I could join you sooner than I thought. I keep going back and forth between thinking that I don't have the energy for another major health challenge and wanting to fight back.

Then something interesting occurred. The same day that I found out about the test result, I also found out that my oldest granddaughter, your niece Victoria, got formally engaged to her long-time boyfriend. Since I don't believe in random coincidences, I immediately thought the universe was giving me a reason to keep on living by giving me the news of her engagement. I now hope that I live long enough to go to her wedding next year (yes—Greek drama—but I can't help it). Cancer, especially at my age, does seem scary, even though with new technology it's no longer the death threat that it used to be. OK, enough about cancer.

Did I already tell you that Robert joined Nicholas in Las Vegas last month for Nicholas's twenty-first birthday extravaganza that Spiros and Olga orchestrated? Isn't it nice how your boys support each other? I know you must be proud. I am.

As always, I love you and miss you. Wish me luck with my new health challenge and keep an eye on me. I truly believe that you and my mother are my afterlife guardians.

June 8, 2019

My Dearest Son,

I had dinner tonight with my longtime friends Uğur and Verdi. I know how much you liked them when you were young. They were born in Turkey, as your dad and I were, but they are not of Greek descent. They are Muslim Turks. Despite the religious difference, we have been close friends for over fifty years. Through the years, they have been the closest thing to a U.S. family for me. They were shocked and saddened last year when I told them of your tragic death. They have tried to be comforting ever since.

Tonight, we didn't talk about you, even though we usually do. They tried to be reassuring about my cancer scare. Uğur is a survivor of breast cancer, and she knows the pitfalls of the disease. Verdi and I usually commiserate about our high blood pressure and our prospective treatments. As usual, it felt nice and comforting to spend that time with my dear friends and to share my fears about my test results.

I couldn't sleep tonight without writing to you. Have I told you that your niece Stacy is now a doctor? She graduated from medical school. The ceremony was in San Antonio, and I couldn't go. I wanted to, but it seemed too difficult to manage with all my health challenges. I was there when she started medical school, when she wore a white coat for the first time, and when she found out in another ceremony the site of her medical residency. Unfortunately, I had to skip her actual graduation from medical school.

When I called her to tell her that I was sorry but would not be able to attend her actual graduation, I also told her how proud I was of her for becoming the first doctor in our family. She thanked me and graciously reminded me that I had already attended all her important educational milestones. She is rewarding herself for finishing her medical studies by going on vacation to the Machu Picchu ruins in Peru with her longtime boyfriend.

I am so proud of all my grandchildren. It pains me to think that you cannot witness all the accomplishments of the younger branch of the family, especially those of your own children. Or, maybe you can from where you are. Who knows? As Shakespeare wisely said through Hamlet, "There are more things in heaven and earth, Horatio / Than are dreamt of in your philosophy."[7]

June 9, 2019

My Dearest Son,

It's that time of the night again. It's 1 a.m., and as usual, I cannot sleep. Tomorrow is my appointment with the specialist. He will probably tell me that I have to undergo a colonoscopy, and I hate the idea already. It doesn't help my attitude to remember that a friend of mine went recently for a colonoscopy and woke up to find that the doctor had inserted a pacemaker in her chest instead. It seems that her heart stopped during the procedure, and they couldn't proceed with the colonoscopy.

When I think about that, my mind immediately goes to what happened to you. Your heart also stopped, sweetheart. Unfortunately, unlike the case with my friend, nobody could save you and resuscitate your heart because nobody knew what was happening. You were alone in the park when your life ended. At least, that was what I was told. My mind and imagination have gone over that scene hundreds of times.

I was told by Leslie that earlier on that fateful day that you fell and hit your head on the ground. They took you to the ER. Why did you go back to the park, I wonder? Did you not have a place to go to besides the streets? It seems that there was a so-called friend with you, and you two had a brawl. He pushed you at one point, and you fell. Did he go away after your fall? Were you too drunk and/or stoned to realize that you needed help? I am so sorry that you died alone, honey, with nobody to hold your hand and comfort you. My fervent hope is that you did not realize what was happening to you and that you were not terrified.

I am so very sad about what happened to you! Once upon a time you were my golden boy who couldn't do anything wrong. You were always an earnest, excellent student with good grades for everything, including behavior. Always the ideal Boy Scout, eager to help others. Your room was a model of cleanliness, with your artifacts lined up perfectly. Your books were even alphabetized. Your father was so proud of you about that.

Then you went to college and law school far away, and we hardly ever saw you again, except for summer vacations. Maybe the fact that your father and I divorced after you left home had something to do with your rare visits home. I don't know, but I wonder.

You were shy as a youngster and had few friends. You were a late bloomer as far as dating was concerned. I don't remember that you even dated while in high school. I know for a fact that a couple of girls asked you about prom, and you turned them down. One of them even called me to tell me how much she liked you. I was rather concerned about your lack of interest, but you told me you were OK and not to worry.

My therapeutic guess now is that you had considerable social anxiety and that probably alcohol and drugs in college enabled you to let go of some of that anxiety. You probably embraced them because of that. Your youth took place during the era of drug experimentation, as well. Unfortunately, your chemical friends later became your enemies, because of the ugly head of addiction, and later ruined your life. I am speculating here, my son, but I think I'm on the right track. Your enemy was a very cunning, powerful villain that knew how to win and did.

You were not alone in this, Jaime. There are millions of people all over the world that fell and still fall victim to similar chemical enemies. I know that I am not the only mother/parent who is suffering the loss of a beloved child due to addiction. We are a small army of parents who stand helplessly by while our children's lives are robbed. We also fall victim to the dreaded disease. We mourn night and day to no avail.

At least your spirit is at peace now. I am glad about that, even as I'm left here on earth to agonize about your death until my dying breath. Don't ever forget that I love you and always will.

June 11, 2019

My Dearest Son,

I was at Spiros and Olga's home tonight for Sunday dinner. Victoria was there, too, showing her beautiful engagement ring and talking about wedding plans. She and Michael (her fiancé) are getting married next summer, and there is already some bickering between mother and daughter about specific wedding plans regarding wedding venue and related issues. Victoria is looking overwhelmed about specific decisions already, and it's only been two weeks since Michael proposed. The wedding will be either here or in Utah.

Michael's parents have a second home in Park City, a resort town in the mountains of Utah, and Victoria loves the place.

I sure hope that I can go to the wedding if it's in Utah. It all depends on how my health is next summer. By the way, the new doctor I went to see last week doesn't think that I have colon cancer, despite the test results. He thinks that it may be a false-positive result. He says that is sometimes the case with older patients. Yea! That's the good news: the not-so-good news is that I have to have a colonoscopy soon, just as I predicted. Talk to the angels on my behalf and maybe the Big Boss, OK, honey? I do want to be able to attend Victoria's wedding. Talking about weddings reminded me of your wedding, Jaime. I loved that you were married in a Greek Orthodox church (the only one of my sons who was).

No, that's not totally true. Your older brother and Olga had a second wedding in a small private ceremony in a Greek chapel just so Spiros could be your best man (*koumbaros*). The church rule is that the *koumbaros* has to be Greek Orthodox by baptism as well as marriage. Since Spiros had been married in a Methodist church ceremony, he had to have a second ceremony in a Greek church.

I never loved Spiros more than I did that day. I was so proud of him for going to such lengths to be your best man. Spiros and Olga even had to undergo premarital counseling, ten years or so after their original wedding. After all the years of bickering and fighting between you and him as kids, it was so heartwarming for me to witness such a demonstration of love and support between the two of you! I don't think you showed as much appreciation for his gestures as they deserved. Maybe you did privately, and I didn't see it. If that's the case, I apologize.

How I wish you were alive to be at Victoria's wedding or your own sons' weddings, for that matter, whenever they occur. You are missing out a lot by having your life cut short by your awful disease. On the other hand, I have to face the fact that if you were alive but still deep in alcoholism, you would not have been able to attend any of these important family gatherings anyway. I have to remind myself to remember your life as it was in the last few years and not to be swept away by sentimental, fantasy scenarios.

How I wish you had been able to find your way into recovery. If you had, then instead of writing these painful letters, I would be talking with you in person and hugging you again and again.

June 15, 2019 (1:30 a.m.)

My Dearest Son,

Here I am again, late at night, trying to converse with you. I know in my head that it's a one-sided conversation, but I can pretend the opposite, can't I? It has been one year and three months since you left me and this earth, and my pain is still raw. Sometimes, during the day, when I'm busy with errands, cooking, and other ordinary activities, life gets a little more mellow. Then nighttime comes, the emotional pain becomes an endless nightmare of my insides bleeding, and all I want to do is scream.

Even during the day there will be surges of acute grief brought on at odd moments by various triggers. I will see a happy-looking mother holding a child close or, at the other end of the spectrum, a desolate mother talking about the death of her child (of any age). Then I start crying and have a hard time stopping.

I'm new at this. I don't know how to grieve in moderation, if there is such a thing. I don't know if the agony of losing a child ever lessens. I see and hear parents in my grief group, including many whose loss happened a long time ago, talk about how they are still inconsolable.

Nowadays, I'm superaware of everybody's mortality and vulnerability, especially of those I love. I worry every time they go on a trip (even though I used to love traveling myself). I don't tell them of my worries, because I don't want them to think of me as a sentimental old fool of a mother and grandmother.

Stacy (Constantine's oldest) went to visit the Machu Picchu ruins recently with her boyfriend, and they mentioned planning to go hiking on the Inca trail on their own without a guide. I was a nervous wreck about the plan. They later had to give up on the idea because Stacy got sick during the trip from something she ate. I breathed a sigh of relief.

Did I already tell you that I have to have a colonoscopy in a few days? I have had numerous tests in my life, including big ones like angioplasty, but I dread the colonoscopy test more than any of the others. It's probably because I've had a vomiting phobia since I was a child, and both times that I've had to prepare for a colonoscopy, I threw up a lot the previous day trying to drink copious amounts of a yucky liquid!

I'm getting a little sleepy now, so I'll go to bed and try to go to sleep. I am hopeful the anticipatory anxiety about the colonoscopy will not keep me up during the night.
All my love,
Mom

June 18, 2019

My Dearest Son,

This is a break from my regular letter writing pattern. I usually write to you late at night, but this is the middle of the day. It's prep day for my colonoscopy tomorrow, and I'm freaking out. I am hungry (can only drink liquids today) and superanxious. Besides the dreaded prep routine, there's also the bigger question of whether I have colon cancer. We'll find out tomorrow.

For a good while after you died, I didn't care if I lived or died. But now I do care and hope I can live somewhat longer so I can accomplish important goals. I do want to attend my granddaughter's wedding next year, but what is more important is that I want to write a book about you. I envision it as a chronicle of your tragic journey of addiction as well as my own journey as one who loved you dearly and always will. In particular, I want the book to reflect on the man you were and the wonderful potential of you that was only partially realized. I want to tell the world of the good person that you used to be: the one with a big heart and a brain to match; the boy with the thirst for knowledge who used to read encyclopedias just for the fun of it; the affectionate son and the loving father who acquired a crippling addiction to alcohol and drugs and went away, leaving loved ones bereft forever. My heart aches for the life interrupted and stopped before its time.

No matter what happens tomorrow or what my test shows, remember that I love you and always will. I will carry you with me no matter where I go.

June 25, 2019

My Dearest Son,

Forgive me for not having written for a while, but I have been busy with medical matters. Please know that even though I didn't write anything down, you were always on my mind.

I had my colonoscopy last week, and even though the preparation was an ordeal, the results were worth the effort. The good news: no evidence of colon cancer. Hallelujah, praise the Lord! The doctor came to the recovery room after I woke up from the anesthesia to tell me the news, and then he added, "Do not take any of those silly tests again." I promised that I wouldn't.

What a relief! Even as I was hoping that the previous test results were wrong, I still worried about the possibility that they were right and that I had colon cancer. I am very glad that the Cologuard test results were wrong.

I keep having flashbacks about my last visit to your home. Leslie told me then that you were verbally abusive to her when you drank and often addressed hurtful, mean remarks to her. I had a very hard time believing that it was you that she was talking about—my wonderful son.

"Please, make him stop," she said. "He loves you and listens to you!" I made a valiant effort to talk with you about what she said. You shrugged your shoulders and told me that she was the sick one and was making up the stuff about abusive remarks. I didn't know which of you to believe. I did see signs that Leslie was severely depressed. She took frequent long naps, let the food burn once too often, and locked one of the bathrooms in the house, telling me that it was very cluttered and the toilet was broken.

When I volunteered to pay to have it fixed, she refused. The dirty dishes sat in the sink for hours unless I washed them. This was certainly not her usual behavior. Whenever I woke up in the middle of the night, there you were, both of you up, casually watching television as if it were daytime.

I realized that you both needed help with your anxiety and depression (as well as ongoing insomnia) and told you so. Looking back, I know for a fact that you ignored my advice and did not get the help you needed. To my everlasting regret, I was not able to convince either one of you to go get the help you desperately needed.

I didn't know at the time how serious the problems were, but I did suspect that they existed (even with all the secrets that you kept from me about your addiction).

My inability to help you, despite all my years of experience and knowledge, adds another layer of distress to my many layers of grief. I keep obsessing over and over again about the fact that I helped hundreds of needy strangers through the years, but I was not able to help my own beloved son.

I am so sorry, Jaime.

June 26, 2019

My Dearest Son,

Today I saw a posting on Facebook (remember Facebook?) about Robert's college graduation. He looked so handsome and proud in his graduation gown. He looked a lot like you did when you were his age, except for a little burlier physique (perhaps from Leslie's Swedish side of the family). Robert has your facial traits, while Nicholas looks more like Leslie but with your type of slim physique. Funny how our children inherit our looks. Nicholas had gone to San Francisco to support his brother on his big day. There is a strong bond between the brothers that I am very happy to see.

Leslie did the picture posting. I was surprised to see that she flew from Minnesota to San Francisco to attend Robert's graduation because I know that there is still some estrangement between her and your boys. I read the posting remarks that she made and thought that some of them did not make any sense to me. I wondered about how well she was really doing. That thought retriggered my old anger at her for not supporting my intervention efforts two years ago. She complained a lot about your behavior, but when the chips were down, she refused to participate in my efforts to help you.

I am so sad, honey, that you could not attend your older son's graduation. I hope that you were there in spirit.

Nicholas is going to New York this week to start his financial internship. He is being flown there by his boss in his private plane. Yes, you read that right, your younger son has become quite a traveler these days. That is primarily due to Spiros's influential support. He helped him secure the internship by introducing him to some of his wealthy clients and friends. Of course, your brother is no fool. He knows that Nicholas is smart and will work hard to deliver the goods. Otherwise, he would never have facilitated his internship.

Speaking of Nicholas, he texted me yesterday that he was accepted at the University of Texas in Austin for his final two college years. I was very happy for him. He had been so fearful that he would not be accepted. "I don't come from a wealthy family," he had told me, "and I'm new to Texas. They won't want me."

I tried to quiet his doubts and fears. "Just tell them the truth about your life," I said, "the whole truth: the dismal senior year at the Los Angeles high school, the loss of your home, and the subsequent homelessness. Tell how you used to take three busses each way, every day, just to make it to classes. Make sure you tell them how you turned your life around in the last two years in Houston and how you attended community college (making top grades) while also working part-time as a valet attendant."

"I don't want to write about all that sad stuff," he said. "I don't want their pity."

"They won't pity you," I replied. "Instead, they will admire your determination, resiliency, and all your accomplishments, despite all the trauma and challenges of the last two years. Just tell the truth about your life, Nicholas, and I promise you that you will be accepted in college. Remember that I was a psychotherapist for many years. I know something about human nature."

He finally agreed to write the essay the way I advised him to, and I'm happy to say that I was right (even though I didn't say that to him). Not only did UT accept him for the fall semester, but even the University of Southern California, which is notoriously difficult to get into, accepted him for the spring semester.

I know you must be happy, Jaime, to find out how well Nicholas and Robert are doing. You told me, on my last visit with you, that your kids were fine. You were right, honey. Your kids are fine, despite all the challenges they have faced. I dearly hope that they stay fine.

July 2, 2019

My Dearest Son,

We are in the second year after your passing into another reality, and I still ache with your loss. Not a day goes by without something reminding me of you.

I was watching the Democratic debates last night, and your brother Constantine and I were texting observations and comments back and forth. As much as I was enjoying our meeting of minds and our exchanges, there were numerous times when I thought, "How I wish I could exchange some thoughts with Jamie as well!"

Yes, I do remember that you were a Libertarian (and not an ardent Democrat like Constantine is and like I am) and that we had many discussions—or debates—throughout the years about that. I kept telling you that you were wasting your votes and that I didn't understand the point of your voting pattern. Your response was that it was a matter of principle, and you didn't want the government to tell you what to do. I would agree to disagree about this issue, and I respected your choice regardless.

The truth is, Jaime, that a big part of you always rebelled against rules and regulations, despite your model behavior as a child. Another truth about you is that, even though you had many admirable qualities and traits, you did tend to be rather stubborn. Unfortunately, your stubbornness may have contributed to your premature death. Knowing your personality, my guess is that you probably thought, to your detriment, that you could beat alcoholism all on your own.

Last time we met was the day of intervention. You told me then that you knew that you drank too much (your words) and that you had tried to quit cold turkey, with disastrous results. Did they tell you in the ER that you had cirrhosis of the liver, or did you already know? Somehow you never told me about it.

Maybe you found out the dreaded diagnosis when you landed in jail for two DWI's and unpaid fines. I knew nothing about your first time in jail. You kept that a secret. The first inkling I had of the awful trajectory of your life was when I received numerous pleading phone calls for bail money before the second jail term. I have already shared with you in previous letters my

217

feelings of agony of that day. It was so awfully hard to say, "No, I can't help you." It broke my heart.

I never knew that tough love principles would be so painful. I truly believe that refusing your pleas that day was the hardest thing I've ever done. I finally had to disconnect my phone so as not to hear your urgent pleas anymore.

I cried the rest of the day and for many days afterwards. I earnestly believed that jail would be such a horrible experience for you that you would seek help and turn your life around. Unfortunately, I was wrong.

I hoped, and still hope, that somehow, even in your foggy alcoholic state, that you understood why I couldn't send you any bail money and that you still believed that I loved you. You were so angry with me that day. You told me that you would never speak with me again. You never did.

As I'm writing this, I have this terrible lump in my throat that's almost choking me. Back then, I thought that this was surely the worst day of my life. I was wrong about that as well.

The worst day was still to come. It was March 13, 2018, the day your heart stopped and crashed my world forever.

July 3, 2019

My Dearest Son,

I was listening to singer-songwriter Brandi Carlile who performed on "Austin City Limits," the PBS music show. She started singing a song she wrote, "I am the Mother of Evangeline," and as she sang the lyrics, I started crying. At the end of the song, a cute little girl came on stage and gave Carlile (her mother) a kiss, and I cried even harder.

So many things remind me of you and of my loss and so many things make me cry these days. Every time I see mothers with their children on television, especially if they are being affectionate with each other, it touches me deeply. If they talk about losing a child, that brings a cascade of tears. At times, my pain becomes so great that I cannot bear it, and I turn off the television.

Reading about the loss of a child has a different effect on me. It is still painful, but it can be a little comforting as well to read about feelings similar to my own.

The book *Lincoln in the Bardo* by George Saunders is a good example. I read it two years ago for the first time because I had read some glowing reviews and because it had won some literary prizes. At that time, I thought that the book, which told the story of the death of President Lincoln's eleven-year-old son during the Civil War, was thoughtful and well written. Then recently, I read it again. What a difference in my reaction to the book! This time around, my own experience of losing a child, albeit a much older child, made the book *Lincoln in the Bardo* come alive in a much stronger way.

I marveled at the wisdom of the author. How true his words sounded! President Lincoln lost an eleven-year-old son. You were not small when you died, but you were certainly, at the end anyway, weak and vulnerable. I too was and still am overwhelmed by doubt and regret as well as guilt for having failed to protect you from your disease of addiction. A friend, who also lost an adult son around the same time I lost you, tells me that her son was her most affectionate child. I tell her that you were my most affectionate one as well. The irony here is that when you were a little boy, you were not very fond of hugs and embraces. You tolerated your grandmother Anastasia's hugs more than anybody else's. You understood that you were her favorite grandson (she was not very subtle about that), and maybe you were proud and happy that she thought that you were so special. Nicholas told me recently that you always carried a picture of your grandmother in your wallet. I was surprised and pleased to hear that, but I admit I felt a touch of jealousy as well! Even though you saw your grandmother only every other year for a couple of months or so, you must have held her in high esteem and affection.

Here is another example of how you felt. Despite being homeless and penniless in the last couple of years before the end, you kept and never sold a valuable antique Greek Orthodox icon of the Virgin Mary that I gave you. I told you at the time I gave it to you that it had belonged to your grandmother Anastasia, and I asked you to take good care of it because she highly valued it. Well, you did. Despite being in the grip of the highly destructive disease of addiction, you held on to your grandmother's icon and gave it to a family friend for safekeeping. I don't know where the icon is now, but the fact that you respected my gift and did not give it up for alcohol or other drugs means a lot to me. I loved that icon and regret losing it, but it's only an object and cannot replace you. Nothing can replace you.

I derive some comfort from watching your boys do well. I hope and pray that they stay healthy and happy. They certainly deserve that after all the trauma that they went through. Keep a close watch on them, Jaime. They still need your spiritual guidance and they always will.

I recently saw in Nicholas's room a lovely picture of you. It's a picture of a much younger version of you. You have Nicholas hoisted on your shoulders, while you also hold Robert's hand. We only see your back in the picture, as you are all on a beach and moving toward your beloved ocean. I get a lump in my throat every time I look at that picture. You were such a loving dad, gone too soon from their lives.

July 6, 2019

My Dearest Son,

There was a big earthquake in California yesterday. It was thirty minutes away from Los Angeles, but I got scared when I heard the news because Nicholas was there, visiting some old friends. They were all planning to go to Catalina Island for a week. I believe Robert will join them there as well. I am glad that your boys are keeping in touch with their childhood friends, but I was concerned about the earthquake.

I texted Nicholas right away. He quickly texted me back that he was okay. The pool shook, he wrote, and there were a lot of waves in the sea, but otherwise things were fine. This earthquake reminded me of the one many years ago that was so fateful for you. You were a newlywed then, and you had your bad accident on the freeway while riding your motorcycle.

When the car in front of you suddenly stopped because of a crack in the highway, you couldn't stop in time and crashed over the car—motorcycle and all—and landed on the concrete. I'm sure you still remember all the details. You told me at the time got really scared because you couldn't move. You tried to make the sign of the cross while on the ground, and you were unable to lift your hands. That intensified your fear, and you appealed to your late grandmother Anastasia for help. That was a close call.

Doctors told you later that you could have been easily paralyzed by the crash or even died. The new helmet that you wore (that you despised) helped save your life. You were lucky you just broke your hip, they added.

You didn't feel so lucky. That fractured hip gave you pain for many years after the accident. I wonder, did you get addicted to the pain pills that they gave you for the hip injury? Knowing your history and addictive personality, my guess would be that those pain pills were the start of a lifelong addiction.

That's one reason, among many others, why I refuse to take pain pills. I have severe osteoarthritis. A rheumatologist told me a few years ago that my arthritis was so severe, that it was close to rheumatoid arthritis. I always seem to be hurting, especially at night, but all I take is some Tylenol and recently CBD (cannabidiol). I took some pain pills after my knee-replacement surgery because the pain was very intense. Because the pills made me feel weird, I stopped them as quickly as I could, and I certainly did not want to get dependent on them. I have seen too many examples through the years of the price one pays for those pills.

Water aerobics at the YMCA used to be my go-to for relief for my arthritis pain for many years, but unfortunately some acute health problems have kept me lately from attending. The aerobics sessions used to help me sleep as well. I miss the sessions greatly.

I realize that my grief over losing you is playing a major role in my semisleepless nights, but I keep hoping that one of these days I can go back to more restful sleep. I used to wonder why so many elderly people had a hard time sleeping. Now, I don't wonder any more. I know how life events as well as body deterioration can do a number on one's sleep. I do wish there was more medical research done on vital geriatric issues and concerns, but I don't see that much. Maybe there's no money in it.

Well, enough philosophizing. I'm going back to bed and try to get some of that blessed sleep.

As always, I love you and achingly miss you, Mom

July 11, 2019

My Dearest Son,

Here I am again, writing at 1:15 a.m. I went to bed around midnight, and then I lay there wide awake. After some time passed and realizing it was not too helpful to keep tossing and turning in bed while sleep eluded me, I gave up and got up to write to you.

How are you, my boy? Do spirits have a variety of moods, or is it always calm and peaceful where you are? I surely hope that you are in a nice place. Maybe it's not the fairy tale heaven that people fantasize about, but if we have a loving, compassionate God or Goddess as the ultimate power over the universe (as I believe), then you should be all right. Do not worry about us and the ones you left behind or our mundane, worldly problems.

Come to think of it, the problems we face on earth and its corroding environment are not so mundane after all, but I don't believe that spirits worry about such things. I wish people would get it through their thick heads that we have to fix the earth's problems while we are still alive.

A friend said to me the other day, "Froso, stop worrying so much. Except for voting, there's hardly anything you can do about the world's problems."

I don't totally agree with my friend. There are some things we can do as individuals, small as they may be, and I do worry. I'm sure that my grief and depression about losing you makes matters seem much worse than they are. Be that as it may, it's very hard to be optimistic about the current state of affairs in the United States and the world.

I always used to be the optimistic one during my twenty-four–year marriage. My ex-husband was chronically depressed, so it was easy to take on the optimistic mantle. Nowadays, it's a different story. I worry about my future as well as my grandchildren's future. I'm sorry, sweetheart. I shouldn't be burdening you with my fears and worries. After all, you deserve your peace after all the suffering that your addiction put you through.

I thought I would distract myself by watching a romantic comedy of about fifteen years ago called *Notting Hill*. I remembered that I had liked it a lot when it first came out. It was funny, touching, and charming—just the kind of smart movie that I enjoy. When the movie was over, I found myself crying, even though it had a happy ending. I'm not sure exactly sure why I was crying. I think it was because it reminded me of my unfulfilled dream of finding a soulmate for life. There's no escaping the fact that I am eighty-five years old, alone except for my little dog, and frequently dealing with health issues instead of romance.

You see, unrealistic as it may be, the longing for romance is still there. Sometimes, it manifests itself in romantic dreams. I wake up and the bittersweet feelings are right there on the surface. Occasionally, there are sexual feelings as well. They went away for some time after you died. I'm sure the immense grief I was feeling drove them away, but now they come back once in a while. Are you shouting, "TMI, Mom!" Is that too much information for a son to hear or read? Sorry, I got carried away some.

On another front, I keep hoping that I will have more dreams of you. So far, I have had only a few precious segments. I don't understand why they are so rare. After all, you are constantly in my mind and heart.

Freud said that dreams are expressions of feelings that are not totally conscious to the individual as yet. Maybe that's the reason that I don't dream of you more often. After all, there's nothing unconscious or semiconscious about my feelings for you. They are very clear and very real. Since they are totally visible, maybe I don't need to work on them in my sleep. That's the psychotherapist in me. I would still love to see you again, even if it's only in a dream!
Sending you lots of love, Mom

July 15, 2019

My Dearest Son,

I saw Nicholas last night at Spiros and Olga's Sunday night family dinner. He was just back from trips to New York and Los Angeles. The trip to New York was a business trip that he took as a finance intern before he goes to the University of Texas in the fall. Your son was very impressed by the fact that he flew on a private plane. "Mema, that's the way to travel," he said to me. "It was super cool."

Then Victoria popped in: "Dad, maybe you can ask your friend if he can fly Mims to my wedding in Utah next June so she doesn't have to deal with a commercial flight," she said. I laughed and so did Spiros. "I don't own the plane, you know," he told his daughter.

Have I already told you the big news? Your niece Victoria is getting married next summer in Park City, Utah, where her fiancé's family has a vacation home. She says that it's a beautiful mountain town and she loves it there. I hope I'm healthy enough next summer to be able to make the trip, even though I doubt very much that I will be going on a private plane. It was sweet of Victoria to think of me and to want me there, though.

Olga is taking her role as her daughter's wedding planner very seriously, and every time the family gets together, there are frequent discussions about wedding plans. It seems that an elegant wedding (and I know Olga well enough to know that it will be an elegant wedding) is a very complicated affair, requiring myriad decisions be made. These discussions sometimes end up in disagreements between the principals, and that makes me start to dread family meetings. Sometimes I get flashes of memory from my own weddings to your father. Yes, we were married twice—first in a civil ceremony by a judge and, second, a month later, by a Greek Orthodox priest. They were happy occasions, but I couldn't call either ceremony elegant. We had to be married twice because the priest was on his honeymoon (Greek priests, unlike Catholic ones, are allowed to get married), and since he was the only Greek Orthodox priest in the vicinity, we had to wait for his return. As for the urgency concerned, I had a deadline to meet about leaving the Louisiana State University dormitory. Given the moral customs and decrees of 1956 in Louisiana, I was not allowed to stay outside the campus unless I was married. The school authorities explained to me that because I was a foreign student, they had to act as my moral guardians (in the absence of family). What nonsense! Nevertheless, I had to obey their decree.

Anyway, both my weddings were low-key affairs. I wore a suit on both occasions—no wedding gown, no veil, and sadly no family in attendance. We had five guests, all foreign students of diverse ethnic backgrounds and religions. We spent the night of my first wedding in the Louisiana State University football stadium watching a playoff game. Since this was my first football game, I had no idea what was happening on the field. We had a flat tire on the second wedding day, so we had to hitchhike to New Orleans where the Greek priest was waiting for us for the religious ceremony. As I said before, neither wedding was exactly an elegant affair.

Jaime, are you getting a chuckle from all this reminiscing? I certainly hope so. How I wish you were alive and well and could attend Victoria's wedding.

Of course, attending her wedding pales in comparison with not being able to attend your sons' weddings, if and when they take place. They are not ready for weddings yet, but I'm already anticipating that I will grieve your absence when they do happen. Of course, if they take a long time to get married, I may not be present either. We'll see what happens and what kismet has in store for me.

Enjoy your eternal peace, my beloved son, and remember that you are indeed beloved. Always!

July 20, 2019

My Dearest Son,

A friend texted me that her son had a bad accident. A big dog lunged at him and broke six bones in his left leg. I sent her a comforting text and then I cried, thinking of you. What I really wanted to tell her but didn't was "At least he's alive, and the bones will eventually heal." I couldn't tell her my true thoughts because I was afraid that I would appear insensitive. The last time I said something similar to that, the person I was addressing got very angry with me and totally misunderstood my intent. She told me that I was comparing you with her son and minimizing her pain about her son who was an addict going to jail.

I felt very hurt when she told me that because it was certainly not my intent to minimize her distress over her son. The basic thought behind my words to her was that as long as he is still alive, there is always hope that things will change for the better. That may sound like a Pollyannaish cliché, but that has always been my belief. Was I comparing her son with you? Probably, but only because of my deep emotional pain about losing you. Things were never the same between my friend and me after that exchange, and eventually I lost that friend. I felt—and still feel—sad about that, because at my age and social semi-isolation, friendships are rare and hard to replace.

How I wish you were still alive and had a chance to heal from broken bones and illness. Yes, honey, I know that you had an illness, a severe, debilitating illness that unfortunately does not respond to surgery or antibiotics or any other kind of medications. It is the kind of illness that attacks both the body and the mind. It's a powerful, sneaky disease that tricks the mind into thinking that it's OK and that other people are to blame for a bad situation. That's how it victimizes millions of individuals and families. That's how it made victims out of you and me.

I believe that a part of you had an inkling of understanding about what I'm talking about because you told me during our last meeting that you knew you drank too much and that it was probably not good for you. You added that you couldn't imagine never drinking again. Then you slipped into what is known as "addict denial" and said, "Mom, you need to know that it's not alcohol or drugs that caused me to lose my house or end up in this crummy motel!"

Later you told me that you knew you had to cut down on your drinking, but that it was very, very hard, given that your anxiety was very high. How my heart sank as I heard you speak! I ached to hold you in my arms and shield you from all the chemical demons agitating inside you and all the nonsense that they were producing in your brain. Unfortunately, you were a middle-aged adult, not a child. Even though you will always be my baby, I couldn't shield or protect you, no matter how I tried. Your addiction disease defeated both of us, and I knew it. All I can do now is lament what happened and make a valiant effort to retrieve and cherish the happy memories of what used to be.

July 21, 2019

My Dearest Son,

It's 2 a.m., and here I am again, writing to you instead of sleeping. I hope you are not getting tired of all these letters that I have been writing. I try not to make them nagging or bitter or give you a guilt trip about dying and leaving me so desolate. You probably didn't expect to die in your fifties, Jaime, even though you must have known on some level that all the alcohol (and probably other drugs here and there) that you were absorbing was bound to hurt you. I just don't think that you believed (or wanted to believe) that the chemicals you were addicted to would eventually kill you.

I remember that when your younger brother, Constantine, was a teenager and having problems functioning because of pot and LSD, he ended up being hospitalized. You were not in Houston anymore; you were in LA. You had questioned my hospitalizing your brother and told me that he didn't need to be in a hospital. In later years, you told me that you felt guilty about Constantine's problems because you had introduced him to pot when he was a young teenager. Constantine went on to marry, raise three children, and maintain good health. I believe that getting him to treatment and even hospitalizing him helped save his life.

I wish I could have done the same for you. Unfortunately, by the time I realized the severity of your substance abuse, you were a middle-aged adult and much too old for me to have the leverage or ability to hospitalize you. All I could do was to come to you and attempt an intervention that didn't have the desired effect of motivating you to seek help. All it seemed to accomplish was to get you to admit that you were an alcoholic. "I promise you Mom, that since you came all this way for this, I will get help," you said.

I looked at you, and even though my brain was telling me that you probably were not going to do it, my aching loving heart was telling me that maybe a miracle would happen and you would keep your promise. What followed was a year of hell when you would not communicate with me or respond to my numerous phone calls and texts. I was on the verge of tears constantly, and I kept hearing bad news from LA about your situation—the foreclosure of your home, loss of your law practice, and eventually your surrender to being on the streets.

The year and a half since you left this world has been another kind of hell. This time, sadness, grief, and regrets have kept me in a tight grip and are running my life. I read a while ago that the limitless grief one experiences after losing a loved one makes living feel like wading through a boundless ocean. That's exactly how I feel and have felt for some time now. I want out of it, even though I know it's not possible right now. For all I know, it may never be possible to get out of that boundless ocean.

I want to transform grief into something more positive and worthwhile. Since I can no longer practice as a therapist and help others by my knowledge and personal experience, I need to find a purpose to my life, a goal to strive for. I just don't want to merely exist or be swallowed by all my grief. I tell myself that there has to be something left in my life to keep me going instead of making me a shadow of my former self.

More and more, I keep thinking that maybe I should write a book. My advanced age and various health issues would be challenges, but not insurmountable ones. I tell myself I did it five years ago, and I could do it again. At the time that I wrote and self-published my memoir about growing up Greek in Turkey, I truly thought that it would be my one and only book. Of course, I did not know at the time that the world of addiction would tear our lives apart. Maybe some healing and some good can come from our terrible experience. Yet, I do not know if I have the emotional strength and energy that it would take to do the work. The pain is still so great that I do not believe that I could go back and relive the agonizing events of the last two years. Recalling the time when hope that you would turn your life around was still alive in my heart would be too wrenching. I don't know if I could bear it. Maybe someday I'll be able to do it. I hope so.

I do know one thing with conviction: I am very glad that you are not suffering anymore. No more pain (physical and emotional). No more shame. No more anxiety. No mother (or father) wants to see her child suffer, and I certainly do not, even if it means having to let you go. I love you and always will. How I wish I could hear your booming laugh just one more time!

July 22, 2019

My Dearest Son,

Do you remember the Armenian lady who owned a deli in Los Angeles? I remembered her today as I was watching a show on Netflix about the Armenian genocide in Turkey's Anatolia region of the early 1900s. I thought of our visit to her deli and how you introduced me to her during one of my yearly visits to see you and my grandkids.

I don't remember her name, but I can still visualize her smiling face and her stately white hair. She must have been at least as old as I (if not older), but she still managed the deli. You told her that I also was born in Turkey in a Greek family, and her smile widened. She immediately told me a few words in Turkish, and I responded in the same language. She beamed.

You told her that you had loved visiting Turkey when you were ten years old, and she nodded her head, telling us that she never forgot her childhood there, many, many years ago.

We bought some pieces of halvah and baklava and some special bread that she had baked that reminded me of the Greek *tsoureki* (Easter bread). Despite her advanced age, she told us she had baked all those specialties herself.

The visit was bittersweet for me. It was nice to meet the Armenian lady, while at the same time it saddened me to remember all the Christian minorities, including me, who used to call Turkey home and were now scattered all over the world. Happy to make a new life, while homesick for the old.

On the way back to your house, loaded with our Middle Eastern specialties, I told you how much I enjoyed our little trip to the deli. You smiled, squeezed my hand, and said, "I knew that you were going to like her and her baked treats, Mom."

I hope that I also told you how I loved all the little trips and adventures that you planned for me during my many visits to LA. Even as I deeply enjoyed being with your whole family, the times that made me the happiest were when you and I went to places together—just the two of us. Those trips made up some for all the years that you were gone from Houston. I do believe that children are supposed to leave the nest and fly away when they grow up and find their own special place. After all, my own mother allowed me to do just that. All the same, I missed you a lot through the years and often wished you were closer.

There was that serendipitous, surprising meeting that you and I had on a hill in Paris, of all places. There I was with a girlfriend, visiting one of my favorite cities in the world, and there you were walking toward us, with your girlfriend. You had told me you were planning to go to Europe, but I had no idea of any specific dates.

My friend Betty and I had just left our hotel and were walking down a hill, when she turned to me and said, "That guy walking toward us sure looks like your son Jaime." I looked and, to my amazement, there you were—an apparition out of nowhere. It was such an amazing coincidence. Not only were we in Paris at the same time, but we were walking on the same hill, in a city full of hills, amid millions of residents and countless visitors. What are the odds?

Since I don't believe in coincidence in life, I would like to believe that our meeting on that hill in Paris on a beautiful September day was a divine gift from above.

All my love, Mom

July 25, 2019

My Dearest Son,

I am spending a week in Baton Rouge, Louisiana, with my dear longtime friends from Turkey, Uğur and Verdi.

I am thinking of you every day, every hour. My friends have known you since you were a tiny baby, so memories of your childhood and of our long history of friendship come fast and furiously. They were shocked last year when they heard of your untimely death, and I truly believe that they were very fond of you and quite sincere in grieving about you. The best part for me is that they are not reluctant to talk about you. Most people I know, including family at home, avoid any mention of you, probably because of a mistaken belief that it would upset me. Actually, the opposite is true. It is unfortunate but true that our society does not like to talk about death or even think about it.

I recently visited a Vietnamese-American home, and one of the first things I noticed was an altar in a prominent place of the living room. The altar was dedicated to the deceased husband of the owner of the house. I was told that honoring departed loved ones is a valued tradition in Vietnam. Citizens of other counties, especially Latin American ones, have other vivid memorials for the family members who have died. I think we could learn from all of them and not treat death as a taboo subject.

Anyway, it's nice to have friends like the ones I'm visiting this week who go back a long way and actually want to share common history and memories. For many years during your childhood, your father and I used to travel back and forth to Uğur and Verdi's home on every holiday, especially on Christmas (even though they were not Christians). For your father and me, this was the equivalent of going home for the holidays, since neither one of us had any biological family in the United States. Our Turkish friends represented our families here. They too traveled to see us. We did this back-and-forth traveling, even when we lived far apart (Maryland for us, and Louisiana for them).

You told me once, while I was reading parts of my memoir about my childhood in Turkey, that the happiest you ever saw your father and me (predivorce) was when we were with these same friends. We keep talking and laughing, and I laugh through my tears.

I showed Verdi a photo on my phone that has significance to both of us. It is a picture of a large tree in the front yard of our old house on Ashford Street in Houston. You were about ten years old when we moved into that house after relocating from Baltimore. You looked at the big, bare yard of the new house and started telling your father and me that we needed to plant a tree in the front yard. We were busy with moving-in chores and told you to be patient and to stop bugging us about tree planting.

Soon after our move, the Turkish-American friends that I'm currently visiting came from Baton Rouge to visit us and see our new house. You told Verdi that our house looked "yucky" without any trees. He didn't laugh at your remarks. He immediately got up from his chair and said, "Come with me, Jaime. Let's go find a nice tree for your new house." You were beaming through the whole experience. I had never seen you so happy, not even at Christmas.

Forty-seven years later, that little tree that you two planted has a huge presence and a large trunk that covers practically half of the front yard of our old house. Another family owns and enjoys the shade of that tree nowadays, but I have the history and the sweet memory of how that tree came into being. Verdi looked at the picture visibly touched. My own eyes were misty with tears.

July 29, 2019

My Dearest Son,

Today I kept seeing your darling face in my mind all day long. Don't know why. Perhaps because a group of us—all part of your family—are planning to go to Galveston on Sunday to scatter your ashes. Nicholas has kept them in his closet for more than a year now and wants to disperse them in a meaningful manner.

He and Robert scattered half of them in Los Angeles last summer when they were both there. The Galveston plan is Nicholas's idea. He texted me last July about it, just as I came back from the Alaska cruise that I had gone on with Victoria and Stuart. I saw the relevant texts at 1 a.m. in the baggage department of the Houston airport, when I was totally exhausted. I had a public meltdown right there and then. I believe I wrote to you earlier about that scene.

Nicholas brought up the subject of the ashes a few times throughout the year. He wanted to disperse them before he went to the campus of the University of Texas next month, and he wanted the rest of the family involved in the process. So, we finally made a plan to meet next Sunday, when all the principal family members were available.

Have I already told you that he was accepted at the University of Texas as a junior? Even the University of California, Los Angeles (notoriously hard to get into), accepted him for the spring semester, but he didn't want to wait so he decided to accept UT's offer. We are all very proud of him.

Going back to this coming Sunday, I don't know how I'm going to be. I already know or guess that it's going to be a very emotional day for me. At the same time, I'm glad that we are doing this. I never got to say goodbye to you and neither did your boys or the rest of your family. A short prayer service that I arranged in the Greek Chapel was all the closure we had. Nicholas and I have been wanting the ash-scattering vigil for some time now, but I have to admit that I'm dreading it at the same time. I have no idea how I am going to handle the surge of grief that I'm expecting to engulf me.

They say that time heals, but I do not believe that the cliché saying applies to grieving parents. Your father was lucky in a way. He died before you did and did not have to endure all the terrible grief of mourning one's child.

I know that this notion is kind of foolish, but I find myself angry with him at times for dying before you did and leaving me as the sole parent to grieve for you. On the other hand, he had Alzheimer's disease during the last years of his life, so maybe he wouldn't have known what was going on anyway.

I still haven't forgiven him for abandoning you in your adulthood and not ever coming to visit you in LA after your marriage. He missed getting to know your children (his grandchildren), so it was his loss as well. You told me numerous times how hurtful his abandonment was to you. I'm so sorry that his actions were hurtful to you.

I'm getting kind of sleepy. I'm going to stop writing, Jaime, and try to go to sleep. Good night, sweetheart!

August 5, 2019

My Dearest Son,

We scattered your ashes today. Nicholas and I—who planned this awful event—thought of Galveston as the most appropriate place for them, given your love of the sea. Spiros, to everyone's surprise, made a very meaningful addition to the plan. Without telling anyone, he went and asked the current owner of our old house if we could scatter some of your ashes by the trunk of the big tree in the middle of the front yard. This is the same tree that you and Verdi planted many years ago, when you were ten years old. It was a seedling at the time, but now it stands tall and majestic. Your tree proved to be a very strong one. It withstood numerous disasters, including major hurricanes like Harvey, that demolished many houses and trees.

I had not seen our old home or tree in many years. I was very surprised and very touched by Spiros's action. Not typical at all for him to do something like that. I also realized that I was wrong to resent him about not publicly sharing my grief over your death. Even though he didn't talk about it, his actions made it clear to me that he did grieve for you in his own way. That was a revelation for me.

By the time our group (Spiros, Olga, Constantine, Nicholas, and I) arrived at the site of our former home, I was crying nonstop. I was so overwhelmed by my emotions that I was literally incapable of getting out of the car to join in the scattering of the ashes by the tree. Olga, trying to comfort me, stayed with me in the car and did not join the rest of the group either. I was sobbing so hard that I couldn't grasp everything that she was telling me, but I did hear her say that she didn't believe in this kind of ritual and that your spirit had already left the earth, so what is the point? I told her—between sobs—that I agreed with her that your spirit had left our earth, but I still found the ash-scattering ritual moving and meaningful. I also told her that I deeply appreciated Spiros's gesture.

After the ceremony by your tree, we went to Galveston, with Spiros driving, so we could scatter the rest of your ashes. We drove around for quite a while, trying to find a spot by the water that was kind of remote and not full of people. Olga, in the meantime, took out of her purse an official-looking pamphlet and started reading out loud the official state rules about scattering ashes of human remains.

She started telling us that the spot we chose had to be three miles from shore, and then she added a whole lot of other bureaucratic regulations.

I was too distressed to pay much attention to what she was reading, but I was surprised and kind of bemused by her seeming resistance to what we were doing. I chose not to be resentful of her attitude, remembering how empathetic she had been to my whole grief process. By this time, it must have become clear to the rest of the group also that she did not totally approve of our ritual, so we silently put aside some of her stated objections and found a suitable spot in a remote part of the Galveston beach. By this time, my sobbing had subsided some, and I was able to get out of the car and participate in the group activity. Your ashes felt strange in my hand and rougher than I had expected. The truth is that, not having ever touched ashes before, I had no idea what to expect. I tried not to dwell on what I was holding but instead focus my feelings on the deeply emotional and meaningful experience of saying goodbye.

I also love the sea as you did, honey, and always get a thrill by my first sight of the ocean. Today, I felt a different kind of emotion. I threw your ashes in the water while imagining you alive as you swam in the ocean or as you joyfully jumped into your pool numerous times during the day. I hoped that your ashes found a welcome home in your beloved body of water. Along with your ashes, I threw in a white rose that I had brought with me for this moment. I smiled through my tears and wished you a final goodbye.

Since I had not been able to tell you goodbye before you died or to have any kind of closure, it was comforting and healing to do this small, but meaningful, ritual. Nicholas came over—as I stood by the water, crying silent tears—and gave me a hug. His eyes were also full of tears. I thanked him for insisting—over a year ago—that we do this. During my acute grief at that time, I had wanted no part of this. I had agreed to the plan, mainly to please him. In fact, I had been dreading it, thinking that it couldn't possibly help me or comfort me in any way.

I was very wrong. Goodbye, my lovely boy!

NOTES

1. "Al-Anon's three Cs—I didn't cause it, I can't control it, and I can't cure it—removed the blame . . . ," on Al-Anon Family Groups' website, n.d. (https://al-anon.org/blog/al-anons three cs).

2. This song has been recorded under multiple titles. The recording by Dinah Washington on the Mercury label in 1959 was inducted into the Grammy Hall of Fame (https://www.grammy.com/artists/dinah-washington/15599).

3. The saying "Nothing fools you better than the lie you tell yourself" may have come to the attention of twenty-first–century American readers in an online story by the silent partner in the magician duo Penn and Teller: Teller, "Teller Reveals His Secrets," *Smithsonian Magazine*, March 2012 (https://www.smithsonianmag.com/arts-culture/teller-reveals-his-secrets-100744801/).

4. Shaunda Kennedy Wenger and Janet Kay Jensen, *The Book Lover's Cookbook: Recipes Inspired by Celebrated Works of Literature and the Passages That Feature Them* (New York: Random House, 2003).

5. "Know thyself" is inscribed on Apollo's temple at Delphi, according to the *Oxford Dictionary of Quotations*, which reports that Plato credited the saying to the Seven Wise Men. See *Oxford Dictionary of Quotations*, 5th ed. (1999), "Know thyself," s.v. "Proverbs."

6. George Saunders, *Lincoln in the Bardo* (New York: Random House, 2017), 232–233.

7. *Shakespeare,* ed. Hardin Craig (Chicago: Scott, Foresman and Company, 1931), *Hamlet,* 1.5.187–188.

Made in the USA
Middletown, DE
24 May 2024

54693032R00137